The
WILEY
advantage

Dear Valued Customer,

We realize you're a busy professional with deadlines to hit. Whether your goal is to learn a new technology or solve a critical problem, we want to be there to lend you a hand. Our primary objective is to provide you with the insight and knowledge you need to stay atop the highly competitive and ever-changing technology industry.

Wiley Publishing, Inc. offers books on a wide variety of technical categories, including security, data warehousing, software development tools, and networking - everything you need to reach your peak. Regardless of your level of expertise, the Wiley family of books has you covered.

- For Dummies – The *fun* and *easy* way to learn
- The Weekend Crash Course –The *fastest* way to learn a new tool or technology
- Visual – For those who prefer to learn a new topic *visually*
- The Bible – The *100% comprehensive* tutorial and reference
- The Wiley Professional list – *Practical* and *reliable* resources for IT professionals

The book you hold now, *Advanced CISSP Prep Guide: Exam Q&A*, is the first in-depth guide to advanced CISSP exam study. Whether you are CISSP certified already and seeking recertification, boning up to take the demanding test for the first time, or seeking to upgrade your information security expertise, *Advanced CISSP Prep Guide: Exam Q&A* gives you what you need. Organized around the ten domains, each answer is designed to be a learning activity to help you review and reinforce key principles.

Our commitment to you does not end at the last page of this book. We'd like to open a dialog with you to see what other solutions we can provide. Please be sure to visit us at www.wiley.com/compbooks to review our complete title list and explore the other resources we offer. If you have a comment, suggestion or any other inquiry, please locate the "contact us" link at www.wiley.com.

Finally, we encourage you to review the following page for a list of additional titles from our list that provide more information on related topics. Thank you for your support and we look forward to hearing from you and serving your needs again in the future.

Sincerely,

Richard K. Swadley

Richard K. Swadley
Vice President & Executive Group Publisher
Wiley Publishing, Inc.

15 HOUR WEEKEND CRASH COURSE

Visual

DUMMIES

WILEY
Independent Thinkers

more information
on related titles

Advanced CISSP®
Prep Guide:
Exam Q & A

Advanced CISSP®
Prep Guide:
Exam Q & A

Ronald L. Krutz
Russell Dean Vines

Wiley Publishing, Inc.

Publisher: Robert Ipsen
Executive Editor: Carol Long
Managing Editor: Angela Smith
New Media Editor: Brian Snapp
Text Design & Composition: D&G Limited, LLC

Designations used by companies to distinguish their products are often claimed as trademarks. In all instances where Wiley Publishing, Inc., is aware of a claim, the product names appear in initial capital or ALL CAPITAL LETTERS. Readers, however, should contact the appropriate companies for more complete information regarding trademarks and registration.

This book is printed on acid-free paper. ∞

For general information on our other products and services please contact our Customer Care Department within the United States at (800) 762-2974, outside the United States at (317) 572-3993 or fax (317) 572-4002.

Wiley also publishes its books in a variety of electronic formats. Some content that appears in print may not be available in electronic versions.

For more information about Wiley products, visit our Web site at www.wiley.com.

Library of Congress Cataloging-in-Publication Data:

ISBN 0471-23663-2

Printed in the United States of America.

10 9 8 7 6 5 4 3 2 1

I dedicate this book to Louis J. Napolitano, my father-in-law, who always gave of himself and who is sorely missed by all . . .

His friends and relatives knew him to be willing and helpful;

His grandchildren knew him to be a juvenile delinquent in senior citizen's skin;

His daughters and sons-in-law knew him to be a rock of strength;

His wife, Rose, knew him to be a devoted and loving husband;

God knows him to be a Precious Child of His.

RLK

In memory of Dave Van Ronk (1936–2002), a fine finger-style guitarist and incomparable song stylist. Over the years, he generously made his couch and table available to newly arrived New Yorkers from Bob Dylan to Russ Vines.

RDV

Contents

Acknowledgments

I want to acknowledge the patience and encouragement of my wife, Hilda, while I was engaged in this project.

I also wish to acknowledge the support and guidance of Carol Long, our executive editor. Her ideas and recommendations were instrumental in ensuring the quality of this work. In addition, I want to extend my appreciation to Micheline Frederick and Adaobi Obi Tulton for their excellent editorial support and Erica Weinstein for her coordination efforts at Wiley.

RLK

I would like to acknowledge the help and support of my wife, Elzy Kolb, for her invaluable assistance throughout the book process. And, I appreciate the great assistance of the editors at Wiley, in particular Carol Long, Micheline Frederick, Adaobi Obi Tulton, and Erica Weinstein.

RDV

About the Authors

Ronald L. Krutz, Ph.D., P.E., CISSP. Dr. Krutz is Director of Privacy with Corbett Technologies, Inc. He also directs the Capability Maturity Model (CMM) engagements for Corbett Technologies and led the development of Corbett's HIPAA-CMM assessment methodology. He has more than 40 years of experience in distributed computing systems, computer architectures, real-time systems, information assurance methodologies, and information security training. He has been an information security consultant at REALTECH Systems Corporation, an associate director of the Carnegie Mellon Research Institute (CMRI), and a Professor in the Carnegie Mellon University Department of Electrical and Computer Engineering. Dr. Krutz founded the CMRI Cybersecurity Center and was founder and director of the CMRI Computer, Automation, and Robotics Group. He was also a lead instructor for the ISC2 CISSP Common Body of Knowledge review seminars. Prior to his 24 years at Carnegie Mellon University, Dr. Krutz was a department director in the Singer Corporate R&D Laboratories and a senior engineer at Gulf Research and Development Company.

Dr. Krutz conducted sponsored-applied research and development in the areas of computer security, artificial intelligence, networking, modeling and simulation, robotics, and real-time computer applications. He is the author of three textbooks in the areas of microcomputer system design, computer interfacing, and computer architecture and is the coauthor of the *CISSP Prep Guide: Mastering the 10 Domains of Computer Security*. Dr. Krutz is the holder of seven patents in the area of digital systems. He is a Distinguished Visiting Lecturer in the University of New Haven Computer Forensics Program and is a part-time instructor in the University of Pittsburgh Computer Engineering Program, where he teaches courses in information system security and computer organization. Dr. Krutz is a Certified Information Systems Security Professional (CISSP) and a Registered Professional Engineer.

Russell Dean Vines, CISSP, CCNA, MCSE, MCNE. President and founder of The RDV Group, Inc., a New York City-based security consulting services firm, Mr. Vines has been active in the prevention, detection, and remediation of security vulnerabilities for international corporations, including government, finance, and new media organizations, for many years.

Mr. Vines is coauthor of the best-selling *CISSP Prep Guide: Mastering the 10 Domains of Computer Security*, and author of *Wireless Security Essentials*, both published by John Wiley and Sons. He frequently addresses classes, professional groups, and corporate clients on privacy, security awareness, and best practices in the information industry.

Mr. Vines has been active in computer engineering since the start of the personal computer revolution. He holds high-level certifications in Cisco, 3Com, Ascend, Microsoft, and Novell technologies and has been trained in the National Security Agency's ISSO Information Assessment Methodology. He has headed computer security departments and managed worldwide information systems networks for prominent technology, entertainment, and non-profit corporations based in New York. He formerly directed the Security Consulting Services Group for Realtech Systems Corporation; designed, implemented, and managed international information networks for CBS/Fox Video, Inc.; and was Director of MIS for the Children's Aid Society in New York.

Mr. Vines's early professional years were illuminated not by the flicker of a computer monitor, but by the bright lights of Nevada casino show rooms. After receiving a *Down Beat* magazine scholarship to Boston's Berklee College of Music, he performed as a sideman for a variety of well-known entertainers, including George Benson, John Denver, Sammy Davis, Jr., and Dean Martin. Mr. Vines composed and arranged hundreds of pieces of jazz and contemporary music that have been recorded and performed by his own big band and others; he also founded and managed a scholastic music publishing company and worked as an artist-in-residence for the National Endowment for the Arts in communities throughout the West. He still performs and teaches music in the New York City area and is a member of Local #802, American Federation of Musicians.

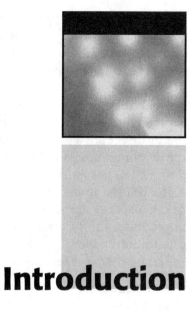

Introduction

The *Advanced CISSP Prep Guide: Exam Q & A* pulls together the key elements of the Common Body of Knowledge (CBK) in a format that tests the candidate's knowledge of the CBK prior to sitting for the CISSP examination. The advanced questions address the 10 domains of the CBK, which are

- Security Management Practices
- Access Control Systems
- Telecommunications and Network Security
- Cryptography
- Security Architecture and Models
- Operations Security
- Applications and Systems Development
- Business Continuity Planning and Disaster Recovery Planning
- Law, Investigation, and Ethics
- Physical Security

A recommended approach is to use this text as one of the final steps in consolidating previously studied CISSP examination-related information. For example, after studying the *CISSP Prep Guide* and completing its list of review questions, the *Advanced CISSP Prep Guide: Exam Q & A* can be used to evaluate the candidate's true understanding of the material by posing questions of greater difficulty. However, the answers to these advanced questions are explained in great detail to consolidate the information on the subject. Even the incorrect answers are discussed in length, where appropriate, to enhance the learning process. The *Advanced CISSP Prep Guide: Exam Q & A* was designed to be complementary to the *CISSP Prep Guide*.

In addition to serving as a tutorial for the subject matter of the advanced questions, the *Advanced CISSP Prep Guide: Exam Q & A* incorporates additional information on the topics and new information that has emerged since the publication of the *CISSP Prep Guide*.

The new subjects addressed include

- Carnivore
- Echelon
- The U.S. Patriot Act
- The Digital Millennium Copyright Act (DMCA) and recent rulings
- The European Union Electronic Signature Directive
- The Advanced Encryption Standard
- Biometrics
- The Software Capability Maturity Model (CMM)
- Genetic algorithms
- Wireless security models
- New threat and countermeasure information

In summary, this text will tell you if you have effectively grasped the key concepts associated with the 10 domains of the CBK and will help you identify and review the areas in which more work is required. In addition, this text will give you information on the latest developments in information security through advanced questions and answers focusing on those topics.

Advanced CISSP®
Prep Guide:
Exam Q & A

CHAPTER

1

Security Management

This chapter is supplemental to and coordinated with the Security Management chapter in the *CISSP Prep Guide*. The fundamentals of security management are covered in Chapter 1 of the *CISSP Prep Guide* at a level on par with that of the CISSP Examination.

It is assumed that the reader has a basic knowledge of the material contained in Chapter 1 and has the CISSP *Prep Guide* available to provide background information for the advanced questions pertaining to the Security Management chapter.

In the Security Management questions areas we will discuss data classification, security awareness, risk analysis, information system policies, and roles in information protection.

Advanced Sample Questions

1. Which choice below most accurately reflects the goals of risk mitigation?

   a. Defining the acceptable level of risk the organization can tolerate, and reducing risk to that level

   b. Analyzing and removing all vulnerabilities and threats to security within the organization

   c. Defining the acceptable level of risk the organization can tolerate, and assigning any costs associated with loss or disruption to a third party, such as an insurance carrier

   d. Analyzing the effects of a business disruption and preparing the company's response

2. Which answer below is the BEST description of a Single Loss Expectancy (SLE)?

   a. An algorithm that represents the magnitude of a loss to an asset from a threat

   b. An algorithm that expresses the annual frequency with which a threat is expected to occur

   c. An algorithm used to determine the monetary impact of each occurrence of a threat

   d. An algorithm that determines the expected annual loss to an organization from a threat

3. Which choice below is the BEST description of an Annualized Loss Expectancy (ALE)?

   a. The expected risk factor of an annual threat event, derived by multiplying the SLE by its ARO

   b. An estimate of how often a given threat event may occur annually

   c. The percentile of the value of the asset expected to be lost, used to calculate the SLE

   d. A value determined by multiplying the value of the asset by its exposure factor

4. Which choice below is NOT an example of appropriate security management practice?

   a. Reviewing access logs for unauthorized behavior

   b. Monitoring employee performance in the workplace

   c. Researching information on new intrusion exploits

   d. Promoting and implementing security awareness programs

5. Which choice below is an accurate statement about standards?

    a. Standards are the high-level statements made by senior management in support of information systems security.

    b. Standards are the first element created in an effective security policy program.

    c. Standards are used to describe how policies will be implemented within an organization.

    d. Standards are senior management's directives to create a computer security program.

6. Which choice below is a role of the Information Systems Security Officer?

    a. The ISO establishes the overall goals of the organization's computer security program.

    b. The ISO is responsible for day-to-day security administration.

    c. The ISO is responsible for examining systems to see whether they are meeting stated security requirements.

    d. The ISO is responsible for following security procedures and reporting security problems.

7. Which statement below is NOT true about security awareness, training, and educational programs?

    a. Awareness and training help users become more accountable for their actions.

    b. Security education assists management in determining who should be promoted.

    c. Security improves the users' awareness of the need to protect information resources.

    d. Security education assists management in developing the in-house expertise to manage security programs.

8. Which choice below is NOT an accurate description of an information policy?

    a. Information policy is senior management's directive to create a computer security program.

    b. An information policy could be a decision pertaining to use of the organization's fax.

    c. Information policy is a documentation of computer security decisions.

    d. Information policies are created after the system's infrastructure has been designed and built.

9. Which choice below MOST accurately describes the organization's responsibilities during an unfriendly termination?

   a. System access should be removed as quickly as possible after termination.

   b. The employee should be given time to remove whatever files he needs from the network.

   c. Cryptographic keys can remain the employee's property.

   d. Physical removal from the offices would never be necessary.

10. Which choice below is NOT an example of an issue-specific policy?

    a. E-mail privacy policy

    b. Virus-checking disk policy

    c. Defined router ACLs

    d. Unfriendly employee termination policy

11. Who has the final responsibility for the preservation of the organization's information?

    a. Technology providers

    b. Senior management

    c. Users

    d. Application owners

12. Which choice below is NOT a generally accepted benefit of security awareness, training, and education?

    a. A security awareness program can help operators understand the value of the information.

    b. A security education program can help system administrators recognize unauthorized intrusion attempts.

    c. A security awareness and training program will help prevent natural disasters from occurring.

    d. A security awareness and training program can help an organization reduce the number and severity of errors and omissions.

13. Which choice below is NOT a common information-gathering technique when performing a risk analysis?

    a. Distributing a questionnaire

    b. Employing automated risk assessment tools

    c. Reviewing existing policy documents

    d. Interviewing terminated employees

14. Which choice below is an incorrect description of a control?

    a. Detective controls discover attacks and trigger preventative or corrective controls.

    b. Corrective controls reduce the likelihood of a deliberate attack.

    c. Corrective controls reduce the effect of an attack.

    d. Controls are the countermeasures for vulnerabilities.

15. Which statement below is accurate about the reasons to implement a layered security architecture?

    a. A layered security approach is not necessary when using COTS products.

    b. A good packet-filtering router will eliminate the need to implement a layered security architecture.

    c. A layered security approach is intended to increase the work-factor for an attacker.

    d. A layered approach doesn't really improve the security posture of the organization.

16. Which choice below represents an application or system demonstrating a need for a high level of confidentiality protection and controls?

    a. Unavailability of the system could result in inability to meet payroll obligations and could cause work stoppage and failure of user organizations to meet critical mission requirements. The system requires 24-hour access.

    b. The application contains proprietary business information and other financial information, which if disclosed to unauthorized sources, could cause an unfair advantage for vendors, contractors, or individuals and could result in financial loss or adverse legal action to user organizations.

    c. Destruction of the information would require significant expenditures of time and effort to replace. Although corrupted information would present an inconvenience to the staff, most information, and all vital information, is either backed up by paper documentation or on disk.

    d. The mission of this system is to produce local weather forecast information that is made available to the news media forecasters and the general public at all times. None of the information requires protection against disclosure.

17. Which choice below is an accurate statement about the difference between monitoring and auditing?

    a. Monitoring is a one-time event to evaluate security.

    b. A system audit is an ongoing "real-time" activity that examines a system.

c. A system audit cannot be automated.

d. Monitoring is an ongoing activity that examines either the system or the users.

18. Which statement below is accurate about the difference between issue-specific and system-specific policies?

a. Issue-specific policy is much more technically focused.

b. System-specific policy is much more technically focused.

c. System-specific policy is similar to program policy.

d. Issue-specific policy commonly addresses only one system.

19. Which statement below MOST accurately describes the difference between security awareness, security training, and security education?

a. Security training teaches the skills that will help employees to perform their jobs more securely.

b. Security education is required for all system operators.

c. Security awareness is not necessary for high-level senior executives.

d. Security training is more in depth than security education.

20. Which choice below BEST describes the difference between the System Owner and the Information Owner?

a. There is a one-to-one relationship between system owners and information owners.

b. One system could have multiple information owners.

c. The Information Owner is responsible for defining the system's operating parameters.

d. The System Owner is responsible for establishing the rules for appropriate use of the information.

21. Which choice below is NOT an accurate statement about an organization's incident-handling capability?

a. The organization's incident-handling capability should be used to detect and punish senior-level executive wrong-doing.

b. It should be used to prevent future damage from incidents.

c. It should be used to provide the ability to respond quickly and effectively to an incident.

d. The organization's incident-handling capability should be used to contain and repair damage done from incidents.

22. Place the data classification scheme in order, from the least secure to the most:

_____ a. Sensitive

_____ b. Public

_____ c. Private

_____ d. Confidential

23. Place the five system security life-cycle phases in order:

    _____ a. Implementation phase

    _____ b. Development/acquisition phase

    _____ c. Disposal phase

    _____ d. Operation/maintenance phase

    _____ e. Initiation phase

24. How often should an independent review of the security controls be performed, according to OMB Circular A-130?

    a. Every year

    b. Every three years

    c. Every five years

    d. Never

25. Which choice below is NOT one of NIST's 33 IT security principles?

    a. Implement least privilege.

    b. Assume that external systems are insecure.

    c. Totally eliminate any level of risk.

    d. Minimize the system elements to be trusted.

26. Which choice below would NOT be considered an element of proper user account management?

    a. Users should never be rotated out of their current duties.

    b. The users' accounts should be reviewed periodically.

    c. A process for tracking access authorizations should be implemented.

    d. Periodically re-screen personnel in sensitive positions.

27. Which question below is NOT accurate regarding the process of Risk Assessment?

    a. The likelihood of a threat must be determined as an element of the risk assessment.

    b. The level of impact of a threat must be determined as an element of the risk assessment.

    c. Risk assessment is the first process in the risk management methodology.

    d. Risk assessment is the final result of the risk management methodology.

28. Which choice below is NOT an accurate statement about the visibility of IT security policy?

    a. The IT security policy should not be afforded high visibility.

    b. The IT security policy could be visible through panel discussions with guest speakers.

    c. The IT security policy should be afforded high visibility.

    d. Include the IT security policy as a regular topic at staff meetings at all levels of the organization.

29. According to NIST, which choice below is not an accepted security self-testing technique?

    a. War Dialing

    b. Virus Distribution

    c. Password Cracking

    d. Virus Detection

30. Which choice below is NOT a concern of policy development at the high level?

    a. Identifying the key business resources

    b. Identifying the types of firewalls to be used for perimeter security

    c. Defining roles in the organization

    d. Determining the capability and functionality of each role.

CHAPTER

2

Access Control

This chapter is supplemental to and coordinated with the Access Control chapter in the *CISSP Prep Guide*. The fundamentals of access control are covered in Chapter 2 of the *CISSP Prep Guide* at a level commensurate with that of the CISSP Examination.

This chapter includes advanced material relative to trusted networks, remote access, biometrics, database security (including relational and object models), operating system security, Kerberos, single sign-on, authentication (including mobile authentication) and Enterprise Access Management (EAM).

It is assumed that the reader has a basic knowledge of the material contained in Chapter 2 and has the *CISSP Prep Guide* available to provide background information for the advanced questions pertaining to access control. These questions and answers build upon the questions and answers covered in Chapter 2 of the *CISSP Prep Guide*.

Advanced Sample Questions

1. The concept of limiting the routes that can be taken between a workstation and a computer resource on a network is called:

   a. Path limitation

   b. An enforced path

   c. A security perimeter

   d. A trusted path

2. An important control that should be in place for external connections to a network that uses call back schemes is:

   a. Breaking of a dial-up connection at the remote user's side of the line

   b. Call forwarding

   c. Call enhancement

   d. Breaking of a dial-up connection at the organization's computing resource side of the line

3. When logging on to a workstation, the log-on process should:

   a. Validate the log-on only after all input data has been supplied.

   b. Provide a Help mechanism that provides log-on assistance.

   c. Place no limits on the time allotted for log-on or on the number of unsuccessful log-on attempts.

   d. Not provide information on the previous successful log-on and on previous unsuccessful log-on attempts.

4. A group of processes that share access to the same resources is called:

   a. An access control list

   b. An access control triple

   c. A protection domain

   d. A Trusted Computing Base (TCB)

5. What part of an access control matrix shows capabilities that one user has to multiple resources?

   a. Columns

   b. Rows

   c. Rows and columns

   d. Access control list

6. A type of preventive/physical access control is:

   a. Biometrics for authentication

   b. Motion detectors

   c. Biometrics for identification

   d. An intrusion detection system

7. In addition to accuracy, a biometric system has additional factors that determine its effectiveness. Which one of the following listed items is NOT one of these additional factors?

   a. Throughput rate

   b. Acceptability

   c. Corpus

   d. Enrollment time

8. Access control that is a function of factors such as location, time of day, and previous access history is called:

   a. Positive

   b. Content-dependent

   c. Context-dependent

   d. Information flow

9. A persistent collection of data items that form relations among each other is called a:

   a. Database management system (DBMS)

   b. Data description language (DDL)

   c. Schema

   d. Database

10. A relational database can provide security through *view* relations. Views enforce what information security principle?

   a. Aggregation

   b. Least privilege

   c. Separation of duties

   d. Inference

11. A software interface to the operating system that implements access control by limiting the system commands that are available to a user is called a(n):

   a. Restricted shell·

   b. Interrupt

c. Physically constrained user interface

d. View

12. Controlling access to information systems and associated networks is necessary for the preservation of their confidentiality, integrity and availability. Which of the following is NOT a goal of integrity?

   a. Prevention of the modification of information by unauthorized users

   b. Prevention of the unauthorized or unintentional modification of information by authorized users

   c. Prevention of authorized modifications by unauthorized users

   d. Preservation of the internal and external consistency of the information

13. In a Kerberos exchange involving a message with an authenticator, the authenticator contains the client ID and which of the following?

   a. Ticket Granting Ticket (TGT)

   b. Timestamp

   c. Client/TGS session key

   d. Client network address

14. Which one of the following security areas is directly addressed by Kerberos?

   a. Confidentiality

   b. Frequency analysis

   c. Availability

   d. Physical attacks

15. The Secure European System for Applications in a Multivendor Environment (SESAME) implements a Kerberos-like distribution of secret keys. Which of the following is NOT a characteristic of SESAME?

   a. Uses a trusted authentication server at each host

   b. Uses secret key cryptography for the distribution of secret keys

   c. Incorporates two certificates or tickets, one for authentication and one defining access privileges

   d. Uses public key cryptography for the distribution of secret keys

16. Windows 2000 uses which of the following as the primary mechanism for authenticating users requesting access to a network?

   a. Hash functions

   b. Kerberos

    c. SESAME

    d. Public key certificates

17. A protection mechanism to limit inferencing of information in statistical database queries is:

    a. Specifying a maximum query set size

    b. Specifying a minimum query set size

    c. Specifying a minimum query set size, but prohibiting the querying of all but one of the records in the database

    d. Specifying a maximum query set size, but prohibiting the querying of all but one of the records in the database

18. In SQL, a relation that is actually existent in the database is called a(n):

    a. Base relation

    b. View

    c. Attribute

    d. Domain

19. A type of access control that supports the management of access rights for groups of subjects is:

    a. Role-based

    b. Discretionary

    c. Mandatory

    d. Rule-based

20. The Simple Security Property and the Star Property are key principles in which type of access control?

    a. Role-based

    b. Rule-based

    c. Discretionary

    d. Mandatory

21. Which of the following items is NOT used to determine the types of access controls to be applied in an organization?

    a. Least privilege

    b. Separation of duties

    c. Relational categories

    d. Organizational policies

22. Kerberos provides an integrity check service for messages between two entities through the use of:

    a. A checksum

    b. Credentials

    c. Tickets

    d. A trusted, third-party authentication server

23. The Open Group has defined functional objectives in support of a user single sign-on (SSO) interface. Which of the following is NOT one of those objectives and would possibly represent a vulnerability?

    a. The interface shall be independent of the type of authentication information handled.

    b. Provision for user-initiated change of nonuser configured authentication information.

    c. It shall not predefine the timing of secondary sign-on operations.

    d. Support shall be provided for a subject to establish a default user profile.

24. There are some correlations between relational database terminology and object-oriented database terminology. Which of the following relational model terms, respectively, correspond to the object model terms of class, attribute, and instance object?

    a. Domain, relation, and column

    b. Relation, domain, and column

    c. Relation, tuple, and column

    d. Relation, column, and tuple

25. A *reference monitor* is a system component that enforces access controls on an object. Specifically, the *reference monitor concept* is an abstract machine that mediates all access of subjects to objects. The hardware, firmware, and software elements of a trusted computing base that implement the reference monitor concept are called:

    a. The authorization database

    b. Identification and authentication (I & A) mechanisms

    c. The auditing subsystem

    d. The security kernel

26. Authentication in which a random value is presented to a user, who then returns a calculated number based on that random value is called:

    a. Man-in-the-middle

    b. Challenge-response

    c. One-time password

    d. Personal identification number (PIN) protocol

27. Which of the following is NOT a criterion for access control?

    a. Identity

    b. Role

    c. Keystroke monitoring

    d. Transactions

28. Which of the following is typically NOT a consideration in the design of passwords?

    a. Lifetime

    b. Composition

    c. Authentication period

    d. Electronic monitoring

29. A distributed system using passwords as the authentication means can use a number of techniques to make the password system stronger. Which of the following is NOT one of these techniques?

    a. Password generators

    b. Regular password reuse

    c. Password file protection

    d. Limiting the number or frequency of log-on attempts

30. Enterprise Access Management (EAM) provides access control management services to Web-based enterprise systems. Which of the following functions is NOT normally provided by extant EAM approaches?

    a. Single sign-on

    b. Accommodation of a variety of authentication mechanisms

    c. Role-based access control

    d. Interoperability among EAM implementations

31. The main approach to obtaining the true biometric information from a collected sample of an individual's physiological or behavioral characteristics is:

    a. Feature extraction

    b. Enrollment

    c. False rejection

    d. Digraphs

32. In a wireless General Packet Radio Services (GPRS) Virtual Private Network (VPN) application, which of the following security protocols is commonly used?

   a. SSL

   b. IPSEC

   c. TLS

   d. WTP

33. How is authentication implemented in GSM?

   a. Using public key cryptography

   b. It is not implemented in GSM

   c. Using secret key cryptography

   d. Out of band verification

CHAPTER

3

Telecommunications and Network Security

This chapter is supplemental to and coordinated with the Telecommunications and Network Security chapter in the *CISSP Prep Guide*. The fundamentals of telecommunications and network security are covered in Chapter 3 of the *CISSP Prep Guide* at a level on par with that of the CISSP Examination.

It is assumed that the reader has a basic knowledge of the material contained in Chapter 3 and has the *CISSP Prep Guide* available to provide background information for the advanced questions pertaining to the Telecommunications and Network Security chapter.

In the Telecommunications and Network Security areas we will discuss protocols, layers, firewalls, IP addressing, and other network concepts.

Advanced Sample Questions

1. Which of the choices below is NOT an OSI reference model Session Layer protocol, standard, or interface?

   a. SQL

   b. RPC

   c. MIDI

   d. ASP

   e. DNA SCP

2. Which part of the 48-bit, 12-digit hexadecimal number known as the Media Access Control (MAC) address identifies the manufacturer of the network device?

   a. The first three bytes

   b. The first two bytes

   c. The second half of the MAC address

   d. The last three bytes

3. Which IEEE protocol defines the Spanning Tree protocol?

   a. IEEE 802.5

   b. IEEE 802.3

   c. IEEE 802.11

   d. IEEE 802.1D

4. Which choice below is NOT one of the legal IP address ranges specified by RFC1976 and reserved by the Internet Assigned Numbers Authority (IANA) for non-routable private addresses?

   a. 10.0.0.0–10.255.255.255

   b. 127.0.0.0–127.0.255.255

   c. 172.16.0.0–172.31.255.255

   d. 192.168.0.0–192.168.255.255

5. Which statement is correct about ISDN Basic Rate Interface?

   a. It offers 23 B channels and 1 D channel.

   b. It offers 2 B channels and 1 D channel.

   c. It offers 30 B channels and 1 D channel.

   d. It offers 1 B channel and 2 D channels.

6. In the DoD reference model, which layer conforms to the OSI transport layer?

   a. Process/Application Layer

   b. Host-to-Host Layer

    c. Internet Layer

    d. Network Access Layer

7. What is the Network Layer of the OSI reference model primarily responsible for?

    a. Internetwork packet routing

    b. LAN bridging

    c. SMTP Gateway services

    d. Signal regeneration and repeating

8. Which IEEE protocol defines wireless transmission in the 5 GHz band with data rates up to 54 Mbps?

    a. IEEE 802.11a

    b. IEEE 802.11b

    c. IEEE 802.11g

    d. IEEE 802.15

9. Which category of UTP wiring is rated for 100BaseT Ethernet networks?

    a. Category 1

    b. Category 2

    c. Category 3

    d. Category 4

    e. Category 5

10. Which choice below is the earliest and the most commonly found Interior Gateway Protocol?

    a. RIP

    b. OSPF

    c. IGRP

    d. EAP

11. The data transmission method in which data is sent continuously and doesn't use either an internal clocking source or start/stop bits for timing is known as:

    a. Asynchronous

    b. Synchronous

    c. Isochronous

    d. Pleisiochronous

12. Which level of RAID is commonly referred to as "disk mirroring"?

    a. RAID 0

    b. RAID 1

    c. RAID 3

    d. RAID 5

13. Which network attack below would NOT be considered a Denial of Service attack?

    a. Ping of Death

    b. SMURF

    c. Brute Force

    d. TCP SYN

14. Which choice below is NOT an element of IPSec?

    a. Authentication Header

    b. Layer Two Tunneling Protocol

    c. Security Association

    d. Encapsulating Security Payload

15. Which statement below is NOT true about the difference between cut-through and store-and-forward switching?

    a. A store-and-forward switch reads the whole packet and checks its validity before sending it to the next destination.

    b. Both methods operate at layer two of the OSI reference model.

    c. A cut-through switch reads only the header on the incoming data packet.

    d. A cut-through switch introduces more latency than a store-and-forward switch.

16. Which statement is NOT true about the SOCKS protocol?

    a. It is sometimes referred to as an application-level proxy.

    b. It uses an ESP for authentication and encryption.

    c. It operates in the transport layer of the OSI model.

    d. Network applications need to be SOCKS-ified to operate.

17. Which choice below does NOT relate to analog dial-up hacking?

    a. War Dialing

    b. War Walking

    c. Demon Dialing

    d. ToneLoc

18. Which choice below is NOT a way to get Windows NT passwords?

    a. Obtain the backup SAM from the repair directory.

    b. Boot the NT server with a floppy containing an alternate operating system.

    c. Obtain root access to the /etc/passwd file.

    d. Use pwdump2 to dump the password hashes directly from the registry.

19. A "back door" into a network refers to what?

    a. Socially engineering passwords from a subject

    b. Mechanisms created by hackers to gain network access at a later time

    c. Undocumented instructions used by programmers to debug applications

    d. Monitoring programs implemented on dummy applications to lure intruders

20. Which protocol below does NOT pertain to e-mail?

    a. SMTP

    b. POP

    c. CHAP

    d. IMAP

21. The IP address, 178.22.90.1, is considered to be in which class of address?

    a. Class A

    b. Class B

    c. Class C

    d. Class D

22. What type of firewall architecture employs two network cards and a single screening router?

    a. A screened-host firewall

    b. A dual-homed host firewall

    c. A screened-subnet firewall

    d. An application-level proxy server

23. What is one of the most common drawbacks to using a dual-homed host firewall?

    a. The examination of the packet at the Network layer introduces latency.

    b. The examination of the packet at the Application layer introduces latency.

   c. The ACLs must be manually maintained on the host.

   d. Internal routing may accidentally become enabled.

24. Which firewall type below uses a dynamic state table to inspect the content of packets?

   a. A packet-filtering firewall

   b. An application-level firewall

   c. A circuit-level firewall

   d. A stateful-inspection firewall

25. Which attack type below does NOT exploit TCP vulnerabilities?

   a. Sequence Number attack

   b. SYN attack

   c. Ping of Death

   d. land.c attack

26. Which utility below can create a server-spoofing attack?

   a. DNS poisoning

   b. C2MYAZZ

   c. Snort

   d. BO2K

27. Which LAN topology below is MOST vulnerable to a single point of failure?

   a. Ethernet Bus

   b. Physical Star

   c. FDDI

   d. Logical Ring

28. Which choice below does NOT accurately describe the difference between multi-mode and single-mode fiber optic cabling?

   a. Multi-mode fiber propagates light waves through many paths, single-mode fiber propagates a single light ray only.

   b. Multi-mode fiber has a longer allowable maximum transmission distance than single-mode fiber.

   c. Single-mode fiber has a longer allowable maximum transmission distance than multi-mode fiber.

   d. Both types have a longer allowable maximum transmission distance than UTP Cat 5.

29. Which statement below is correct regarding VLANs?
    a. A VLAN restricts flooding to only those ports included in the VLAN.
    b. A VLAN is a network segmented physically, not logically.
    c. A VLAN is less secure when implemented in conjunction with private port switching.
    d. A "closed" VLAN configuration is the least secure VLAN configuration.

30. Which choice below denotes a packet-switched connectionless wide area network (WAN) technology?
    a. X.25
    b. Frame Relay
    c. SMDS
    d. ATM

31. Which statement below is accurate about the difference between Ethernet II and 802.3 frame formats?
    a. 802.3 uses a "Length" field, whereas Ethernet II uses a "Type" field.
    b. 802.3 uses a "Type" field, whereas Ethernet II uses a "Length" field.
    c. Ethernet II uses a 4-byte FCS field, whereas 802.3 uses an 8-byte Preamble field.
    d. Ethernet II uses an 8-byte Preamble field, whereas 802.3 uses a 4-byte FCS field.

32. Which standard below does NOT specify fiber optic cabling as its physical media?
    a. 100BaseFX
    b. 1000BaseCX
    c. 1000BaseLX
    d. 1000BaseSX

33. Which type of routing below commonly broadcasts its routing table information to all other routers every minute?
    a. Static Routing
    b. Distance Vector Routing
    c. Link State Routing
    d. Dynamic Control Protocol Routing

34. Which protocol is used to resolve a known IP address to an unknown MAC address?
    a. ARP
    b. RARP

    c. ICMP

    d. TFTP

35. Which statement accurately describes the difference between 802.11b WLAN ad hoc and infrastructure modes?

    a. The ad hoc mode requires an Access Point to communicate to the wired network.

    b. Wireless nodes can communicate peer-to-peer in the infrastructure mode.

    c. Wireless nodes can communicate peer-to-peer in the ad hoc mode.

    d. Access points are rarely used in 802.11b WLANs.

36. Which type of cabling below is the most common type for recent Ethernet installations?

    a. ThickNet

    b. ThinNet

    c. Twinax

    d. Twisted Pair

37. Which choice below most accurately describes SSL?

    a. It's a widely used standard of securing e-mail at the Application level.

    b. It gives a user remote access to a command prompt across a secure, encrypted session.

    c. It uses two protocols, the Authentication Header and the Encapsulating Security Payload.

    d. It allows an application to have authenticated, encrypted communications across a network.

38. Which backup method listed below will probably require the backup operator to use the most number of tapes for a complete system restoration, if a different tape is used every night in a five-day rotation?

    a. Full Backup Method

    b. Differential Backup Method

    c. Incremental Backup Method

    d. Ad Hoc Backup Method

39. Which choice below is NOT an element of a fiber optic cable?

    a. Core

    b. BNC

    c. Jacket

    d. Cladding

40. Given an IP address of 172.16.0.0, which subnet mask below would allow us to divide the network into the maximum number of subnets with at least 600 host addresses per subnet?

    a. 255.255.224.0

    b. 255.255.240.0

    c. 255.255.248.0

    d. 255.255.252.0

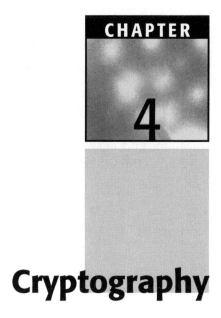

CHAPTER

4

Cryptography

This chapter is supplemental to and coordinated with the Cryptography chapter in the *CISSP Prep Guide*. The fundamentals of cryptography are covered in Chapter 4 of the *CISSP Prep Guide* at a level commensurate with that of the CISSP Examination.

Topics covered in this chapter include:

- British Standard 7799/ISO Standard 17799
- Digital cash
- Digital certificates
- Digital signatures
- Elliptic curves
- Escrowed encryption
- Quantum computing
- The 802.11 Wireless LAN Standard
- The Advanced Encryption Standard (Rijndael)
- The Wireless Application Protocol (WAP)
- Transport Layer Security (TLS)

- Triple DES
- Wired Equivalency Privacy (WEP)
- Wireless Transport Layer Security (WTLS)

It is assumed that the reader has a basic knowledge of the material contained in Chapter 4 and has the *CISSP Prep Guide* available to provide background information for the advanced cryptography questions. These questions and answers build upon the cryptography questions and answers covered in the *CISSP Prep Guide*.

Advanced Sample Questions

1. A cryptographic algorithm is also known as:
   a. A cryptosystem
   b. Cryptanalysis
   c. A cipher
   d. A key

2. Which of the following is NOT an issue with secret key cryptography?
   a. Security of the certification authority.
   b. A networked group of m users with separate keys for each pair of users will require m (m-1)/2 keys.
   c. Secure distribution of the keys.
   d. Compromise of the keys can enable the attacker to impersonate the key owners and, therefore, read and send false messages.

3. Which of the following is NOT a characteristic of the ElGamal public key cryptosystem?
   a. It can perform encryption.
   b. It can be used to generate digital signatures.
   c. It is based on the discrete logarithm problem.
   d. It can perform encryption, but not digital signatures.

4. The Transport Layer Security (TLS) 1.0 protocol is based on which Protocol Specification?
   a. SSH-2
   b. SSL-3.0
   c. IPSEC
   d. TCP/IP

5. The primary goal of the TLS Protocol is to provide:
   a. Privacy and authentication between two communicating applications
   b. Privacy and data integrity between two communicating applications
   c. Authentication and data integrity between two communicating applications
   d. Privacy, authentication, and data integrity between two communicating applications

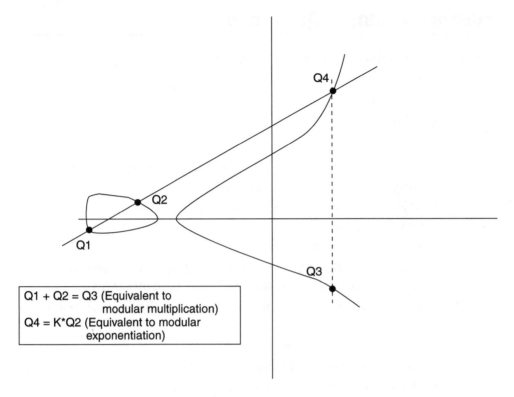

Figure 4.1 Graph of the function $y^2 = x^3 + ax + b$.

6. The graph in Figure 4.1, which depicts the equation $y^2 = x^3 + ax + b$, denotes the:

   a. Elliptic curve and the elliptic curve discrete logarithm problem

   b. RSA Factoring problem

   c. ElGamal discrete logarithm problem

   d. Knapsack problem

7. In communications between two parties, encrypting the hash function of a message with a symmetric key algorithm is equivalent to:

   a. Generating a digital signature

   b. Providing for secrecy of the message

   c. Generating a one-way function

   d. Generating a keyed Message Authentication Code (MAC)

8. Which of the following is NOT a characteristic of a cryptographic hash function, H (m), where m denotes the message being hashed by the function H?

   a. H (m) is collision-free.

   b. H (m) is difficult to compute for any given m.

   c. The output is of fixed length.

   d. H (m) is a one-way function.

9. Which one of the following statements BEST describes the operation of the Digital Signature Algorithm (DSA) (National Institute of Standards and Technology, NIST FIPS PUB 186, "Digital Signature Standard," U.S. Department of Commerce, May 1994) at the transmitting end of a communication between two parties?

   a. A message of $< 2^{64}$ bits is input to the DSA, and the resultant message digest of 160 bits is fed into the Secure Hash Algorithm (SHA), which generates the digital signature of the message.

   b. A message of $< 2^{64}$ bits is input to the Secure Hash Algorithm (SHA), and the resultant message digest of 128 bits is fed into the DSA, which generates the digital signature of the message.

   c. A message of $< 2^{64}$ bits is input to the Secure Hash Algorithm (SHA), and the resultant message digest of 160 bits is used as the digital signature of the message.

   d. A message of $< 2^{64}$ bits is input to the Secure Hash Algorithm (SHA), and the resultant message digest of 160 bits is fed into the DSA, which generates the digital signature of the message.

10. If the application of a hash function results in an m-bit fixed length output, an attack on the hash function that attempts to achieve a collision after $2^{m/2}$ possible trial input values is called a(n):

    a. Adaptive-chosen-plaintext attack

    b. Chosen-ciphertext attack

    c. Birthday attack

    d. Meet-in-the-middle attack

11. The minimum information necessary on a digital certificate is:

    a. Name, expiration date, digital signature of the certifier

    b. Name, expiration date, public key

    c. Name, serial number, private key

    d. Name, public key, digital signature of the certifier

12. What do the message digest algorithms MD2, MD4, and MD5 have in common?

    a. They all take a message of arbitrary length and produce a message digest of 160-bits.

    b. They all take a message of arbitrary length and produce a message digest of 128-bits.

    c. They are all optimized for 32-bit machines.

    d. They are all used in the Secure Hash Algorithm (SHA).

13. What is the correct sequence which enables an authorized agency to use the Law Enforcement Access Field (LEAF) to decrypt a message sent by using the Clipper Chip? (The following designations are used for the respective keys involved—K_f, the family key; K_s, the session key; U, a unique identifier for each Clipper Chip, and K_u, the unit key that is unique to each Clipper Chip.)

    a. Obtain a court order to acquire the two halves of K_u, the unit key. Recover K_u. Decrypt the LEAF with K_u and then recover K_s, the session key. Use the session key to decrypt the message.

    b. Decrypt the LEAF with the family key, K_f; recover U; obtain a court order to obtain the two halves of K_u; recover K_u; and then recover K_s, the session key. Use the session key to decrypt the message.

    c. Decrypt the LEAF with the family key, K_f; recover U; obtain a court order to obtain K_s, the session key. Use the session key to decrypt the message.

    d. Obtain a court order to acquire the family key, K_f; recover U and K_u; then recover K_s, the session key. Use the session key to decrypt the message.

14. What BEST describes the National Security Agency-developed Capstone?

    a. A device for intercepting electromagnetic emissions

    b. The PC Card implementation of the Clipper Chip system

    c. A chip that implements the U. S. Escrowed Encryption Standard

    d. A one-way function for implementation of public key encryption

15. Which of the following BEST describes a block cipher?

    a. A symmetric key algorithm that operates on a variable-length block of plaintext and transforms it into a fixed-length block of ciphertext

    b. A symmetric key algorithm that operates on a fixed-length block of plaintext and transforms it into a fixed-length block of ciphertext

    c. An asymmetric key algorithm that operates on a variable-length block of plaintext and transforms it into a fixed-length block of ciphertext

    d. An asymmetric key algorithm that operates on a fixed-length block of plaintext and transforms it into a fixed-length block of ciphertext

16. An iterated block cipher encrypts by breaking the plaintext block into two halves and, with a subkey, applying a "round" transformation to one of the halves. Then, the output of this transformation is XORed with the remaining half. The round is completed by swapping the two halves. This type of cipher is known as:

    a. RC4

    b. Diffie-Hellman

    c. RC6

    d. Feistel

17. A key schedule is:

    a. A list of cryptographic keys to be used at specified dates and times

    b. A method of generating keys by the use of random numbers

    c. A set of subkeys derived from a secret key

    d. Using distributed computing resources to conduct a brute force attack on a symmetric algorithm

18. The Wireless Transport Layer Security (WTLS) Protocol in the Wireless Application Protocol (WAP) stack is based on which Internet Security Protocol?

    a. S-HTTP

    b. TLS

    c. SET

    d. IPSEC

19. The Advanced Encryption Standard (Rijndael) block cipher requirements regarding keys and block sizes have now evolved to which configuration?

    a. Both the key and block sizes can be 128, 192, and 256 bits each.

    b. The key size is 128 bits, and the block size can be 128, 192, or 256 bits.

    c. The block size is 128 bits, and the key can be 128, 192, or 256 bits.

    d. The block size is 128 bits, and the key size is 128 bits.

20. The Wireless Transport Layer Security Protocol (WTLS) in the Wireless Application Protocol (WAP) stack provides for security:

    a. Between the WAP gateway and the content server

    b. Between the WAP client and the gateway

    c. Between the Internet and the content server

    d. Between the WAP content server and the WAP client

21. What is a protocol that adds digital signatures and encryption to Internet MIME (Multipurpose Internet Mail Extensions)?

    a. IPSEC

    b. PGP

c. S/MIME

d. SET/MIME

22. Digital cash refers to the electronic transfer of funds from one party to another. When digital cash is referred to as anonymous or identified, it means that:

a. Anonymous—the identity of the cash holder is not known; Identified—the identity of the cash holder is known

b. Anonymous—the identity of merchant is withheld; Identified—the identity of the merchant is not withheld

c. Anonymous—the identity of the bank is withheld; Identified—the identity of the bank is not withheld

d. Anonymous—the identity of the cash holder is not known; Identified—the identity of the merchant is known

23. Which of the following is NOT a key recovery method?

a. A message is encrypted with a session key and the session key is, in turn, encrypted with the public key of a trustee agent. The encrypted session key is sent along with the encrypted message. The trustee, when authorized, can then decrypt the message by recovering the session key with the trustee's private key.

b. A message is encrypted with a session key. The session key, in turn, is broken into parts and each part is encrypted with the public key of a different trustee agent. The encrypted parts of the session key are sent along with the encrypted message. The trustees, when authorized, can then decrypt their portion of the session key and provide their respective parts of the session key to a central agent. The central agent can then decrypt the message by reconstructing the session key from the individual components.

c. A secret key or a private key is broken into a number of parts and each part is deposited with a trustee agent. The agents can then provide their parts of the key to a central authority, when presented with appropriate authorization. The key can then be reconstructed and used to decrypt messages encrypted with that key.

d. A message is encrypted with a session key and the session key is, in turn, encrypted with the private key of a trustee agent. The encrypted session key is sent along with the encrypted message. The trustee, when authorized, can then decrypt the message by recovering the session key with the trustee's public key.

24. Theoretically, quantum computing offers the possibility of factoring the products of large prime numbers and calculating discreet logarithms in

polynomial time. These calculations can be accomplished in such a compressed time frame because:

   a. Information can be transformed into quantum light waves that travel through fiber optic channels. Computations can be performed on the associated data by passing the light waves through various types of optical filters and solid-state materials with varying indices of refraction, thus drastically increasing the throughput over conventional computations.

   b. A quantum bit in a quantum computer is actually a linear superposition of both the one and zero states and, therefore, can theoretically represent both values in parallel. This phenomenon allows computation that usually takes exponential time to be accomplished in polynomial time since different values of the binary pattern of the solution can be calculated simultaneously.

   c. A quantum computer takes advantage of quantum tunneling in molecular scale transistors. This mode permits ultra high-speed switching to take place, thus exponentially increasing the speed of computations.

   d. A quantum computer exploits the time-space relationship that changes as particles approach the speed of light. At that interface, the resistance of conducting materials effectively is zero and exponential speed computations are possible.

25. Which of the following statements BEST describes the Public Key Cryptography Standards (PKCS)?

   a. A set of public-key cryptography standards that support algorithms such as Diffie-Hellman and RSA as well as algorithm-independent standards

   b. A set of public-key cryptography standards that support only "standard" algorithms such as Diffie-Hellman and RSA

   c. A set of public-key cryptography standards that support only algorithm-independent implementations

   d. A set of public-key cryptography standards that support encryption algorithms such as Diffie-Hellman and RSA, but does not address digital signatures

26. An interface to a library of software functions that provide security and cryptography services is called:

   a. A security application programming interface (SAPI)

   b. An assurance application programming interface (AAPI)

   c. A cryptographic application programming interface (CAPI)

   d. A confidentiality, integrity, and availability application programming interface (CIAAPI)

27. The British Standard 7799/ISO Standard 17799 discusses cryptographic policies. It states, "An organization should develop a policy on its use of cryptographic controls for protection of its information. . . . When developing a policy, the following should be considered:" (Which of the following items would most likely NOT be listed?)

    a. The management approach toward the use of cryptographic controls across the organization

    b. The approach to key management, including methods to deal with the recovery of encrypted information in the case of lost, compromised or damaged keys

    c. Roles and responsibilities

    d. The encryption schemes to be used

28. The Number Field Sieve (NFS) is a:

    a. General purpose factoring algorithm that can be used to factor large numbers

    b. General purpose algorithm to calculate discreet logarithms

    c. General purpose algorithm used for brute force attacks on secret key cryptosystems

    d. General purpose hash algorithm

29. DESX is a variant of DES in which:

    a. Input plaintext is bitwise XORed with 64 bits of additional key material before encryption with DES.

    b. Input plaintext is bitwise XORed with 64 bits of additional key material before encryption with DES, and the output of DES is also bitwise XORed with another 64 bits of key material.

    c. The output of DES is bitwise XORed with 64 bits of key material.

    d. The input plaintext is encrypted X times with the DES algorithm using different keys for each encryption.

30. The ANSI X9.52 standard defines a variant of DES encryption with keys k1, k2, and k3 as:

    $C = E_{k3} [D_{k2} [E_{k1} [M]]]$

    What is this DES variant?

    a. DESX

    b. Triple DES in the EEE mode

    c. Double DES with an encryption and decryption with different keys

    d. Triple DES in the EDE mode

31. Using a modulo 26 substitution cipher where the letters A to Z of the alphabet are given a value of 0 to 25, respectively, encrypt the message "OVER-

LORD BEGINS." Use the key K = NEW and D = 3 where D is the number of repeating letters representing the key. The encrypted message is:

a. BFAEQKEH XRKFAW

b. BFAEPKEH XRKFAW

c. BFAEPKEH XRKEAW

d. BFAERKEH XRKEAW

32. The algorithm of the 802.11 Wireless LAN Standard that is used to protect transmitted information from disclosure is called:

a. Wireless Application Environment (WAE)

b. Wired Equivalency Privacy (WEP)

c. Wireless Transaction Protocol (WTP)

d. Wireless Transport Layer Security Protocol (WTLS)

33. The Wired Equivalency Privacy algorithm (WEP) of the 802.11 Wireless LAN Standard uses which of the following to protect the confidentiality of information being transmitted on the LAN?

a. A secret key that is shared between a mobile station (e.g., a laptop with a wireless Ethernet card) and a base station access point

b. A public/private key pair that is shared between a mobile station (e.g., a laptop with a wireless Ethernet card) and a base station access point

c. Frequency shift keying (FSK) of the message that is sent between a mobile station (e.g., a laptop with a wireless Ethernet card) and a base station access point

d. A digital signature that is sent between a mobile station (e.g., a laptop with a wireless Ethernet card) and a base station access point

34. In a block cipher, diffusion can be accomplished through:

a. Substitution

b. XORing

c. Non-linear S-boxes

d. Permutation

35. The National Computer Security Center (NCSC) is:

a. A division of the National Institute of Standards and Technology (NIST) that issues standards for cryptographic functions and publishes them as Federal Information Processing Standards (FIPS)

b. A branch of the National Security Agency (NSA) that initiates research and develops and publishes standards and criteria for trusted information systems

    c. A joint enterprise between the NSA and NIST for developing cryptographic algorithms and standards

    d. An activity within the U.S. Department of Commerce that provides information security awareness training and develops standards for protecting sensitive but unclassified information

36. A portion of a Vigenère cipher square is given below using five (1, 2, 14, 16, 22) of the possible 26 alphabets. Using the key word bow, which of the following is the encryption of the word "advance" using the Vigenère cipher in Table 4.1?

    a. b r r b b y h

    b. b r r b j y f

    c. b r r b b y f

    d. b r r b c y f

37. There are two fundamental security protocols in IPSEC. These are the Authentication Header (AH) and the Encapsulating Security Payload (ESP). Which of the following correctly describes the functions of each?

    a. ESP—data encrypting protocol that also validates the integrity of the transmitted data; AH—source authenticating protocol that also validates the integrity of the transmitted data

    b. ESP—data encrypting and source authenticating protocol; AH—source authenticating protocol that also validates the integrity of the transmitted data

    c. ESP—data encrypting and source authenticating protocol that also validates the integrity of the transmitted data; AH—source authenticating protocol

    d. ESP—data encrypting and source authenticating protocol that also validates the integrity of the transmitted data; AH—source authenticating protocol that also validates the integrity of the transmitted data

38. Which of the following is NOT an advantage of a stream cipher?

    a. The same equipment can be used for encryption and decryption.

    b. It is amenable to hardware implementations that result in higher speeds.

    c. Since encryption takes place bit by bit, there is no error propagation.

    d. The receiver and transmitter must be synchronized.

39. Which of the following is NOT a property of a public key cryptosystem? (Let P represent the private key, Q represent the public key, and M the plaintext message.)

    a. $Q[P(M)] = M$

    b. $P[Q(M)] = M$

Table **4.1** Vigenère Cipher

PLAINTEXT	A	B	C	D	E	F	G	H	I	J	K	L	M	N	O	P	Q	R	S	T	U	V	W	X	Y	Z
1	b	c	d	e	f	g	h	i	j	k	l	m	n	o	p	q	r	s	t	u	v	w	x	y	z	a
2	c	d	e	f	g	h	i	j	k	l	m	n	o	p	q	r	s	t	u	v	w	x	y	z	a	b
14	o	p	q	r	s	t	u	v	w	x	y	z	a	b	c	d	e	f	g	h	i	j	k	l	m	n
16	q	r	s	t	u	v	w	x	y	z	a	b	c	d	e	f	g	h	i	j	k	l	m	n	o	p
22	w	x	y	z	a	b	c	d	e	f	g	h	i	j	k	l	m	n	o	p	q	r	s	t	u	v

c. It is computationally infeasible to derive P from Q.

d. P and Q are difficult to generate from a particular key value.

40. A form of digital signature where the signer is not privy to the content of the message is called a:

a. Zero knowledge proof

b. Blind signature

c. Masked signature

d. Encrypted signature

41. The following compilation represents what facet of cryptanalysis?

A	8.2	N	6.7
B	1.5	O	7.5
C	2.8	P	1.9
D	4.3	Q	0.1
E	12.7	R	6.0
F	2.2	S	6.3
G	2.0	T	9.1
H	6.1	U	2.8
I	7.0	V	1.0
J	0.2	W	2.4
K	0.8	X	0.2
L	4.0	Y	2.0
M	2.4		

a. Z 0.1 Period analysis

b. Frequency analysis

c. Cilly analysis

d. Cartouche analysis

CHAPTER

5

Security Architecture and Models

This chapter is supplemental to and coordinated with the Security Architecture and Models chapter in the *CISSP Prep Guide*. The fundamentals of security architecture and models are covered in Chapter 5 of the *CISSP Prep Guide* at a level commensurate with that of the CISSP Examination.

This chapter includes advanced material relative to computer architectures, computer hardware, the Java security model, multilevel security, security models and their properties, Trusted Computer Systems, the Common Criteria, ITSEC, TCSEC, HIPAA privacy, HIPAA security, HIPAA transactions, HIPAA code sets, the Gramm-Leach-Bliley Act, privacy, NIACAP, DITSCAP, P3P and FedCIRC.

It is assumed that the reader has a basic knowledge of the material contained in Chapter 5 and has the *CISSP Prep Guide* available to provide background information for the advanced questions pertaining to security architecture and models. These questions and answers build upon the questions and answers covered in Chapter 5 of the *CISSP Prep Guide*.

Advanced Sample Questions

1. When microcomputers were first developed, the instruction fetch time was much longer than the instruction execution time because of the relatively slow speed of memory accesses. This situation led to the design of the:

   a. Reduced Instruction Set Computer (RISC)

   b. Complex Instruction Set Computer (CISC)

   c. Superscalar processor

   d. Very-long-instruction-word (VLIW) processor

2. The main objective of the Java Security Model (JSM) is to:

   a. Protect the user from hostile, network mobile code

   b. Protect a web server from hostile, client code

   c. Protect the local client from hostile, user-input code

   d. Provide accountability for events

3. Which of the following would NOT be a component of a general enterprise security architecture model for an organization?

   a. Information and resources to ensure the appropriate level of risk management

   b. Consideration of all the items that comprise information security, including distributed systems, software, hardware, communications systems and networks

   c. A systematic and unified approach for evaluating the organization's information systems security infrastructure and defining approaches to implementation and deployment of information security controls

   d. IT system auditing

4. In a multilevel security system (MLS), the Pump is:

   a. A two-way information flow device

   b. A one-way information flow device

   c. Compartmented Mode Workstation (CMW)

   d. A device that implements role-based access control

5. The Bell-LaPadula model addresses which one of the following items?

   a. Covert channels

   b. The creation and destruction of subjects and objects

   c. Information flow from high to low

   d. Definition of a secure state transition

6. In order to recognize the practical aspects of multilevel security in which, for example, an unclassified paragraph in a Secret document has to be moved to an Unclassified document, the Bell-LaPadula model introduces the concept of a:

   a. Simple security property

   b. Secure exchange

   c. Data flow

   d. Trusted subject

7. In a refinement of the Bell–LaPadula model, the *strong tranquility property* states that:

   a. Objects never change their security level.

   b. Objects never change their security level in a way that would violate the system security policy.

   c. Objects can change their security level in an unconstrained fashion.

   d. Subjects can read up.

8. As an analog of confidentiality labels, integrity labels in the Biba model are assigned according to which of the following rules?

   a. Objects are assigned integrity labels identical to the corresponding confidentiality labels.

   b. Objects are assigned integrity labels according to their trustworthiness; subjects are assigned classes according to the harm that would be done if the data were modified improperly.

   c. Subjects are assigned classes according to their trustworthiness; objects are assigned integrity labels according to the harm that would be done if the data were modified improperly.

   d. Integrity labels are assigned according to the harm that would occur from unauthorized disclosure of the information.

9. The Clark-Wilson Integrity Model (D. Clark, D. Wilson, "A Comparison of Commercial and Military Computer Security Policies," *Proceedings of the 1987 IEEE Computer Society Symposium on Research in Security and Privacy, Los Alamitos, CA, IEEE Computer Society Press, 1987*) focuses on what two concepts?

   a. Separation of duty and well-formed transactions

   b. Least privilege and well-formed transactions

   c. Capability lists and domains

   d. Well-formed transactions and denial of service

10. The model that addresses the situation wherein one group is not affected by another group using specific commands is called the:

    a. Information flow model

    b. Non-interference model

    c. Composition model

    d. Clark-Wilson model

11. The secure path between a user and the Trusted Computing Base (TCB) is called:

    a. Trusted distribution

    b. Trusted path

    c. Trusted facility management

    d. The security perimeter

12. The Common Criteria terminology for the degree of examination of the product to be tested is:

    a. Target of Evaluation (TOE)

    b. Protection Profile (PP)

    c. Functionality (F)

    d. Evaluation Assurance Level (EAL)

13. A difference between the Information Technology Security Evaluation Criteria (ITSEC) and the Trusted Computer System Evaluation Criteria (TCSEC) is:

    a. TCSEC addresses availability as well as confidentiality

    b. ITSEC addresses confidentiality only

    c. ITSEC addresses integrity and availability as well as confidentiality

    d. TCSEC separates functionality and assurance

14. Which of the following items BEST describes the standards addressed by Title II, Administrative Simplification, of the Health Insurance Portability and Accountability Act (U.S. *Kennedy-Kassenbaum Health Insurance and Portability Accountability Act -HIPAA-Public Law 104-19)*?

    a. Transaction Standards, to include Code Sets; Unique Health Identifiers; Security and Electronic Signatures and Privacy

    b. Transaction Standards, to include Code Sets; Security and Electronic Signatures and Privacy

    c. Unique Health Identifiers; Security and Electronic Signatures and Privacy

    d. Security and Electronic Signatures and Privacy

15. Which one of the following is generally NOT considered a covered entity under Title II, Administrative Simplification, of the HIPAA law?
    a. Health care providers who transmit health information electronically in connection with standard transactions
    b. Health plans
    c. Employers
    d. Health care clearinghouses

16. The principles of Notice, Choice, Access, Security, and Enforcement refer to which of the following?
    a. Authorization
    b. Privacy
    c. Nonrepudiation
    d. Authentication

17. The simple security property of which one of the following models is described as:

    "A user has access to a client company's information, c, if and only if for all other information, o, that the user can read, either $x(c) \neq z(o)$ or $x(c) = x(o)$, where $x(c)$ is the client's company and $z(o)$ are the competitors of $x(c)$."

    a. Biba
    b. Lattice
    c. Bell-LaPadula
    d. Chinese wall

18. The two categories of the policy of *separation of duty* are:
    a. Span of control and functional separation
    b. Inference control and functional separation
    c. Dual control and functional separation
    d. Dual control and aggregation control

19. In the National Information Assurance Certification and Accreditation Process (NIACAP), a *type accreditation* performs which one of the following functions?
    a. Evaluates a major application or general support system
    b. Verifies the evolving or modified system's compliance with the information agreed on in the System Security Authorization Agreement (SSAA)
    c. Evaluates an application or system that is distributed to a number of different locations
    d. Evaluates the applications and systems at a specific, self-contained location

20. Which of the following processes establishes the minimum national standards for certifying and accrediting national security systems?

    a. CIAP

    b. DITSCAP

    c. NIACAP

    d. Defense audit

21. Which of the following terms is NOT associated with a Read Only Memory (ROM)?

    a. Flash memory

    b. Field Programmable Gate Array (FPGA)

    c. Static RAM (SRAM)

    d. Firmware

22. Serial data transmission in which information can be transmitted in two directions, but only one direction at a time is called:

    a. Simplex

    b. Half-duplex

    c. Synchronized

    d. Full-duplex

23. The ANSI ASC X12 (American National Standards Institute Accredited Standards Committee X12) Standard version 4010 applies to which one of the following HIPAA categories?

    a. Privacy

    b. Code sets

    c. Transactions

    d. Security

24. A 1999 law that addresses privacy issues related to health care, insurance, and finance and that will implemented by the states is:

    a. Gramm-Leach-Bliley (GLB)

    b. Kennedy-Kassebaum

    c. the Medical Action Bill

    d. the Insurance Reform Act

25. The Platform for Privacy Preferences (P3P) was developed by the World Wide Web Consortium (W3C) for what purpose?

    a. To implement public key cryptography for transactions

    b. To evaluate a client's privacy practices

    c. To monitor users

    d. To implement privacy practices on Web sites

26. What process is used to accomplish high-speed data transfer between a peripheral device and computer memory, bypassing the Central Processing Unit (CPU)?

    a. Direct memory access

    b. Interrupt processing

    c. Transfer under program control

    d. Direct access control

27. An associative memory operates in which one of the following ways?

    a. Uses indirect addressing only

    b. Searches for values in memory exceeding a specified value

    c. Searches for a specific data value in memory

    d. Returns values stored in a memory address location specified in the CPU address register

28. The following concerns usually apply to what type of architecture?

    ■ Desktop systems can contain sensitive information that may be at risk of being exposed.

    ■ Users may generally lack security awareness.

    ■ Modems present a vulnerability to dial-in attacks.

    ■ Lack of proper backup may exist.

    a. Distributed

    b. Centralized

    c. Open system

    d. Symmetric

29. The definition "A relatively small amount (when compared to primary memory) of very high speed RAM, which holds the instructions and data from primary memory, that has a high probability of being accessed during the currently executing portion of a program" refers to what category of computer memory?

    a. Secondary

    b. Real

    c. Cache

    d. Virtual

30. The organization that "establishes a collaborative partnership of computer incident response, security and law enforcement professionals who work together to handle computer security incidents and to provide both proactive and reactive security services for the U.S. Federal government" is called:

    a. CERT/CC

    b. Center for Infrastructure Protection

    c. Federal CIO Council

    d. Federal Computer Incident Response Center

CHAPTER

6

Operations Security

This chapter is supplemental to and coordinated with the Operations Security chapter in the *CISSP Prep Guide*. The fundamentals of operations security are covered in Chapter 6 of the *CISSP Prep Guide* at a level on par with that of the CISSP Examination.

It is assumed that the reader has a basic knowledge of the material contained in Chapter 6 and has the *CISSP Prep Guide* available to provide background information for the advanced questions pertaining to the Operations Security chapter.

In the Operations Security questions areas we will discuss the Rainbow series, data remanence, the Common Criteria, configuration management, and various security terminology.

Advanced Sample Questions

1. Which book of the Rainbow series addresses the Trusted Network Interpretation (TNI)?

    a. Red Book

    b. Orange Book

    c. Green Book

    d. Purple Book

2. Which choice describes the Forest Green Book?

    a. It is a tool that assists vendors in data gathering for certifiers.

    b. It is a Rainbow series book that defines the secure handling of storage media.

    c. It is a Rainbow series book that defines guidelines for implementing access control lists.

    d. It does not exist; there is no "Forest Green Book."

3. Which term below BEST describes the concept of "least privilege"?

    a. Each user is granted the lowest clearance required for their tasks.

    b. A formal separation of command, program, and interface functions.

    c. A combination of classification and categories that represents the sensitivity of information.

    d. Active monitoring of facility entry access points.

4. Which general TCSEC security class category describes that mandatory access policies be enforced in the TCB?

    a. A

    b. B

    c. C

    d. D

5. Which statement below is the BEST definition of "need-to-know"?

    a. Need-to-know ensures that no single individual (acting alone) can compromise security controls.

    b. Need-to-know grants each user the lowest clearance required for their tasks.

    c. Need-to-know limits the time an operator performs a task.

    d. Need-to-know requires that the operator have the minimum knowledge of the system necessary to perform his task.

6. Place the four systems security modes of operation in order, from the most secure to the least:

   _____ a. Dedicated Mode

   _____ b. Multilevel Mode

   _____ c. Compartmented Mode

   _____ d. System High Mode

7. Which media control below is the BEST choice to prevent data remanence on magnetic tapes or floppy disks?

   a. Overwriting the media with new application data

   b. Degaussing the media

   c. Applying a concentration of hydriodic acid (55% to 58% solution) to the gamma ferric oxide disk surface

   d. Making sure the disk is re-circulated as quickly as possible to prevent object reuse

8. Which choice below is the BEST description of an audit trail?

   a. Audit trails are used to detect penetration of a computer system and to reveal usage that identifies misuse.

   b. An audit trail is a device that permits simultaneous data processing of two or more security levels without risk of compromise.

   c. An audit trail mediates all access to objects within the network by subjects within the network.

   d. Audit trails are used to prevent access to sensitive systems by unauthorized personnel.

9. Which TCSEC security class category below specifies "trusted recovery" controls?

   a. C2

   b. B1

   c. B2

   d. B3

10. Which choice does NOT describe an element of configuration management?

    a. Configuration management involves information capture and version control.

    b. Configuration management reports the status of change processing.

    c. Configuration management is the decomposition process of a verification system into Configuration Items (CIs).

    d. Configuration management documents the functional and physical characteristics of each configuration item.

11. Which choice below does NOT accurately describe a task of the Configuration Control Board?

    a. The CCB should meet periodically to discuss configuration status accounting reports.

    b. The CCB is responsible for documenting the status of configuration control activities.

    c. The CCB is responsible for assuring that changes made do not jeopardize the soundness of the verification system.

    d. The CCB assures that the changes made are approved, tested, documented, and implemented correctly.

12. Which choice below is NOT a security goal of an audit mechanism?

    a. Deter perpetrators' attempts to bypass the system protection mechanisms

    b. Review employee production output records

    c. Review patterns of access to individual objects

    d. Discover when a user assumes a functionality with privileges greater than his own

13. Which choice below is NOT a common element of user account administration?

    a. Periodically verifying the legitimacy of current accounts and access authorizations

    b. Authorizing the request for a user's system account

    c. Tracking users and their respective access authorizations

    d. Establishing, issuing, and closing user accounts

14. Which element of Configuration Management listed below involves the use of Configuration Items (CIs)?

    a. Configuration Accounting

    b. Configuration Audit

    c. Configuration Control

    d. Configuration Identification

15. Which standard defines the International Standard for the Common Criteria?

    a. IS15408

    b. BS7799

    c. DoD 5200.28-STD

    d. CSC-STD-002-85

16. Which statement below is NOT correct about reviewing user accounts?

    a. User account reviews cannot be conducted by outside auditors.

    b. User account reviews can examine conformity with least privilege.

    c. User account reviews may be conducted on a system-wide basis.

    d. User account reviews may be conducted on an application-by-application basis.

17. Which statement below MOST accurately describes configuration control?

    a. The decomposition process of a verification system into CIs

    b. Assuring that only the proposed and approved system changes are implemented

    c. Tracking the status of current changes as they move through the configuration control process

    d. Verifying that all configuration management policies are being followed

18. Which term below MOST accurately describes the Trusted Computing Base (TCB)?

    a. A computer that controls all access to objects by subjects

    b. A piece of information that represents the security level of an object

    c. Formal proofs used to demonstrate the consistency between a system's specification and a security model

    d. The totality of protection mechanisms within a computer system

19. Which choice below would NOT be considered a benefit of employing incident-handling capability?

    a. An individual acting alone would not be able to subvert a security process or control.

    b. It enhances internal communications and the readiness of the organization to respond to incidents.

    c. It assists an organization in preventing damage from future incidents.

    d. Security training personnel would have a better understanding of users' knowledge of security issues.

20. Which statement below is accurate about Evaluation Assurance Levels (EALs) in the Common Criteria (CC)?

    a. A security level equal to the security level of the objects to which the subject has both read and write access

    b. A statement of intent to counter specified threats

c. Requirements that specify the security behavior of an IT product or system

d. Predefined packages of assurance components that make up the security confidence rating scale

21. Which choice below is the BEST description of operational assurance?

a. Operational assurance is the process of examining audit logs to reveal usage that identifies misuse.

b. Operational assurance has the benefit of containing and repairing damage from incidents.

c. Operational assurance is the process of reviewing an operational system to see that security controls are functioning correctly.

d. Operational assurance is the process of performing pre-employment background screening.

22. Which choice below MOST accurately describes a Covert Storage Channel?

a. A process that manipulates observable system resources in a way that affects response time

b. An information transfer path within a system

c. A communication channel that allows a process to transfer information in a manner that violates the system's security policy

d. An information transfer that involves the direct or indirect writing of a storage location by one process and the direct or indirect reading of the storage location by another process

23. Which choice below is the BEST description of a Protection Profile (PP), as defined by the Common Criteria (CC)?

a. A statement of security claims for a particular IT security product

b. A reusable definition of product security requirements

c. An intermediate combination of security requirement components

d. The IT product or system to be evaluated

24. Which choice below is NOT one of the four major aspects of configuration management?

a. Configuration status accounting

b. Configuration product evaluation

c. Configuration auditing

d. Configuration identification

25. Which choice below MOST accurately describes "partitioned security mode"?

a. All personnel have the clearance and formal access approval.

b. All personnel have the clearance but not necessarily formal access approval.

    c. The only state in which certain privileged instructions may be executed.

    d. A system containing information accessed by personnel with different security clearances.

26. Which choice below is NOT an example of a media control?

    a. Sanitizing the media before disposition

    b. Printing to a printer in a secured room

    c. Physically protecting copies of backup media

    d. Conducting background checks on individuals

27. Which statement below is the BEST example of "separation of duties"?

    a. An activity that checks on the system, its users, or the environment.

    b. Getting users to divulge their passwords.

    c. One person initiates a request for a payment and another authorizes that same payment.

    d. A data entry clerk may not have access to run database analysis reports.

28. Which minimum TCSEC security class category specifies "trusted distribution" controls?

    a. C2

    b. B2

    c. B3

    d. A1

29. Which statement is accurate about "trusted facility management"?

    a. The role of a security administrator shall be identified and auditable in C2 systems and above.

    b. The role of a security administrator shall be identified and auditable in B2 systems and above.

    c. The TCB shall support separate operator and administrator functions for C2 systems and above.

    d. The TCB shall support separate operator and administrator functions for B2 systems and above.

30. Which statement below is accurate about the concept of Object Reuse?

    a. Object reuse protects against physical attacks on the storage medium.

    b. Object reuse ensures that users do not obtain residual information from system resources.

    c. Object reuse applies to removable media only.

    d. Object reuse controls the granting of access rights to objects.

Applications and Systems Development

This chapter is supplemental to and coordinated with the Applications and Systems Development chapter in the *CISSP Prep Guide*. The fundamentals of applications and systems development are covered in Chapter 7 of the *CISSP Prep Guide* at a level commensurate with that of the CISSP Examination.

This chapter includes advanced material relative to software engineering, software development, the software capability maturity model (CMM), object-oriented systems, expert systems, neural networks, genetic algorithms, databases, the data warehouse, data mining, the Common Object Model (COM), client/server architecture and distributed data processing.

It is assumed that the reader has a basic knowledge of the material contained in Chapter 7 and has the *CISSP Prep Guide* available to provide background information for the advanced questions pertaining to applications and systems development. These questions and answers build upon the questions and answers covered in Chapter 7 of the *CISSP Prep Guide*.

Advanced Sample Questions

1. The definition "the science and art of specifying, designing, implementing and evolving programs, documentation and operating procedures whereby computers can be made useful to man" is that of:

   a. Structured analysis/structured design (SA/SD)

   b. Software engineering

   c. An object-oriented system

   d. Functional programming

2. In software engineering, the term *verification* is defined as:

   a. To establish the truth of correspondence between a software product and its specification

   b. A complete, validated specification of the required functions, interfaces, and performance for the software product

   c. To establish the fitness or worth of a software product for its operational mission

   d. A complete, verified specification of the overall hardware-software architecture, control structure, and data structure for the product

3. The discipline of identifying the components of a continually evolving system for the purposes of controlling changes to those components and maintaining integrity and traceability throughout the life cycle is called:

   a. Change control

   b. Request control

   c. Release control

   d. Configuration management

4. The basic version of the Construction Cost Model (COCOMO), which proposes quantitative, life-cycle relationships, performs what function?

   a. Estimates software development effort based on user function categories

   b. Estimates software development effort and cost as a function of the size of the software product in source instructions

   c. Estimates software development effort and cost as a function of the size of the software product in source instructions modified by manpower buildup and productivity factors

   d. Estimates software development effort and cost as a function of the size of the software product in source instructions modified by hardware and input functions

5. A refinement to the basic Waterfall Model that states that software should be developed in increments of functional capability is called:

   a. Functional refinement

   b. Functional development

   c. Incremental refinement

   d. Incremental development

6. The Spiral Model of the software development process (B.W. Boehm, "A Spiral Model of Software Development and Enhancement," *IEEE Computer*, May 1988) uses the following metric relative to the spiral:

   a. The radial dimension represents the cost of each phase

   b. The radial dimension represents progress made in completing each cycle

   c. The angular dimension represents cumulative cost

   d. The radial dimension represents cumulative cost

7. In the Capability Maturity Model (CMM) for software, the definition "describes the range of expected results that can be achieved by following a software process" is that of:

   a. Structured analysis/structured design (SA/SD)

   b. Software process capability

   c. Software process performance

   d. Software process maturity

8. Which of the following is NOT a Software CMM maturity level?

   a. Initial

   b. Repeatable

   c. Behavioral

   d. Managed

9. The main differences between a *software process assessment* and a *software capability evaluation* are:

   a. Software process assessments determine the state of an organization's current software process and are used to gain support from within the organization for a software process improvement program; software capability evaluations are used to identify contractors who are qualified to develop software or to monitor the state of the software process in a current software project.

   b. Software capability evaluations determine the state of an organization's current software process and are used to gain support from within the organization for a software process improvement program; software process assessments are used to identify contractors who are qualified to develop software or to monitor the state of the software process in a current software project.

c. Software process assessments are used to develop a risk profile for source selection; software capability evaluations are used to develop an action plan for continuous process improvement.

d. Software process assessments and software capability evaluations are, essentially, identical and there are no major differences between the two.

10. Which of the following is NOT a common term in object-oriented systems?

a. Behavior

b. Message

c. Method

d. Function

11. In object-oriented programming, when all the methods of one class are passed on to a subclass, this is called:

a. Forward chaining

b. Inheritance

c. Multiple Inheritance

d. Delegation

12. Which of the following languages is NOT an object-oriented language?

a. Smalltalk

b. Simula 67

c. Lisp

d. C++

13. Which of the following items is NOT a component of a knowledge-based system (KBS)?

a. Knowledge base

b. Procedural code

c. Inference Engine

d. Interface between the user and the system

14. In an expert system, the process of beginning with a possible solution and using the knowledge in the knowledge base to justify the solution based on the raw input data is called:

a. Dynamic reasoning

b. Forward chaining

c. Backward chaining

d. A blackboard solution

15. An off-the-shelf software package that implements an inference engine, a mechanism for entering knowledge, a user interface, and a system to provide explanations of the reasoning used to generate a solution is called:

    a. An expert system shell

    b. A knowledge base

    c. A neural network

    d. A knowledge acquisition system

16. What key professional or professionals are required to develop an expert system?

    a. Knowledge engineer and object designer

    b. Knowledge engineer and domain expert

    c. Domain expert

    d. Domain expert and object designer

17. An expert system that has rules of the form "If w is low and x is high then y is intermediate," where w and x are input variables and y is the output variable, is called a:

    a. Neural network

    b. Realistic expert system

    c. Boolean expert system

    d. Fuzzy expert system

18. What is a "subject-oriented, integrated, time-variant, nonvolatile collection of data in support of management's decision-making process"?

    a. Data mart

    b. Data warehouse

    c. Data model

    d. Data architecture

19. The process of analyzing large data sets in a data warehouse to find nonobvious patterns is called:

    a. Data mining

    b. Data scanning

    c. Data administration

    d. Derived data

20. The equation $Z = f\,[\sum w_n\,i_n\,]$, where Z is the output, w_n are weighting functions and i_n is a set of inputs describes:

    a. An expert system

    b. A knowledge-based system

    c. An artificial neural network (ANN)

    d. A knowledge acquisition system

21. A database that comprises tools to support the analysis, design and development of software and support good software engineering practices is called a:

    a. Data model

    b. Database management system (DBMS)

    c. Data dictionary

    d. Data type dictionary

22. Another type of artificial intelligence technology involves genetic algorithms. Genetic algorithms are part of the general class known as:

    a. Neural networks

    b. Suboptimal computing

    c. Evolutionary computing

    d. Biological computing

23. The Object Request Architecture (ORA) is a high-level framework for a distributed environment. It consists of four components. Which of the following items is NOT one of those components?

    a. Object Request Brokers (ORBs)

    b. Object Services

    c. Application Objects

    d. Application Services

24. A standard that uses the Object Request Broker (ORB) to implement exchanges among objects in a heterogeneous, distributed environment is called:

    a. The Object Management Group (OMG) Object Model

    b. A Common Object Request Broker Architecture (CORBA)

    c. Open Architecture

    d. An Interface Definition Language (IDL)

25. Another model that allows two software components to communicate with each other independent of their platforms' operating systems and languages of implementation is:

    a. Common Object Model (COM)

    b. Sandbox

    c. Basic Object Model (BOM)

    d. Spiral Model

26. A distributed object model that has similarities to the Common Object Request Broker Architecture (CORBA) is:

    a. Distributed Component Object Model (DCOM)

    b. The Chinese Wall Model

    c. Inference Model

    d. Distributed Data Model

27. Which of the following is NOT a characteristic of a client in the client/server model?

    a. Extensive user interface

    b. May be diskless

    c. Data entry screens

    d. Systems backup and database protection

28. A client/server implementation approach in which any platform may act as a client or server or both is called:

    a. Simple file transfer

    b. Peer-to-peer

    c. Application Programming Interface (API)

    d. Graphical User Interface (GUI)

29. Which of the following is NOT a characteristic of a distributed data processing (DDP) approach?

    a. Consists of multiple processing locations that can provide alternatives for computing in the event of a site becoming inoperative.

    b. Distances from user to processing resource are transparent to the user.

    c. Security is enhanced because of networked systems.

    d. Data stored at multiple, geographically separate locations is easily available to the user.

30. A database management system (DBMS) is useful in situations where:

   a. Rapid development of applications is required and preprogrammed functions can be used to provide those applications along with other support features such as security, error recovery, and access control.

   b. Data are processed infrequently and results are not urgently needed.

   c. Large amounts of data are to be processed in time-critical situations.

   d. The operations to be performed on the data are modified infrequently and the operations are relatively straightforward.

CHAPTER

8

Business Continuity Planning— Disaster Recovery Planning

This chapter is supplemental to and coordinated with the Business Continuity Planning—Disaster Recovery Planning Chapter in the *CISSP Prep Guide*. The fundamentals of business continuity planning-disaster recovery planning are covered in Chapter 8 of the *CISSP Prep Guide* at a level on par with that of the CISSP Examination.

It is assumed that the reader has a basic knowledge of the material contained in Chapter 8 and has the *CISSP Prep Guide* available to provide background information for the advanced questions pertaining to the Business Continuity Planning—Disaster Recovery Planning chapter. Here we'll discuss business continuity, business resumption, disaster recovery, emergency management, and vulnerability assessments.

Advanced Sample Questions

1. Which choice below is the MOST accurate description of a warm site?

    a. A backup processing facility with adequate electrical wiring and air conditioning, but no hardware or software installed

    b. A backup processing facility with most hardware and software installed, which can be operational within a matter of days

    c. A backup processing facility with all hardware and software installed and 100% compatible with the original site, operational within hours

    d. A mobile trailer with portable generators and air conditioning

2. Which choice below is NOT an accurate description or element of remote sensing technology?

    a. Photographic, radar, infrared, or multi-spectral imagery from manned or unmanned aircraft.

    b. Photographic, radar, infrared, or multi-spectral imagery from land-based tracking stations.

    c. Photographic, radar, infrared, or multi-spectral imagery from geostationary or orbiting satellites.

    d. RS intelligence may be integrated into geographic information systems (GIS) to produce map-based products.

3. Which disaster recovery/emergency management plan testing type below is considered the most cost-effective and efficient way to identify areas of overlap in the plan before conducting more demanding training exercises?

    a. Full-scale exercise

    b. Walk-through drill

    c. Table-top exercise test

    d. Evacuation drill

4. Which task below would normally be considered a BCP task, rather than a DRP task?

    a. Life safety processes

    b. Project scoping

    c. Restoration procedures

    d. Recovery procedures

5. Which choice below is NOT a role or responsibility of the person designated to manage the contingency planning process?

    a. Providing direction to senior management

    b. Providing stress reduction programs to employees after an event

    c. Ensuring the identification of all critical business functions

    d. Integrating the planning process across business units

6. Which choice below is NOT an emergency management procedure directly relating to financial decision making?

    a. Establishing accounting procedures to track the costs of emergencies

    b. Establishing procedures for the continuance of payroll

    c. Establishing critical incident stress procedures

    d. Establishing program procurement procedures

7. Which choice below is NOT considered an appropriate role for senior management in the business continuity and disaster recovery process?

    a. Delegate recovery roles

    b. Publicly praise successes

    c. Closely control media and analyst communications

    d. Assess the adequacy of information security during the disaster recovery

8. Which choice below is NOT considered a potential hazard resulting from natural events?

    a. Earthquake/land shift

    b. Forest fire

    c. Arson

    d. Urban fire

9. Which choice below represents the most important first step in creating a business resumption plan?

    a. Performing a risk analysis

    b. Obtaining senior management support

    c. Analyzing the business impact

    d. Planning recovery strategies

10. Which choice below would NOT be a valid reason for testing the disaster recovery plan?

    a. Testing provides the contingency planner with recent documentation.

    b. Testing verifies the accuracy of the recovery procedures.

c. Testing prepares the personnel to properly execute their emergency duties.

d. Testing identifies deficiencies within the recovery procedures.

11. Which choice below is NOT a commonly accepted definition for a disaster?

a. An occurrence that is outside the normal computing function

b. An occurrence or imminent threat to the entity of widespread or severe damage, injury, loss of life, or loss of property

c. An emergency that is beyond the normal response resources of the entity

d. A suddenly occurring event that has a long-term negative impact on social life

12. Which choice below is NOT considered an appropriate role for Financial Management in the business continuity and disaster recovery process?

a. Tracking the recovery costs

b. Monitoring employee morale and guarding against employee burnout

c. Formally notifying insurers of claims

d. Reassessing cash flow projections

13. Which choice below most accurately describes a business continuity program?

a. Ongoing process to ensure that the necessary steps are taken to identify the impact of potential losses and maintain viable recovery

b. A program that implements the mission, vision, and strategic goals of the organization

c. A determination of the effects of a disaster on human, physical, economic, and natural resources

d. A standard that allows for rapid recovery during system interruption and data loss

14. What is the responsibility of the contingency planner regarding LAN backup and recovery if the LAN is part of a building server environment?

a. Getting a copy of the recovery procedures from the building server administrator

b. Recovering client/server systems owned and supported by internal staff

c. Classifying the recovery time frame of the business unit LAN

d. Identifying essential business functions

15. Which choice below is the correct definition of a Mutual Aid Agreement?

    a. A management-level analysis that identifies the impact of losing an entity's resources

    b. An appraisal or determination of the effects of a disaster on human, physical, economic, and natural resources

    c. A prearranged agreement to render assistance to the parties of the agreement

    d. Activities taken to eliminate or reduce the degree of risk to life and property

16. In which order should the following steps be taken to create an emergency management plan?

    _____ a. Implement the plan

    _____ b. Form a planning team

    _____ c. Develop a plan

    _____ d. Conduct a vulnerability assessment

17. Place the BRP groups below in their properly tiered organizational structure, from highest to lowest:

    _____ a. Policy group

    _____ b. Senior executives

    _____ c. Emergency response team

    _____ d. Disaster management team

18. Which choice below most accurately describes a business impact analysis (BIA)?

    a. A program that implements the strategic goals of the organization

    b. A management-level analysis that identifies the impact of losing an entity's resources

    c. A prearranged agreement between two or more entities to provide assistance

    d. Activities designed to return an organization to an acceptable operating condition

19. In which order should the following steps be taken to perform a vulnerability assessment?

    _____ a. List potential emergencies

    _____ b. Estimate probability

    _____ c. Assess external and internal resources

    _____ d. Assess potential impact

20. According to FEMA, which choice below is NOT a recommended way to purify water after a disaster?

    a. Adding 16 drops per gallon of household liquid bleach to the water

    b. Boiling from 3 to 5 minutes

    c. Adding water treatment tablets to the water

    d. Distilling the water for twenty minutes

21. Which choice below is NOT a recommended step to take when resuming normal operations after an emergency?

    a. Re-occupy the damaged building as soon as possible.

    b. Account for all damage-related costs.

    c. Protect undamaged property.

    d. Conduct an investigation.

22. In developing a emergency or recovery plan, which choice below would NOT be considered a short-term objective?

    a. Priorities for restoration

    b. Acceptable downtime before restoration

    c. Minimum resources needed to accomplish the restoration

    d. The organization's strategic plan

23. When should security isolation of the incident scene start?

    a. Immediately after the emergency is discovered

    b. As soon as the disaster plan is implemented

    c. After all personnel have been evacuated

    d. When hazardous materials have been discovered at the site

24. Place the following backup processing alternatives in order, from the most expensive solution to the least expensive:

    _____ a. Warm site

    _____ b. Hot site

    _____ c. Cold site

    _____ d. Mutual aid agreement

25. Which choice below is incorrect regarding when a BCP, DRP, or emergency management plan should be evaluated and modified?

    a. Never; once it has been tested it should not be changed.

    b. Annually, in a scheduled review.

    c. After training drills, tests, or exercises.

    d. After an emergency or disaster response.

26. Which choice below refers to a business asset?
    a. Events or situations that could cause a financial or operational impact to the organization
    b. Protection devices or procedures in place that reduce the effects of threats
    c. Competitive advantage, credibility or good will
    d. Personnel compensation and retirement programs

27. Which choice below is an example of a potential hazard due to a technological event, rather than a human event?
    a. Sabotage
    b. Financial collapse
    c. Mass hysteria
    d. Enemy attack

28. When should the public and media be informed about a disaster?
    a. Whenever site emergencies extend beyond the facility
    b. When any emergency occurs at the facility, internally or externally
    c. When the public's health or safety is in danger
    d. When the disaster has been contained

29. Which choice below is the first priority in an emergency?
    a. Communicating with employees' families the status of the emergency
    b. Notifying external support resources for recovery and restoration
    c. Protecting the health and safety of everyone in the facility
    d. Warning customers and contactors of a potential interruption of service

CHAPTER

9

Law, Investigation, and Ethics

This chapter is supplemental to and coordinated with the Law, Investigation, and Ethics chapter in the *CISSP Prep Guide*. The fundamentals of law, investigation, and ethics are covered in Chapter 9 of the *CISSP Prep Guide* at a level commensurate with that of the CISSP Examination.

This chapter includes advanced material relative to computer law, investigation, and ethics both in the U.S. and internationally. Questions address the recently passed U.S. Patriot Act, international copyright issues, computer forensics, changes in search and seizure laws, Internet monitoring, electronic signatures, and the U.S. Health Information Portability and Accountability Act (HIPAA).

It is assumed that the reader has a basic knowledge of the material contained in Chapter 9 and has the *CISSP Prep Guide* available to provide background information for the advanced questions pertaining to the law, ethics, and information security chapter. These questions and answers build upon the questions and answers covered in Chapter 9 of the Prep Guide.

Advanced Sample Questions

1. In the legal field, there is a term that is used to describe a computer system so that everyone can agree on a common definition. The term describes a computer for the purposes of computer security as "any assembly of electronic equipment, hardware, software and firmware configured to collect, create, communicate, disseminate, process, store and control data or information." This definition includes peripheral items such as keyboards, printers, and additional memory. The term that corresponds to this definition is:

   a. A central processing unit (CPU)

   b. A microprocessor

   c. An arithmetic logic unit (ALU)

   d. An automated information system (AIS)

2. In general, computer crimes fall into two major categories and two additional related categories. Which of the following categories is NOT one of these four?

   a. The computer as a target of the crime

   b. Crimes using the computer

   c. Malfeasance by computer

   d. Crimes associated with the prevalence of computers

3. Which of the following is NOT a valid legal issue associated with computer crime?

   a. Electronic Data Interchange (EDI) makes it easier to relate a crime to an individual.

   b. It may be difficult to prove criminal intent.

   c. It may be difficult to obtain a trail of evidence of activities performed on the computer.

   d. It may be difficult to show causation.

4. The Federal Intelligence Surveillance Act (FISA) of 1978, the Electronic Communications Privacy Act (ECPA) of 1986, and the Communications Assistance for Law Enforcement Act (CALEA) of 1994 are legislative acts passed by the United States Congress. These acts all address what major information security issue?

   a. Computer fraud

   b. Wiretapping

   c. Malicious code

   d. Unlawful use of and access to government computers and networks

5. A *pen register* is a:
   a. Device that identifies the cell in which a mobile phone is operating
   b. Device that records the URLs accessed by an individual
   c. Device that records the caller-ID of incoming calls
   d. Device that records all the numbers dialed from a specific telephone line

6. A device that is used to monitor Internet Service Provider (ISP) data traffic is called:
   a. Carnivore
   b. Echelon
   c. Escrowed encryption
   d. Key manager

7. In 1996, the World Intellectual Property Organization (WIPO) sponsored a treaty under which participating countries would standardize treatment of digital copyrights. One of the items of standardization was the prohibition of altering copyright management information (CMI) that is included with the copyrighted material. CMI is:
   a. An encryption algorithm
   b. Product description information
   c. A listing of Public keys
   d. Licensing and ownership information

8. The European Union (EU) has enacted a Conditional Access Directive (CAD) that addresses which of the following?
   a. Access to and use of copyrighted material
   b. Reverse engineering
   c. Unauthorized access to Internet subscription sites and pay TV services
   d. Use of copyrighted material by libraries

9. Which of the following actions by the U.S. government are NOT permitted or required by the U.S. Patriot Act, signed into law on October 26, 2001?
   a. Subpoena of electronic records
   b. Monitoring of Internet communications
   c. Search and seizure of information on live systems (including routers and servers), backups, and archives
   d. Reporting of cash and wire transfers of $5,000 or more

10. The U.S. Uniform Computer Information Transactions Act (UCITA) is a:

    a. Model act that is intended to apply uniform legislation to software licensing

    b. Model act that addresses digital signatures

    c. Model act that is intended to apply uniform legislation to electronic credit transactions

    d. Model act that addresses electronic transactions conducted by financial institutions

11. The European Union Electronic Signature Directive of January, 2000, defines an "advanced electronic signature." This signature must meet all of the following requirements except that:

    a. It must be uniquely linked to the signatory.

    b. It must be created using means that are generally accessible and available.

    c. It must be capable of identifying the signatory.

    d. It must be linked to the data to which it relates in such a manner that any subsequent change of the data is detectable.

12. On June 30, 2000, the U.S. Congress enacted the Electronic Signatures in Global and National Commerce Act (ESIGN) "to facilitate the use of electronic records and signatures in interstate and foreign commerce by ensuring the validity and legal effect of contracts entered into electronically." An important provision of the Act requires that:

    a. Businesses obtain electronic consent or confirmation from consumers to receive information electronically that a law normally requires to be in writing.

    b. The e-commerce businesses do not have to determine whether the consumer has the ability to receive an electronic notice before transmitting the legally required notices to the consumer.

    c. Businesses have the ability to use product price to persuade consumers to accept electronic records instead of paper.

    d. Specific technologies be used to ensure technical compatibility.

13. Under Civil Law, the victim is NOT entitled to which of the following types of damages?

    a. Statutory

    b. Punitive

    c. Compensatory

    d. Imprisonment of the offender

14. Which of the following is NOT one of the European Union (EU) privacy principles?

    a. Individuals are entitled to receive a report on the information that is held about them.

    b. Data transmission of personal information to locations where "equivalent" personal data protection cannot be assured is prohibited.

    c. Information collected about an individual can be disclosed to other organizations or individuals unless specifically prohibited by the individual.

    d. Individuals have the right to correct errors contained in their personal data.

15. Which of the following is NOT a goal of the Kennedy-Kassebaum Health Insurance Portability and Accountability Act (HIPAA) of 1996?

    a. Provide for restricted access by the patient to personal healthcare information

    b. Administrative simplification

    c. Enable the portability of health insurance

    d. Establish strong penalties for healthcare fraud

16. The proposed HIPAA Security Rule mandates the protection of the confidentiality, integrity, and availability of protected health information (PHI) through three of the following activities. Which of the activities is NOT included under the proposed HIPAA Security Rule?

    a. Administrative procedures

    b. Physical safeguards

    c. Technical services and mechanisms

    d. Appointment of a Privacy Officer

17. Individual privacy rights as defined in the HIPAA Privacy Rule include consent and authorization by the patient for the release of PHI. The difference between consent and authorization as used in the Privacy Rule is:

    a. Consent grants general permission to use or disclose PHI, and authorization limits permission to the purposes and the parties specified in the authorization.

    b. Authorization grants general permission to use or disclose PHI, and consent limits permission to the purposes and the parties specified in the consent.

c. Consent grants general permission to use or disclose PHI, and authorization limits permission to the purposes specified in the authorization.

d. Consent grants general permission to use or disclose PHI, and authorization limits permission to the parties specified in the authorization.

18. Because of the nature of information that is stored on the computer, the investigation and prosecution of computer criminal cases have specific characteristics, one of which is:

   a. Investigators and prosecutors have a longer time frame for the investigation.

   b. The information is intangible.

   c. The investigation does not usually interfere with the normal conduct of the business of an organization.

   d. Evidence is usually easy to gather.

19. In order for evidence to be admissible in a court of law, it must be relevant, legally permissible, reliable, properly identified, and properly preserved. Reliability of evidence means that:

   a. It must tend to prove a material fact; the evidence is related to the crime in that it shows that the crime has been committed, can provide information describing the crime, can provide information as to the perpetrator's motives, can verify what had occurred, and so on.

   b. The evidence is identified without changing or damaging the evidence.

   c. The evidence has not been tampered with or modified.

   d. The evidence is not subject to damage or destruction.

20. In the U.S. Federal Rules of Evidence, Rule 803 (6) permits an exception to the Hearsay Rule regarding business records and computer records. Which one of the following is NOT a requirement for business or computer records exception under Rule 803 (6)?

   a. Made during the regular conduct of business and authenticated by witnesses familiar with their use

   b. Relied upon in the regular course of business

   c. Made only by a person with knowledge of the records

   d. Made by a person with information transmitted by a person with knowledge

21. Law enforcement officials in the United States, up until passage of the Patriot Act (see Question 9), had extensive restrictions on search and

seizure as established in the Fourth Amendment to the U.S. Constitution. These restrictions are still, essentially, more severe than those on private citizens, who are not agents of a government entity. Thus, internal investigators in an organization or private investigators are not subject to the same restrictions as government officials. Private individuals are not normally held to the same standards regarding search and seizure since they are not conducting an unconstitutional government search. However, there are certain exceptions where the Fourth Amendment applies to private citizens if they act as agents of the government/police. Which of the following is NOT one of these exceptions?

a. The government is aware of the intent to search or is aware of a search conducted by the private individual and does not object to these actions.

b. The private individual performs the search to aid the government.

c. The private individual conducts a search that would require a search warrant if conducted by a government entity.

d. The private individual conducts a warrantless search of company property for the company.

22. One important tool of computer forensics is the disk image backup. The disk image backup is:

a. Copying the system files

b. Conducting a bit-level copy, sector by sector

c. Copying the disk directory

d. Copying and authenticating the system files

23. In the context of legal proceedings and trial practice, *discovery* refers to:

a. The process in which the prosecution presents information it has uncovered to the defense, including potential witnesses, reports resulting from the investigation, evidence, and so on

b. The process undertaken by the investigators to acquire evidence needed for prosecution of a case

c. A step in the computer forensic process

d. The process of obtaining information on potential and existing employees using background checks

24. Which of the following alternatives should NOT be used by law enforcement to gain access to a password?

a. Using password "cracker" software

b. Compelling the suspect to provide the password

    c. Contacting the developer of the software for information to gain access to the computer or network through a back door

    d. Data manipulation and trial procedures applied to the original version of the system hard disk

25. During the investigation of a computer crime, audit trails can be very useful. To ensure that the audit information can be used as evidence, certain procedures must be followed. Which of the following is NOT one of these procedures?

    a. The audit trail information must be used during the normal course of business.

    b. There must be a valid organizational security policy in place and in use that defines the use of the audit information.

    c. Mechanisms should be in place to protect the integrity of the audit trail information.

    d. Audit trails should be viewed prior to the image backup.

26. The Internet Activities Board (IAB) considers which of the following behaviors relative to the Internet as unethical?

    a. Negligence in the conduct of Internet experiments

    b. Record-keeping whose very existence is secret

    c. Record-keeping in which an individual cannot find out what information concerning that individual is in the record

    d. Improper dissemination and use of identifiable personal data

27. Which of the following is NOT a form of computer/network surveillance?

    a. Keyboard monitoring

    b. Use of network sniffers

    c. Use of CCTV cameras

    d. Review of audit logs

28. Which of the following is NOT a definition or characteristic of "Due Care?"

    a. Just, proper, and sufficient care, so far as the circumstances demand it.

    b. That care which an ordinary prudent person would have exercised under the same or similar circumstances.

    c. Implies that a party has been guilty of a violation of the law in relation to the subject matter or transaction.

    d. It may and often does require extraordinary care.

29. The definition "A mark used in the sale or advertising of services to identify the services of one person and distinguish them from the services of others" refers to a:

    a. Trademark

    b. Service mark

    c. Trade name

    d. Copyright

30. It is estimated that the Asia/Pacific region accounts for about $4 billion worth of loss of income to software publishers due to software piracy. As with the Internet, cross-jurisdictional law enforcement issues make investigating and prosecuting such crime difficult. Which of the following items is NOT an issue in stopping overseas software piracy?

    a. Obtaining the cooperation of foreign law enforcement agencies and foreign governments.

    b. The quality of the illegal copies of the software is improving, making it more difficult for purchasers to differentiate between legal and illegal products.

    c. The producers of the illegal copies of software are dealing in larger and larger quantities, resulting in faster deliveries of illicit software.

    d. Lack of a central, nongovernmental organization to address the issue of software piracy.

CHAPTER

10

Physical Security

This chapter is supplemental to and coordinated with the Physical Security chapter in the *CISSP Prep Guide*. The fundamentals of Physical Security are covered in Chapter 10 of the *CISSP Prep Guide* at a level commensurate with that of the CISSP Examination.

These advanced questions and answers build upon the questions and answers covered in Chapter 10 of the *CISSP Prep Guide*. While these questions may be more difficult than the actual questions on the exam, they are good preparation for the concepts covered, such as fire suppression, physical access control, and physical intrusion detection.

Advanced Sample Questions

1. Which choice below is NOT a common biometric method?

   a. Retina pattern devices

   b. Fingerprint devices

   c. Handprint devices

   d. Phrenologic devices

2. According to the NFPA, which choice below is NOT a recommended risk factor to consider when determining the need for protecting the computing environment from fire?

   a. Life safety aspects of the computing function or process

   b. Fire threat of the installation to occupants or exposed property

   c. Distance of the computing facility from a fire station

   d. Economic loss of the equipment's value

3. Which choice below is NOT an example of a Halocarbon Agent?

   a. HFC-23

   b. FC-3-1-10

   c. IG-541

   d. HCFC-22

4. Which choice below is NOT an example of a combustible in a Class B fire?

   a. Grease

   b. Rubber

   c. Oil-base paints

   d. Flammable gases

5. Which statement below most accurately describes a "dry pipe" sprinkler system?

   a. Dry pipe is the most commonly used sprinkler system.

   b. Dry pipe contains air pressure.

   c. Dry pipe sounds an alarm and delays water release.

   d. Dry pipe may contain carbon dioxide.

6. Which choice below is NOT a recommendation for records and materials storage in the computer room, for fire safety?

   a. Green bar printing paper for printers should be stored in the computer room.

   b. Abandoned cables shall not be allowed to accumulate.

   c. Space beneath the raised floor shall not be used for storage purposes.

   d. Only minimum records shall be required for essential and efficient operation.

7. Which choice below is NOT considered an element of two-factor authentication?

   a. Something you know

   b. Something you do

   c. Something you have

   d. Something you are

8. Which choice below is NOT an example of a "clean" fire extinguishing agent?

   a. CO_2

   b. IG-55

   c. IG-01

   d. HCFC-22

9. Which choice below is NOT considered a requirement to install an automatic sprinkler system?

   a. The building is required to be sprinklered.

   b. The computer room is vented to outside offices.

   c. The computer room contains a significant quantity of combustible materials.

   d. A computer system's enclosure contains combustible materials.

10. Which choice below is NOT a type of motion detection system?

   a. Ultrasonic detection system

   b. Microwave detection system

   c. Host-based intrusion detection system

   d. Sonic detection system

11. Which fire extinguishant choice below does NOT create toxic HF levels?

   a. Halon 1301

   b. Halon 1211

   c. IG-01

   d. HCFC-22

12. Which choice below is NOT permitted under computer room raised flooring?

   a. Interconnecting DP cables enclosed in a raceway

   b. Underfloor ventilation for the computer room only

    c. Nonabrasive openings for cables

    d. Underfloor ventilation to the rest of the offices' ventilation system

13. Which choice below represents the BEST reason to control the humidity in computer operations areas?

    a. Computer operators do not perform at their peak if the humidity is too high.

    b. Electrostatic discharges can harm electronic equipment.

    c. Static electricity destroys the electrical efficiency of the circuits.

    d. If the air is too dry, electroplating of conductors may occur.

14. Which statement below is NOT accurate about smoke damage to electronic equipment?

    a. Smoke exposure during a fire for a relatively short period does little immediate damage.

    b. Continuing power to the smoke-exposed equipment can increase the damage.

    c. Moisture and oxygen corrosion constitute the main damage to the equipment.

    d. The primary damage done by smoke exposure is immediate.

15. Which choice below most accurately describes the prime benefit from using guards?

    a. Human guards are less expensive than guard dogs.

    b. Guards can exercise discretionary judgment in a way that automated systems can't.

    c. Automated systems have a greater reliability rate than guards.

    d. Guard dogs cannot discern an intruder's intent.

16. Which choice below is an accurate statement about EMI and RFI?

    a. EMI can contain RFI.

    b. EMI is generated naturally; RFI is man-made.

    c. RFI is generated naturally; EMI is man-made.

    d. Natural sources of EMI pose the greatest threat to electronic equipment.

17. In which proper order should the steps below be taken after electronic equipment or media has been exposed to water?

    _____ a. Place all affected equipment or media in an air-conditioned area, if portable.

    _____ b. Turn off all electrical power to the equipment.

_____ c. Open cabinet doors and remove panels and covers to allow water to run out.

_____ d. Wipe with alcohol or Freon-alcohol solutions or spray with water-displacement aerosol sprays.

18. Which choice below is NOT an example of using a social engineering technique to gain physical access to a secure facility?

   a. Asserting authority or pulling rank

   b. Intimidating or threatening

   c. Praising or flattering

   d. Employing the salami fraud

19. In which proper order should the steps below be taken after electronic equipment or media has been exposed to smoke contaminants?

   _____ a. Turn off power to equipment.

   _____ b. Spray corrosion-inhibiting aerosol to stabilize metal contact surfaces.

   _____ c. Spray connectors, backplanes, and printed circuit boards with Freon or Freon-alcohol solvents.

   _____ d. Move equipment into an air-conditioned and humidity-controlled environment.

20. Which fire suppression medium below is considered to be the MOST toxic to personnel?

   a. CO_2

   b. IG-01

   c. Halon 1301

   d. Halocarbon Agents

21. Which type of personnel control below helps prevent piggybacking?

   a. Man traps

   b. Back doors

   c. Brute force

   d. Maintenance hooks

22. Which type of physical access control method below is best suited for high-security areas?

   a. Deadbolts

   b. Access token

   c. Key locks

   d. Pushbutton locks

23. Which term below refers to a standard used in determining the fire safety of a computer room?

    a. Noncombustible

    b. Fire-resistant

    c. Fire-retardant

    d. Nonflammable

APPENDIX

A

Answers to Sample Questions

Chapter 1—Security Management Practices

1. Which choice below most accurately reflects the goals of risk mitigation?

   a. Defining the acceptable level of risk the organization can tolerate, and reducing risk to that level

   b. Analyzing and removing all vulnerabilities and threats to security within the organization

   c. Defining the acceptable level of risk the organization can tolerate, and assigning any costs associated with loss or disruption to a third party, such as an insurance carrier

   d. Analyzing the effects of a business disruption and preparing the company's response

   Answer: a

   The correct answer is a. The goal of risk mitigation is to reduce risk to a level acceptable to the organization. Therefore risk needs to be defined for the organization through risk analysis, business impact assessment, and/or vulnerability assessment.

Answer b is not possible. Answer c is called risk transference. Answer d is a distracter.

2. Which answer below is the BEST description of a Single Loss Expectancy (SLE)?

   a. An algorithm that represents the magnitude of a loss to an asset from a threat

   b. An algorithm that expresses the annual frequency with which a threat is expected to occur

   c. An algorithm used to determine the monetary impact of each occurrence of a threat

   d. An algorithm that determines the expected annual loss to an organization from a threat

   Answer: c

   The correct answer is c. The Single Loss Expectancy (or Exposure) figure may be created as a result of a Business Impact Assessment (BIA). The SLE represents only the estimated monetary loss of a single occurrence of a specified threat event. The SLE is determined by multiplying the value of the asset by its exposure factor. This gives the expected loss the threat will cause for one occurrence.

   Answer a describes the Exposure Factor (EF). The EF is expressed as a percentile of the expected value or functionality of the asset to be lost due to the realized threat event. This figure is used to calculate the SLE, above.

   Answer b describes the Annualized Rate of Occurrence (ARO). This is an estimate of how often a given threat event may occur annually. For example, a threat expected to occur weekly would have an ARO of 52. A threat expected to occur once every five years has an ARO of 1/5 or .2. This figure is used to determine the ALE.

   Answer d describes the Annualized Loss Expectancy (ALE). The ALE is derived by multiplying the SLE by its ARO. This value represents the expected risk factor of an annual threat event. This figure is then integrated into the risk management process.

3. Which choice below is the BEST description of an Annualized Loss Expectancy (ALE)?

   a. The expected risk factor of an annual threat event, derived by multiplying the SLE by its ARO

   b. An estimate of how often a given threat event may occur annually

c. The percentile of the value of the asset expected to be lost, used to calculate the SLE

d. A value determined by multiplying the value of the asset by its exposure factor

Answer: a

Answer b describes the Annualized Rate of Occurrence (ARO).

Answer c describes the Exposure Factor (EF).

Answer d describes the algorithm to determine the Single Loss Expectancy (SLE) of a threat.

4. Which choice below is NOT an example of appropriate security management practice?

a. Reviewing access logs for unauthorized behavior

b. Monitoring employee performance in the workplace

c. Researching information on new intrusion exploits

d. Promoting and implementing security awareness programs

Answer: b

Monitoring employee performance is not an example of security management, or a job function of the Information Security Officer. Employee performance issues are the domain of human resources and the employee's manager. The other three choices are appropriate practice for the information security area.

5. Which choice below is an accurate statement about standards?

a. Standards are the high-level statements made by senior management in support of information systems security.

b. Standards are the first element created in an effective security policy program.

c. Standards are used to describe how policies will be implemented within an organization.

d. Standards are senior management's directives to create a computer security program.

Answer: c

Answers a, b, and d describe policies. Guidelines, standards, and procedures often accompany policy, but always follow the senior level management's statement of policy. Procedures, standards, and guidelines are used to describe how these policies will be implemented within an organization. Simply put, the three break down as follows:

■ Standards specify the use of specific technologies in a uniform way (for example, the standardization of operating procedures).

- Guidelines are similar to standards but are recommended actions.
- Procedures are the detailed steps that must be performed for any task.

6. Which choice below is a role of the Information Systems Security Officer?

   a. The ISO establishes the overall goals of the organization's computer security program.

   b. The ISO is responsible for day-to-day security administration.

   c. The ISO is responsible for examining systems to see whether they are meeting stated security requirements.

   d. The ISO is responsible for following security procedures and reporting security problems.

   Answer: b

   Answer a is a responsibility of senior management. Answer c is a description of the role of auditing. Answer d is the role of the user, or consumer, of security in an organization.

7. Which statement below is NOT true about security awareness, training, and educational programs?

   a. Awareness and training help users become more accountable for their actions.

   b. Security education assists management in determining who should be promoted.

   c. Security improves the users' awareness of the need to protect information resources.

   d. Security education assists management in developing the in-house expertise to manage security programs.

   Answer: b

   The purpose of computer security awareness, training, and education is to enhance security by:

- Improving awareness of the need to protect system resources
- Developing skills and knowledge so computer users can perform their jobs more securely
- Building in-depth knowledge, as needed, to design, implement, or operate security programs for organizations and systems

   Making computer system users aware of their security responsibilities and teaching them correct practices helps users change their behavior. It also supports individual accountability because without the knowledge of the necessary security measures and to how to use them, users cannot be truly accountable for their actions. Source: *National Institute of Standards and Technology, An Introduction to Computer Security: The NIST Handbook Special Publication 800-12.*

8. Which choice below is NOT an accurate description of an information policy?

    a. Information policy is senior management's directive to create a computer security program.

    b. An information policy could be a decision pertaining to use of the organization's fax.

    c. Information policy is a documentation of computer security decisions.

    d. Information policies are created after the system's infrastructure has been designed and built.

    > *Answer:* d
    >
    > Computer security policy is often defined as the "documentation of computer security decisions." The term "policy" has more than one meaning. Policy is senior management's directives to create a computer security program, establish its goals, and assign responsibilities. The term "policy" is also used to refer to the specific security rules for particular systems. Additionally, policy may refer to entirely different matters, such as the specific managerial decisions setting an organization's e-mail privacy policy or fax security policy.
    >
    > A security policy is an important document to develop while designing an information system, early in the System Development Life Cycle (SDLC). The security policy begins with the organization's basic commitment to information security formulated as a general policy statement. The policy is then applied to all aspects of the system design or security solution. Source: *NIST Special Publication 800-27, Engineering Principles for Information Technology Security (A Baseline for Achieving Security).*

9. Which choice below MOST accurately describes the organization's responsibilities during an unfriendly termination?

    a. System access should be removed as quickly as possible after termination.

    b. The employee should be given time to remove whatever files he needs from the network.

    c. Cryptographic keys can remain the employee's property.

    d. Physical removal from the offices would never be necessary.

    > *Answer:* a

Friendly terminations should be accomplished by implementing a standard set of procedures for outgoing or transferring employees. This normally includes:

- Removal of access privileges, computer accounts, authentication tokens.
- The control of keys.
- The briefing on the continuing responsibilities for confidentiality and privacy.
- Return of property.
- Continued availability of data. In both the manual and the electronic worlds this may involve documenting procedures or filing schemes, such as how documents are stored on the hard disk, and how they are backed up. Employees should be instructed whether or not to "clean up" their PC before leaving.
- If cryptography is used to protect data, the availability of cryptographic keys to management personnel must be ensured.

Given the potential for adverse consequences during an unfriendly termination, organizations should do the following:

- System access should be terminated as quickly as possible when an employee is leaving a position under less-than-friendly terms. If employees are to be fired, system access should be removed at the same time (or just before) the employees are notified of their dismissal.
- When an employee notifies an organization of the resignation and it can be reasonably expected that it is on unfriendly terms, system access should be immediately terminated.
- During the "notice of termination" period, it may be necessary to assign the individual to a restricted area and function. This may be particularly true for employees capable of changing programs or modifying the system or applications.
- In some cases, physical removal from the offices may be necessary.

Source: *NIST Special Publication 800-14 Generally Accepted Principles and Practices for Securing Information Technology Systems.*

10. Which choice below is NOT an example of an issue-specific policy?

a. E-mail privacy policy

b. Virus-checking disk policy

c. Defined router ACLs

d. Unfriendly employee termination policy

Answer: c

Answer c is an example of a system-specific policy, in this case the router's access control lists. The other three answers are examples of issue-specific policy, as defined by NIST. Issue-specific policies are similar to program policies, in that they are not technically focused. While program policy is traditionally more general and strategic (the organization's computer security program, for example), issue-specific policy is a nontechnical policy addressing a single or specific issue of concern to the organization, such as the procedural guidelines for checking disks brought to work or e-mail privacy concerns. System-specific policy is technically focused and addresses only one computer system or device type. Source: *National Institute of Standards and Technology, An Introduction to Computer Security: The NIST Handbook Special Publication 800-12.*

11. Who has the final responsibility for the preservation of the organization's information?

a. Technology providers

b. Senior management

c. Users

d. Application owners

Answer: b

Various officials and organizational offices are typically involved with computer security. They include the following groups:

■ Senior management

■ Program/functional managers/application owners

■ Computer security management

■ Technology providers

■ Supporting organizations

■ Users

Senior management has the final responsibility through due care and due diligence to preserve the capital of the organization and further its business model through the implementation of a security program. While senior management does not have the functional role of managing security procedures, it has the ultimate responsibility to see that business continuity is preserved.

12. Which choice below is NOT a generally accepted benefit of security awareness, training, and education?

    a. A security awareness program can help operators understand the value of the information.

    b. A security education program can help system administrators recognize unauthorized intrusion attempts.

    c. A security awareness and training program will help prevent natural disasters from occurring.

    d. A security awareness and training program can help an organization reduce the number and severity of errors and omissions.

    > *Answer:* c

    > An effective computer security awareness and training program requires proper planning, implementation, maintenance, and periodic evaluation.

    > In general, a computer security awareness and training program should encompass the following seven steps:

    > 1. Identify program scope, goals, and objectives.

    > 2   Identify training staff.

    > 3. Identify target audiences.

    > 4. Motivate management and employees.

    > 5. Administer the program.

    > 6. Maintain the program.

    > 7. Evaluate the program.

    > Source: *NIST Special Publication 800-14, Generally Accepted Principles and Practices for Securing Information Technology Systems.*

13. Which choice below is NOT a common information-gathering technique when performing a risk analysis?

    a. Distributing a questionnaire

    b. Employing automated risk assessment tools

    c. Reviewing existing policy documents

    d. Interviewing terminated employees

    > *Answer:* d

    > Any combination of the following techniques can be used in gathering information relevant to the IT system within its operational boundary:

    > **Questionnaire.** The questionnaire should be distributed to the applicable technical and nontechnical management personnel who are designing or supporting the IT system.

On-site Interviews. On-site visits also allow risk assessment personnel to observe and gather information about the physical, environmental, and operational security of the IT system.

Document Review. Policy documents, system documentation, and security-related documentation can provide good information about the security controls used by and planned for the IT system.

Use of Automated Scanning Tools. Proactive technical methods can be used to collect system information efficiently.

Source: *NIST Special Publication 800-30, Risk Management Guide for Information Technology Systems.*

14. Which choice below is an incorrect description of a control?

    a. Detective controls discover attacks and trigger preventative or corrective controls.

    b. Corrective controls reduce the likelihood of a deliberate attack.

    c. Corrective controls reduce the effect of an attack.

    d. Controls are the countermeasures for vulnerabilities.

    Answer: b

    Controls are the countermeasures for vulnerabilities. There are many kinds, but generally they are categorized into four types:

    ■ Deterrent controls reduce the likelihood of a deliberate attack.

    ■ Preventative controls protect vulnerabilities and make an attack unsuccessful or reduce its impact. Preventative controls inhibit attempts to violate security policy.

    ■ Corrective controls reduce the effect of an attack.

    ■ Detective controls discover attacks and trigger preventative or corrective controls. Detective controls warn of violations or attempted violations of security policy and include such controls as audit trails, intrusion detection methods, and checksums.

    Source: *Introduction to Risk Analysis, C & A Security Risk Analysis Group* and *NIST Special Publication 800-30, Risk Management Guide for Information Technology Systems.*

15. Which statement below is accurate about the reasons to implement a layered security architecture?

    a. A layered security approach is not necessary when using COTS products.

    b. A good packet-filtering router will eliminate the need to implement a layered security architecture.

c. A layered security approach is intended to increase the work-factor for an attacker.

d. A layered approach doesn't really improve the security posture of the organization.

Answer: c

Security designs should consider a layered approach to address or protect against a specific threat or to reduce a vulnerability. For example, the use of a packet-filtering router in conjunction with an application gateway and an intrusion detection system combine to increase the work-factor an attacker must expend to successfully attack the system. The need for layered protections is important when commercial-off-the-shelf (COTS) products are used. The current state-of-the-art for security quality in COTS products do not provide a high degree of protection against sophisticated attacks. It is possible to help mitigate this situation by placing several controls in levels, requiring additional work by attackers to accomplish their goals.

Source: *NIST Special Publication 800-27, Engineering Principles for Information Technology Security (A Baseline for Achieving Security).*

16. Which choice below represents an application or system demonstrating a need for a high level of confidentiality protection and controls?

a. Unavailability of the system could result in inability to meet payroll obligations and could cause work stoppage and failure of user organizations to meet critical mission requirements. The system requires 24-hour access.

b. The application contains proprietary business information and other financial information, which if disclosed to unauthorized sources, could cause an unfair advantage for vendors, contractors, or individuals and could result in financial loss or adverse legal action to user organizations.

c. Destruction of the information would require significant expenditures of time and effort to replace. Although corrupted information would present an inconvenience to the staff, most information, and all vital information, is backed up by either paper documentation or on disk.

d. The mission of this system is to produce local weather forecast information that is made available to the news media forecasters and the general public at all times. None of the information requires protection against disclosure.

Answer: b

Although elements of all of the systems described could require specific controls for confidentiality, given the descriptions above, system b fits the definition most closely of a system requiring a very high level of confidentiality. Answer a is an example of a system requiring high availability. Answer c is an example of a system that requires medium integrity controls. Answer d is a system that requires only a low level of confidentiality.

A system may need protection for one or more of the following reasons:

Confidentiality. The system contains information that requires protection from unauthorized disclosure.

Integrity. The system contains information that must be protected from unauthorized, unanticipated, or unintentional modification.

Availability. The system contains information or provides services which must be available on a timely basis to meet mission requirements or to avoid substantial losses.

Source: *NIST Special Publication 800-18, Guide for Developing Security Plans for Information Technology Systems*

17. Which choice below is an accurate statement about the difference between monitoring and auditing?

a. Monitoring is a one-time event to evaluate security.

b. A system audit is an ongoing "real-time" activity that examines a system.

c. A system audit cannot be automated.

d. Monitoring is an ongoing activity that examines either the system or the users.

Answer: d

System audits and monitoring are the two methods organizations use to maintain operational assurance. Although the terms are used loosely within the computer security community, a system audit is a one-time or periodic event to evaluate security, whereas monitoring refers to an ongoing activity that examines either the system or the users. In general, the more "real-time" an activity is, the more it falls into the category of monitoring. Source: *NIST Special Publication 800-14, Generally Accepted Principles and Practices for Securing Information Technology Systems.*

18. Which statement below is accurate about the difference between issue-specific and system-specific policies?

    a. Issue-specific policy is much more technically focused.

    b. System-specific policy is much more technically focused.

    c. System-specific policy is similar to program policy.

    d. Issue-specific policy commonly addresses only one system.

    Answer: b

    Often, managerial computer system security policies are categorized into three basic types:

    ■ Program policy—used to create an organization's computer security program

    ■ Issue-specific policies—used to address specific issues of concern to the organization

    ■ System-specific policies—technical directives taken by management to protect a particular system

    Program policy and issue-specific policy both address policy from a broad level, usually encompassing the entire organization. However, they do not provide sufficient information or direction, for example, to be used in establishing an access control list or in training users on what actions are permitted. System-specific policy fills this need. System-specific policy is much more focused, since it addresses only one system.

    Table A.1 helps illustrate the difference between these three types of policies. Source: *National Institute of Standards and Technology, An Introduction to Computer Security: The NIST Handbook Special Publication 800-12.*

Table A.1   Security Policy Types

POLICY TYPE	DESCRIPTION	EXAMPLE
Program policy	High-level program policy	Senior-level Management Statement
Issue-specific policy	Addresses single issue	Email privacy policy
System-specific policy	Single-system directives	Router Access Control Lists

19. Which statement below most accurately describes the difference between security awareness, security training, and security education?

    a. Security training teaches the skills that will help employees to perform their jobs more securely.

    b. Security education is required for all system operators.

    c. Security awareness is not necessary for high-level senior executives.

    d. Security training is more in depth than security education.

    > *Answer:* a
    >
    > Awareness is used to reinforce the fact that security supports the mission of the organization by protecting valuable resources. The purpose of training is to teach people the skills that will enable them to perform their jobs more securely. Security education is more in depth than security training and is targeted for security professionals and those whose jobs require expertise in security. Management commitment is necessary because of the resources used in developing and implementing the program and also because the program affects their staff. Source: *National Institute of Standards and Technology, An Introduction to Computer Security: The NIST Handbook Special Publication 800-12.*

20. Which choice below BEST describes the difference between the System Owner and the Information Owner?

    a. There is a one-to-one relationship between system owners and information owners.

    b. One system could have multiple information owners.

    c. The Information Owner is responsible for defining the system's operating parameters.

    d. The System Owner is responsible for establishing the rules for appropriate use of the information.

    > *Answer:* b
    >
    > The System Owner is responsible for ensuring that the security plan is prepared and for implementing the plan and monitoring its effectiveness. The System Owner is responsible for defining the system's operating parameters, authorized functions, and security requirements. The information owner for information stored within, processed by, or transmitted by a system may or may not be the same as the System Owner. Also, a single system may utilize information from multiple Information Owners.
    >
    > The Information Owner is responsible for establishing the rules for appropriate use and protection of the subject data/information (rules of

behavior). The Information Owner retains that responsibility even when the data/information are shared with other organizations. Source: *NIST Special Publication 800-18, Guide for Developing Security Plans for Information Technology Systems.*

21. Which choice below is NOT an accurate statement about an organization's incident-handling capability?

    a. The organization's incident-handling capability should be used to detect and punish senior-level executive wrong-doing.

    b. It should be used to prevent future damage from incidents.

    c. It should be used to provide the ability to respond quickly and effectively to an incident.

    d. The organization's incident-handling capability should be used to contain and repair damage done from incidents.

      Answer: a

      An organization should address computer security incidents by developing an incident-handling capability. The incident-handling capability should be used to:

      ■ Provide the ability to respond quickly and effectively.

      ■ Contain and repair the damage from incidents. When left unchecked, malicious software can significantly harm an organization's computing, depending on the technology and its connectivity. Containing the incident should include an assessment of whether the incident is part of a targeted attack on the organization or an isolated incident.

      ■ Prevent future damage. An incident-handling capability should assist an organization in preventing (or at least minimizing) damage from future incidents. Incidents can be studied internally to gain a better understanding of the organization's threats and vulnerabilities.

      Source: *NIST Special Publication 800-14, Generally Accepted Principles and Practices for Securing Information Technology Systems.*

22. Place the data classification scheme in order, from the least secure to the most:

    a. Sensitive

    b. Public

    c. Private

    d. Confidential

      Answer: b, c, a, and d

      Various formats for categorizing the sensitivity of data exist. Although originally implemented in government systems, data classification is

Table A.2 A Sample H/M/L Data Classification

CATEGORY	DESCRIPTION
High	Could cause loss of life, imprisonment, major financial loss, or require legal action for correction if the information is compromised.
Medium	Could cause significant financial loss or require legal action for correction if the information is compromised.
Low	Would cause only minor financial loss or require only administrative action for correction if the information is compromised.

very useful in determining the sensitivity of business information to threats to confidentiality, integrity, or availability. Often an organization would use the high, medium, or low categories. This simple classification scheme rates each system by its need for protection based upon its C.I.A. needs, and whether it requires high, medium, or low protective controls. For example, a system and its information may require a high degree of integrity and availability, yet have no need for confidentiality.

Or organizations may categorize data into four sensitivity classifications with separate handling requirements, such as Sensitive, Confidential, Private, and Public.

This system would define the categories as follows:

Sensitive. This classification applies to information that requires special precautions to assure the integrity of the information, by protecting it from unauthorized modification or deletion. It is information that requires a higher-than-normal assurance of accuracy and completeness.

Confidential. This classification applies to the most sensitive business information that is intended strictly for use within the organization. Its unauthorized disclosure could seriously and adversely impact the organization, its stockholders, its business partners, and/or its customers. This information is exempt from disclosure under the provisions of the Freedom of Information Act or other applicable federal laws or regulations.

Private. This classification applies to personal information that is intended for use within the organization. Its unauthorized disclosure could seriously and adversely impact the organization and/or its employees.

Public. This classification applies to all other information that does not clearly fit into any of the preceding three classifications. While its unauthorized disclosure is against policy, it is not expected to impact seriously or adversely the organization, its employees, and/or its customers.

The designated owners of information are responsible for determining data classification levels, subject to executive management review. Table A.2 shows a sample H/M/L data classification for sensitive information. Source: *NIST Special Publication 800-26, Security Self-Assessment Guide for Information Technology Systems.*

23. Place the five system security life-cycle phases in order:

_____ a. Implementation phase

_____ b. Development/acquisition phase

_____ c. Disposal phase

_____ d. Operation/maintenance phase

_____ e. Initiation phase

Answer: e, b, a, d, c

Security, like other aspects of an IT system, is best managed if planned for throughout the IT system life cycle. There are many models for the IT system life cycle, but most contain five basic phases: initiation, development/acquisition, implementation, operation, and disposal.

The order of these phases is:

a. Initiation phase—During the initiation phase, the need for a system is expressed and the purpose of the system is documented.

b. Development/acquisition phase—During this phase, the system is designed, purchased, programmed, developed, or otherwise constructed.

c. Implementation phase—During implementation, the system is tested and installed or fielded.

d. Operation/maintenance phase—During this phase, the system performs its work. The system is almost always being continuously modified by the addition of hardware and software and by numerous other events.

e. Disposal phase—The disposal phase of the IT system life cycle involves the disposition of information, hardware, and software.

Source: *NIST Special Publication 800-14, Generally Accepted Principles and Practices for Securing Information Technology Systems.*

24. How often should an independent review of the security controls be performed, according to OMB Circular A-130?

a. Every year

b. Every three years

c. Every five years

d. Never

Answer: b

The correct answer is b. OMB Circular A-130 requires that a review of the security controls for each major government application be performed at least every three years. For general support systems, OMB Circular A-130 requires that the security controls be reviewed either by an independent audit or self review. Audits can be self-administered or independent (either internal or external). The essential difference between a self-audit and an independent audit is objectivity; however, some systems may require a fully independent review. Source: Office of Management and Budget Circular A-130, revised November 30, 2000.

25. Which choice below is NOT one of NIST's 33 IT security principles?

a. Implement least privilege.

b. Assume that external systems are insecure.

c. Totally eliminate any level of risk.

d. Minimize the system elements to be trusted.

Answer: c

Risk can never be totally eliminated. NIST IT security principle #4 states: "Reduce risk to an acceptable level." The National Institute of Standards and Technology's (NIST) Information Technology Laboratory (ITL) released NIST Special Publication (SP) 800-27, "Engineering Principles for Information Technology Security (EP-ITS)" in June 2001 to assist in the secure design, development, deployment, and life-cycle of information systems. It presents 33 security principles which start at the design phase of the information system or application and continue until the system's retirement and secure disposal. Some of the other 33 principles are:

Principle 1. Establish a sound security policy as the "foundation" for design.

Principle 2. Treat security as an integral part of the overall system design.

Principle 5. Assume that external systems are insecure.

Principle 6. Identify potential trade-offs between reducing risk and increased costs and decrease in other aspects of operational effectiveness.

Principle 7. Implement layered security (ensure no single point of vulnerability).

Principle 11. Minimize the system elements to be trusted.

Principle 16. Isolate public access systems from mission critical resources (e.g., data, processes, etc.).

Principle 17. Use boundary mechanisms to separate computing systems and network infrastructures.

Principle 22. Authenticate users and processes to ensure appropriate access control decisions both within and across domains.

Principle 23. Use unique identities to ensure accountability.

Principle 24. Implement least privilege.

Source: *NIST Special Publication 800-27, Engineering Principles for Information Technology Security (A Baseline for Achieving Security)*, and "Federal Systems Level Guidance for Securing Information Systems," James Corrie, August 16, 2001.

26. Which choice below would NOT be considered an element of proper user account management?

a. Users should never be rotated out of their current duties.

b. The users' accounts should be reviewed periodically.

c. A process for tracking access authorizations should be implemented.

d. Periodically re-screen personnel in sensitive positions.

Answer: a

Organizations should ensure effective administration of users' computer access to maintain system security, including user account management, auditing, and the timely modification or removal of access. This includes:

User Account Management. Organizations should have a process for requesting, establishing, issuing, and closing user accounts, tracking users and their respective access authorizations, and managing these functions.

Management Reviews. It is necessary to periodically review user accounts. Reviews should examine the levels of access each individual has, conformity with the concept of least privilege, whether all accounts are still active, whether management authorizations are up-to-date, and whether required training has been completed.

Detecting Unauthorized/Illegal Activities. Mechanisms besides auditing and analysis of audit trails should be used to detect unauthorized and illegal acts, such as rotating employees in sensitive positions, which could expose a scam that required an employee's presence, or periodic re-screening of personnel.

Source: *NIST Special Publication 800-14, Generally Accepted Principles and Practices for Securing Information Technology Systems.*

27. Which question below is NOT accurate regarding the process of risk assessment?
    a. The likelihood of a threat must be determined as an element of the risk assessment.
    b. The level of impact of a threat must be determined as an element of the risk assessment.
    c. Risk assessment is the first process in the risk management methodology
    d. Risk assessment is the final result of the risk management methodology.

    Answer: d

    Risk is a function of the likelihood of a given threat-source's exercising a particular potential vulnerability, and the resulting impact of that adverse event on the organization. Risk assessment is the first process in the risk management methodology. The risk assessment process helps organizations identify appropriate controls for reducing or eliminating risk during the risk mitigation process.

    To determine the likelihood of a future adverse event, threats to an IT system must be analyzed in conjunction with the potential vulnerabilities and the controls in place for the IT system. The likelihood that a potential vulnerability could be exercised by a given threat-source can be described as high, medium, or low. Impact refers to the magnitude of harm that could be caused by a threat's exploitation of a vulnerability. The determination of the level of impact produces a relative value for the IT assets and resources affected. Source: *NIST Special Publication 800-30, Risk Management Guide for Information Technology Systems.*

28. Which choice below is NOT an accurate statement about the visibility of IT security policy?
    a. The IT security policy should not be afforded high visibility.
    b. The IT security policy could be visible through panel discussions with guest speakers.
    c. The IT security policy should be afforded high visibility.
    d. Include the IT security policy as a regular topic at staff meetings at all levels of the organization.

    Answer: a

    Especially high visibility should be afforded the formal issuance of IT security policy. This is because nearly all employees at all levels will in some way be affected, major organizational resources are being addressed, and many new terms, procedures, and activities will be introduced.

Including IT security as a regular topic at staff meetings at all levels of the organization can be helpful. Also, providing visibility through such avenues as management presentations, panel discussions, guest speakers, question/answer forums, and newsletters can be beneficial.

29. According to NIST, which choice below is not an accepted security self-testing technique?

    a. War Dialing

    b. Virus Distribution

    c. Password Cracking

    d. Virus Detection

    Answer: b

    Common types of self-testing techniques include:

    ■ Network Mapping

    ■ Vulnerability Scanning

    ■ Penetration Testing

    ■ Password Cracking

    ■ Log Review

    ■ Virus Detection

    ■ War Dialing

    Some testing techniques are predominantly human-initiated and conducted, while other tests are highly automated and require less human involvement. The staff that initiates and implements in-house security testing should have significant security and networking knowledge. These testing techniques are often combined to gain a more comprehensive assessment of the overall network security posture. For example, penetration testing almost always includes network mapping and vulnerability scanning to identify vulnerable hosts and services that may be targeted for later penetration. None of these tests by themselves will provide a complete picture of the network or its security posture. Source: *NIST Special Publication 800-42, DRAFT Guideline on Network Security Testing.*

30. Which choice below is NOT a concern of policy development at the high level?

    a. Identifying the key business resources

    b. Identifying the type of firewalls to be used for perimeter security

    c. Defining roles in the organization

    d. Determining the capability and functionality of each role

    Answer: b

Answers a, c, and d are elements of policy development at the highest level. Key business resources would have been identified during the risk assessment process. The various roles are then defined to determine the various levels of access to those resources. Answer d is the final step in the policy creation process and combines steps a and c. It determines which group gets access to each resource and what access privileges its members are assigned. Access to resources should be based on roles, not on individual identity. Source: *Surviving Security: How to Integrate People, Process, and Technology* by Mandy Andress (Sams Publishing, 2001).

Chapter 2—Access Control Systems and Methodology

1. The concept of limiting the routes that can be taken between a workstation and a computer resource on a network is called:

   a. Path limitation

   b. An enforced path

   c. A security perimeter

   d. A trusted path

   Answer: b

   Individuals are authorized access to resources on a network through specific paths and the *enforced path* prohibits the user from accessing a resource through a different route than is authorized to that particular user. This prevents the individual from having unauthorized access to sensitive information in areas off limits to that individual. Examples of controls to implement an enforced path include establishing virtual private networks (VPNs) for specific groups within an organization, using firewalls with access control lists, restricting user menu options, and providing specific phone numbers or dedicated lines for remote access. Answer a is a distracter. Answer c, *security perimeter*, refers to the boundary where security controls are in effect to protect assets. This is a general definition and can apply to physical and technical (logical) access controls. In physical security, a fence may define the security perimeter. In technical access control, a security perimeter can be defined in terms of a *Trusted Computing Base (TCB)*. A TCB is the total combination of protection mechanisms within a computer system. These mechanisms include the firmware, hardware, and software that enforce the system security policy. The *security perimeter* is the boundary that separates the TCB from the remainder of the system. In answer d, a *trusted path* is a path that exists to permit the user to access the TCB without being compromised by other processes or users.

2. An important control that should be in place for external connections to a network that uses call-back schemes is:

   a. Breaking of a dial-up connection at the remote user's side of the line

   b. Call forwarding

   c. Call enhancement

   d. Breaking of a dial-up connection at the organization's computing resource side of the line

   Answer: d

One attack that can be applied when call back is used for remote, dial-up connections is that the caller may not hang up. If the caller had been previously authenticated and has completed his/her session, a "live" connection into the remote network will still be maintained. Also, an unauthenticated remote user may hold the line open, acting as if call-back authentication has taken place. Thus, an active disconnect should be effected at the computing resource's side of the line. Answer a is not correct since it involves the caller hanging up. Answer b, call forwarding, is a feature that should be disabled, if possible, when used with call-back schemes. With call back, a cracker can have a call forwarded from a valid phone number to an invalid phone number during the call-back process. Answer c is a distracter.

3. When logging on to a workstation, the log-on process should:

   a. Validate the log-on only after all input data has been supplied.

   b. Provide a Help mechanism that provides log-on assistance.

   c. Place no limits on the time allotted for log-on or on the number of unsuccessful log-on attempts.

   d. Not provide information on the previous successful log-on and on previous unsuccessful log-on attempts.

   Answer: a

   This approach is necessary to ensure that all the information required for a log-on has been submitted and to avoid providing information that would aid a cracker in trying to gain unauthorized access to the workstation or network. If a log-on attempt fails, information as to which part of the requested log-on information was incorrect should not be supplied to the user. Answer b is incorrect since a Help utility would provide help to a cracker trying to gain unauthorized access to the network. For answer c, maximum and minimum time limits should be placed on the log-on process. Also, the log-on process should limit the number of unsuccessful log-on attempts and temporarily suspend the log-on capability if that number is exceeded. One approach is to progressively increase the time interval allowed between unsuccessful log-on attempts. Answer d is incorrect since providing such information will alert an authorized user if someone has been attempting to gain unauthorized access to the network from the user's workstation.

4. A group of processes that share access to the same resources is called:

   a. An access control list

   b. An access control triple

   c. A protection domain

   d. A Trusted Computing Base (TCB)

Answer: c

In answer a, an *access control list (ACL)* is a list denoting which users have what privileges to a particular resource. Table A.3 illustrates an ACL. The table shows the *subjects* or users that have access to the *object*, FILE X and what privileges they have with respect to that file.

For answer b, an *access control triple* consists of the user, program, and file with the corresponding access privileges noted for each user. The TCB, of answer d, is defined in the answers to Question 1 as the total combination of protection mechanisms within a computer system. These mechanisms include the firmware, hardware, and software that enforce the system security policy.

5. What part of an access control matrix shows capabilities that one user has to multiple resources?

   a. Columns

   b. Rows

   c. Rows and columns

   d. Access control list

   Answer: b

   The rows of an access control matrix indicate the capabilities that users have to a number of resources. An example of a row in the access control matrix showing the capabilities of user JIM is given in Table A.4.

   Answer a, columns in the access control matrix, define the access control list described in question 4. Answer c is incorrect since capabilities involve only the rows of the access control matrix. Answer d

Table A.3   Access Control List

USER	FILE X
JIM	READ
PROGRAM Y	READ/WRITE
GAIL	READ/WRITE

Table A.4   Capabilities

USER	PROGRAM X	FILE X	FILE Y
JIM	EXECUTE	READ	READ/ WRITE

is incorrect since an ACL, again, is a column in the access control matrix.

6. A type of preventive/physical access control is:

   a. Biometrics for authentication

   b. Motion detectors

   c. Biometrics for identification

   d. An intrusion detection system

   Answer: c

   Biometrics applied to identification of an individual is a "one-to-many" search where an individual's physiological or behavioral characteristics are compared to a database of stored information. An example would be trying to match a person's fingerprints to a set in a national database of fingerprints. This search differs from the biometrics search for authentication in answer a. That search would be a "one-to-one" comparison of a person's physiological or behavioral characteristics with their corresponding entry in an authentication database. Answer b, motion detectors, is a type of detective physical control and answer d is a detective/technical control.

7. In addition to accuracy, a biometric system has additional factors that determine its effectiveness. Which one of the following listed items is NOT one of these additional factors?

   a. Throughput rate

   b. Acceptability

   c. Corpus

   d. Enrollment time

   Answer: c

   A *corpus* is a biometric term that refers to collected biometric images. The corpus is stored in a database of images. Potential sources of error are the corruption of images during collection and mislabeling or other transcription problems associated with the database. Therefore, the image collection, process and storage must be performed carefully with constant checking. These images are collected during the enrollment process and thus, are critical to the correct operation of the biometric device. In *enrollment*, images are collected and features are extracted, but no comparison occurs. The information is stored for use in future comparison steps. Answer a, the *throughput rate*, refers to the rate at which individuals, once enrolled, can be processed by a biometric system. If an individual is being authenticated, the biometric system will take a sample of the individual's characteristic to be evaluated and compare it to a template. A metric called *distance* is used to determine if the sample matches the template. Distance is the difference between the quantitative measure of the sample and the template. If the distance falls within a threshold value, a match is declared. If not, there is no match. Answer b, *acceptability*, is determined by privacy issues, invasiveness, and psychological and physical comfort when using the biometric system. *Enrollment time*, answer d, is the time it takes to initially "register" with a system by providing samples of the biometric characteristic to be evaluated.

8. Access control that is a function of factors such as location, time of day, and previous access history is called:

   a. Positive

   b. Content-dependent

   c. Context-dependent

   d. Information flow

   > *Answer:* c
   >
   > In answer c, access is determined by the context of the decision as opposed to the information contained in the item being accessed. The latter is referred to as *content-dependent* access control. (Answer b) In content-dependent access control, for example, the manager of a department may be authorized to access employment records of a department employee, but may not be permitted to view the health records of the employee. In answer a, the term "positive" in access control refers to positive access rights, such as read or write. Denial rights, such as denial to write to a file, can also be conferred upon a subject. Information flow, cited in answer d, describes a class of access control models. An *information flow model* is described by the set consisting of object, flow policy, states, and rules describing the transitions among states.

9. A persistent collection of data items that form relations among each other is called a:

   a. Database management system (DBMS)

   b. Data description language (DDL)

   c. Schema

   d. Database

   > *Answer:* d
   >
   > For a database to be viable, the data items must be stored on nonvolatile media and be protected from unauthorized modification. For answer a, a DBMS provides access to the items in the database and maintains the information in the database. The Data description language

(DDL) in answer b provides the means to define the database and answer c, schema, is the description of the database.

10. A relational database can provide security through *view* relations. Views enforce what information security principle?

    a. Aggregation

    b. Least privilege

    c. Separation of duties

    d. Inference

    Answer: b

    The principle of *least privilege* states that a subject is permitted to have access to the minimum amount of information required to perform an authorized task. When related to government security clearances, it is referred to as "need-to-know." Answer a, *aggregation*, is defined as assembling or compiling units of information at one sensitivity level and having the resultant totality of data being of a higher sensitivity level than the individual components. *Separation of duties*, answer c, requires that two or more subjects are necessary to authorize an activity or task. Answer d, *inference*, refers to the ability of a subject to deduce information that is not authorized to be accessed by that subject from information that is authorized to that subject.

11. A software interface to the operating system that implements access control by limiting the system commands that are available to a user is called a(n):

    a. Restricted shell

    b. Interrupt

    c. Physically constrained user interface

    d. View

    Answer: a

    Answer b refers to a software or hardware interrupt to a processor that causes the program to jump to another program to handle the interrupt request. Before leaving the program that was being executed at the time of the interrupt, the CPU must save the state of the computer so that the original program can continue after the interrupt has been serviced. A physically constrained user interface, answer c, is one in which a user's operations are limited by the physical characteristics of the interface device. An example would be a keypad with the choices limited to the operations permitted by each key. Answer d refers to database *views*, which restrict access to information contained in a database through content-dependent access control.

12. Controlling access to information systems and associated networks is necessary for the preservation of their confidentiality, integrity, and availability. Which of the following is NOT a goal of integrity?

   a. Prevention of the modification of information by unauthorized users

   b. Prevention of the unauthorized or unintentional modification of information by authorized users

   c. Prevention of authorized modifications by unauthorized users

   d. Preservation of the internal and external consistency of the information

   > *Answer:* c

   > Answers a, b, and d are the three principles of integrity. Answer c is a distracter and does not make sense. In answer d, internal consistency ensures that internal data correlate. For example, the total number of a particular data item in the database should be the sum of all the individual, non-identical occurrences of that data item in the database. External consistency requires that the database content be consistent with the real world items that it represents.

13. In a Kerberos exchange involving a message with an authenticator, the authenticator contains the client ID and which of the following?

   a. Ticket Granting Ticket (TGT)

   b. Timestamp

   c. Client/TGS session key

   d. Client network address

   > *Answer:* b

   > A *timestamp*, t, is used to check the validity of the accompanying request since a Kerberos ticket is valid for some time window, v, after it is issued. The timestamp indicates when the ticket was issued. Answer a, the TGT, is comprised of the client ID, the client network address, the starting and ending time the ticket is valid (v), and the client/TGS session key. This ticket is used by the client to request the service of a resource on the network from the TGS. In answer c, the client/TGS session key, $K_{c, tgs}$, is the symmetric key used for encrypted communication between the client and TGS for this particular session. For answer d, the client network address is included in the TGT and not in the authenticator.

14. Which one of the following security areas is directly addressed by Kerberos?

    a. Confidentiality

    b. Frequency analysis

    c. Availability

    d. Physical attacks

    Answer: a

    Kerberos directly addresses the confidentiality and also the integrity of information. For answer b, attacks such as frequency analysis are not considered in the basic Kerberos implementation. In addition, the Kerberos protocol does not directly address availability issues. (Answer c.) For answer d, since the Kerberos TGS and the authentication servers hold all the secret keys, these servers are vulnerable to both physical attacks and attacks from malicious code. In the Kerberos exchange, the client workstation temporarily holds the client's secret key, and this key is vulnerable to compromise at the workstation.

15. The Secure European System for Applications in a Multivendor Environment (SESAME) implements a Kerberos-like distribution of secret keys. Which of the following is NOT a characteristic of SESAME?

    a. Uses a trusted authentication server at each host

    b. Uses secret key cryptography for the distribution of secret keys

    c. Incorporates two certificates or tickets, one for authentication and one defining access privileges

    d. Uses public key cryptography for the distribution of secret keys

    Answer: b

    SESAME uses public key cryptography for the distribution of secret keys. In addition, SESAME employs the MD5 and crc32 one-way hash functions. A weakness in SESAME is that, similar to Kerberos, it is subject to password guessing.

16. Windows 2000 uses which of the following as the primary mechanism for authenticating users requesting access to a network?

    a. Hash functions

    b. Kerberos

    c. SESAME

    d. Public key certificates

    Answer: b

While Kerberos is the primary mechanism, system administrators may also use alternative authentication services running under the Security Support Provider Interface (SSPI). Answer a, hash functions, are used for digital signature implementations. Answer c, SESAME, is incorrect. It is the Secure European System for Applications in a Multivendor Environment. SESAME performs similar functions to Kerberos, but uses public key cryptography to distribute the secret keys. Answer d is incorrect, since public key certificates are not used in the Windows 2000 primary authentication approach.

17. A protection mechanism to limit inferencing of information in statistical database queries is:

    a. Specifying a maximum query set size

    b. Specifying a minimum query set size

    c. Specifying a minimum query set size, but prohibiting the querying of all but one of the records in the database

    d. Specifying a maximum query set size, but prohibiting the querying of all but one of the records in the database

    Answer: c

    When querying a database for statistical information, individually identifiable information should be protected. Thus, requiring a minimum size for the query set (greater than one) offers protection against gathering information on one individual. However, an attack may consist of gathering statistics on a query set size M, equal to or greater than the minimum query set size, and then requesting the same statistics on a query set size of M + 1. The second query set would be designed to include the individual whose information is being sought surreptitiously. Thus with answer c, this type of attack could not take place. Answer b is, therefore, incorrect since it leaves open the loophole of the M+1 set size query. Answers a and d are incorrect since the critical metric is the minimum query set size and not the maximum size. Obviously, the maximum query set size cannot be set to a value less than the minimum set size.

18. In SQL, a relation that is actually existent in the database is called a(n):

    a. Base relation

    b. View

    c. Attribute

    d. Domain

    Answer: a

A *base relation* exists in the database while a view, answer b, is a virtual relation that is not stored in the database. A view is derived by the SQL definition and is developed from base relations or, possibly, other views. Answer c, an *attribute*, is a column in a relation table and answer d, a *domain*, is the set of permissible values of an attribute.

19. A type of access control that supports the management of access rights for groups of subjects is:

   a. Role-based

   b. Discretionary

   c. Mandatory

   d. Rule-based

   Answer: a

   Role-based access control assigns identical privileges to groups of users. This approach simplifies the management of access rights, particularly when members of the group change. Thus, access rights are assigned to a role, not to an individual. Individuals are entered as members of specific groups and are assigned the access privileges of that group. In answer b, the access rights to an object are assigned by the owner at the owner's discretion. For large numbers of people whose duties and participation may change frequently, this type of access control can become unwieldy. *Mandatory access control*, answer c, uses security labels or classifications assigned to data items and clearances assigned to users. A user has access rights to data items with a classification equal to or less than the user's clearance. Another restriction is that the user has to have a "need-to-know" the information; this requirement is identical to the principle of least privilege. Answer d, *rule-based* access control, assigns access rights based on stated rules. An example of a rule is "Access to trade-secret data is restricted to corporate officers, the data owner and the legal department."

20. The Simple Security Property and the Star Property are key principles in which type of access control?

   a. Role-based

   b. Rule-based

   c. Discretionary

   d. Mandatory

   Answer: d

   Two properties define fundamental principles of mandatory access control. These properties are:

   Simple Security Property. A user at one clearance level cannot read data from a higher classification level.

Star Property. A user at one clearance level cannot write data to a lower classification level

Answers a, b, and c are discussed in Question 19.

21. Which of the following items is NOT used to determine the types of access controls to be applied in an organization?

   a. Least privilege

   b. Separation of duties

   c. Relational categories

   d. Organizational policies

   Answer: c

   The item, relational categories, is a distracter. Answers a, b, and d are important determinants of access control implementations in an organization.

22. Kerberos provides an integrity check service for messages between two entities through the use of:

   a. A checksum

   b. Credentials

   c. Tickets

   d. A trusted, third-party authentication server

   Answer: a

   A checksum that is derived from a Kerberos message is used to verify the integrity of the message. This checksum may be a message digest resulting from the application of a hash function to the message. At the receiving end of the transmission, the receiving party can calculate the message digest of the received message using the identical hash algorithm as the sender. Then the message digest calculated by the receiver can be compared with the message digest appended to the message by the sender. If the two message digests match, the message has not been modified en route, and its integrity has been preserved. For answers b and c, credentials and tickets are authenticators used in the process of granting user access to services on the network. Answer d is the AS or authentication server that conducts the ticket-granting process.

23. The Open Group has defined functional objectives in support of a user single sign-on (SSO) interface. Which of the following is NOT one of those objectives and would possibly represent a vulnerability?

   a. The interface shall be independent of the type of authentication information handled.

   b. Provision for user-initiated change of nonuser-configured authentication information.

c. It shall not predefine the timing of secondary sign-on operations.

d. Support shall be provided for a subject to establish a default user profile.

Answer: b

User configuration of nonuser-configured authentication mechanisms is not supported by the Open Group SSO interface objectives. Authentication mechanisms include items such as smart cards and magnetic badges. Strict controls must be placed to prevent a user from changing configurations that are set by another authority. Objective a supports the incorporation of a variety of authentication schemes and technologies. Answer c states that the interface functional objectives do not require that all sign-on operations be performed at the same time as the primary sign on. This prevents the creation of user sessions with all the available services even though these services are not needed by the user. For answer d, the creation of a default user profile will make the sign-on more efficient and less time-consuming.

In summary, the scope of the Open Group Single Sign-On Standards is to define services in support of:

■ "The development of applications to provide a common, single end-user sign-on interface for an enterprise.

■ The development of applications for the coordinated management of multiple user account management information bases maintained by an enterprise."

24. There are some correlations between relational data base terminology and object-oriented database terminology. Which of the following relational model terms, respectively, correspond to the object model terms of class, attribute and instance object?

a. Domain, relation, and column

b. Relation, domain, and column

c. Relation, tuple, and column

d. Relation, column, and tuple

Answer: d

Table A.5 shows the correspondence between the two models.

In comparing the two models, a class is similar to a relation; however, a relation does not have the inheritance property of a class. An attribute in the object model is similar to the column of a relational table. The column has limitations on the data types it can hold while an attribute in the object model can use all data types that are supported by the Java and C++ languages. An instance object in the object model corresponds to a tuple in the relational model. Again

Table A.5   Object and Relational Model Correspondence

OBJECT MODEL	RELATIONAL MODEL
CLASS	RELATION
ATTRIBUTE	COLUMN
INSTANCE OBJECT	TUPLE

the data structures of the tuple are limited while those of the instance object can use data structures of Java and C++.

25. A *reference monitor* is a system component that enforces access controls on an object. Specifically, the *reference monitor concept* is an abstract machine that mediates all access of subjects to objects. The hardware, firmware, and software elements of a trusted computing base that implement the reference monitor concept are called:

   a. The authorization database

   b. Identification and authentication (I & A) mechanisms

   c. The auditing subsystem

   d. The security kernel

   Answer: d

   The *security kernel* implements the reference model concept. The reference model must have the following characteristics:

   ■ It must mediate all accesses.

   ■ It must be protected from modification.

   ■ It must be verifiable as correct.

   Answer a, the authorization database, is used by the reference monitor to mediate accesses by subjects to objects. When a request for access is received, the reference monitor refers to entries in the authorization database to verify that the operation requested by a subject for application to an object is permitted. The authorization database has entries or *authorizations* of the form subject, object, access mode. In answer b, the I & A operation is separate from the reference monitor. The user enters his/her identification to the I & A function. Then the user must be authenticated. *Authentication* is verification that the user's claimed identity is valid. Authentication is based on the following three factor types:

   Type 1. Something you know, such as a PIN or password

   Type 2. Something you have, such as an ATM card or smart card

   Type 3. Something you are (physically), such as a fingerprint or retina scan

Answer c, the auditing subsystem, is a key complement to the reference monitor. The auditing subsystem is used by the reference monitor to keep track of the reference monitor's activities. Examples of such activities include the date and time of an access request, identification of the subject and objects involved, the access privileges requested and the result of the request.

26. Authentication in which a random value is presented to a user, who then returns a calculated number based on that random value is called:

   a. Man-in-the-middle

   b. Challenge-response

   c. One-time password

   d. Personal identification number (PIN) protocol

   Answer: b

   In *challenge-response authentication,* the user enters a random value (challenge) sent by the authentication server into a token device. The token device shares knowledge of a cryptographic secret key with the authentication server and calculates a response based on the challenge value and the secret key. This response is entered into the authentication server, which uses the response to authenticate the identity of the user by performing the same calculation and comparing results. Answer a, *man-in-the-middle,* is a type of attack in which a cracker is interposed between the user and authentication server and attempts to gain access to packets for replay in order to impersonate a valid user. A *one-time password,* answer c, is a password that is used only once to gain access to a network or computer system. A typical implementation is through the use of a token that generates a number based on the time of day. The user reads this number and enters it into the authenticating device. The authenticating device calculates the same number based on the time of day and uses the same algorithm used by the token. If the token's number matches that of the authentication server, the identity of the user is validated. Obviously, the token and the authentication server must be time-synchronized for this approach to work. Also, there is allowance for small values of time skew between the authorization device and the token. Answer d refers to a PIN number that is something you know used with something you have, such as an ATM card.

27. Which of the following is NOT a criterion for access control?

   a. Identity

   b. Role

c. Keystroke monitoring

d. Transactions

Answer: c

Keystroke monitoring is associated with the auditing function and not access control. For answer a, the identity of the user is a criterion for access control. The identity must be authenticated as part of the I & A process. Answer b refers to role-based access control where access to information is determined by the user's job function or role in the organization. Transactions, answer d, refer to access control through entering an account number or a transaction number, as may be required for bill payments by telephone, for example.

28. Which of the following is typically NOT a consideration in the design of passwords?

a. Lifetime

b. Composition

c. Authentication period

d. Electronic monitoring

Answer: d

Electronic monitoring is the eavesdropping on passwords that are being transmitted to the authenticating device. This issue is a technical one and is not a consideration in designing passwords. The other answers relate to very important password characteristics that must be taken into account when developing passwords. Password lifetime, in answer a, refers to the maximum period of time that a password is valid. Ideally, a password should be used only once. This approach can be implemented by token password generators and challenge response schemes. However, as a practical matter, passwords on most PC's and workstations are used repeatedly. The time period after which passwords should be changed is a function of the level of protection required for the information being accessed. In typical organizations, passwords may be changed every three to six months. Obviously, passwords should be changed when employees leave an organization or in a situation where a password may have been compromised. Answer b, the composition of a password, defines the characters that can be used in the password. The characters may be letters, numbers, or special symbols. The authentication period in answer c defines the maximum acceptable period between the initial authentication of a user and any subsequent reauthorization process. For example, users may be asked to authenticate themselves again after a specified period of time of being logged on to a server containing critical information.

29. A distributed system using passwords as the authentication means can use a number of techniques to make the password system stronger. Which of the following is NOT one of these techniques?

   a. Password generators
   b. Regular password reuse
   c. Password file protection
   d. Limiting the number or frequency of log-on attempts

   Answer: b

   Passwords should never be reused after the time limit on their use has expired. Answer a, password generators, supply passwords upon request. These passwords are usually comprised of numbers, characters, and sometimes symbols. Passwords provided by password generators are, usually, not easy to remember. For answer c, password file protection may consist of encrypting the password with a one-way hash function and storing it in a password file. A typical brute force attack against this type of protection is to encrypt trial password guesses using the same hash function and to compare the encrypted results with the encrypted passwords stored in the password file. Answer d provides protection in that, after a specified number of unsuccessful log-on attempts, a user may be locked out of trying to log on for a period of time. An alternative is to progressively increase the time between permitted log-on tries after each unsuccessful log-on attempt.

30. Enterprise Access Management (EAM) provides access control management services to Web-based enterprise systems. Which of the following functions is NOT normally provided by extant EAM approaches?

   a. Single sign-on
   b. Accommodation of a variety of authentication mechanisms
   c. Role-based access control
   d. Interoperability among EAM implementations

   Answer: d

   In general, security credentials produced by one EAM solution are not recognized by another implementation. Thus, reauthentication is required when linking from one Web site to another related Web site if the sites have different EAM implementations.   Single sign-on

(SSO), answer a, is approached in a number of ways. For example, SSO can be implemented on Web applications in the same domain residing on different servers by using nonpersistent, encrypted cookies on the client interface. This is accomplished by providing a cookie to each application that the user wishes to access. Another solution is to build a secure credential for each user on a reverse proxy that is situated in front of the Web server. The credential is, then, presented at each instance of a user attempting to access protected Web applications. For answer b, most EAM solutions accommodate a variety of authentication technologies, including tokens, ID/passwords and digital certificates. Similarly, for answer c, EAM solutions support role-based access controls, albeit they may be implemented in different fashions. Enterprise-level roles should be defined in terms that are universally accepted across most e-commerce applications.

31. The main approach to obtaining the true biometric information from a collected sample of an individual's physiological or behavioral characteristics is:

   a. Feature extraction

   b. Enrollment

   c. False rejection

   d. Digraphs

   Answer: a

   Feature extraction algorithms are a subset of signal/image processing and are used to extract the key biometric information from a sample that has been taken from an individual. Usually, the sample is taken in an environment that may have "noise" and other conditions that may affect the raw sample image. Neural networks are an example of a feature extraction approach. Answer b, *enrollment*, refers to the process of collecting samples that are averaged and then stored to use as a reference base against which future samples are compared. False rejection, answer c, refers to the false rejection in biometrics. *False rejection* is the rejection of an authorized user because of a mismatch between the sample and the reference template. Conversely, *false acceptance* is the acceptance of an unauthorized user because of an incorrect match to the template of an authorized user. The corresponding measures in percentage are the False Rejection Rate (FRR) and False Acceptance Rate (FAR). For answer d, diagraphs refer to sets of average values compiled in the biometrics area of keystroke dynamics. *Keystroke dynamics* involves analyzing the characteristics of a user typing on a keyboard. Keystroke duration samples as well as measures of the latency between keystrokes are taken and averaged. These averages for all pairs of keys are called *diagraphs*. *Trigraphs*, sample sets for all key triples, can also be used as biometric samples.

32. In a wireless General Packet Radio Services (GPRS) Virtual Private Network (VPN) application, which of the following security protocols is commonly used?

   a. SSL

   b. IPSEC

   c. TLS

   d. WTP

   Answer: b

   An example is the use of a GPRS-enabled laptop that connects to a corporate intranet via a VPN. The laptop is given an IP address and a RADIUS server authenticates the user. IPSEC is used to create the VPN. As background, GPRS is a second-generation (2G) packet data technology that is overlaid on existing Global System for Mobile communications (GSM). GSM is the wireless analog of the ISDN landline system. The key features of GPRS are that it is always on line (no dial-up needed), existing GSM networks can be upgraded with GPRS, and it can serve as the packet data core of third generation (3G) systems. Answers a and c, SSL and TLS, are similar security protocols that are used on the Internet side of the Wireless Application Protocol (WAP) Gateway. For answer d, WTP is the Wireless Transaction Protocol that is part of the WAP suite of protocols. WTP is a lightweight, message-oriented, transaction protocol that provides more reliable connections than UDP, but does not have the robustness of TCP.

33. How is authentication implemented in GSM?

   a. Using public key cryptography

   b. It is not implemented in GSM

   c. Using secret key cryptography

   d. Out-of-band verification

   Answer: c

   Authentication is effected in GSM through the use of a common secret key, K_s, that is stored in the network operator's Authentication Center (AuC) and in the subscriber's SIM card. The SIM card may be in the subscriber's laptop, and the subscriber is not privy to K_s. To begin the authentication exchange, the home location of the subscriber's mobile station, (MS), generates a 128-bit random number (RAND) and sends it to the MS. Using an algorithm that is known to both the AuC and MS, the RAND is encrypted by both parties using the secret key, K_s. The ciphertext generated at the MS is then sent to the AuC and compared with the ciphertext generated by the AuC. If the two results match, the MS is authenticated and the access request is granted. If they do not match, the access request is denied. Answers a, b, and d are, therefore, incorrect.

Chapter 3—Telecommunications and Network Security

1. Which of the choices below is NOT an OSI reference model Session Layer protocol, standard, or interface?

    a. SQL

    b. RPC

    c. MIDI

    d. ASP

    e. DNA SCP

    Answer: c

    The Musical Instrument Digital Interface (MIDI) standard is a Presentation Layer standard for digitized music. The other answers are all Session layer protocols or standards. Answer a, SQL, refers to the Structured Query Language database standard originally developed by IBM. Answer b, RPC, refers to the Remote Procedure Call redirection mechanism for remote clients. Answer d, ASP, is the AppleTalk Session Protocol; and answer e, DNA SCP, refers to DECnet's Digital Network Architecture Session Control Protocol. Source: *Introduction to Cisco Router Configuration* edited by Laura Chappell (Cisco Press, 1999).

2. Which part of the 48-bit, 12-digit hexadecimal number known as the Media Access Control (MAC) address identifies the manufacturer of the network device?

    a. The first three bytes

    b. The first two bytes

    c. The second half of the MAC address

    d. The last three bytes

    Answer: a

    The first three bytes (or first half) of the six-byte MAC address is the manufacturer's identifier (see Table A.6). This can be a good troubleshooting aid if a network device is acting up, as it will isolate the brand of the failing device. The other answers are distracters. Source: *Mastering Network Security* by Chris Brenton (Sybex, 1999).

3. Which IEEE protocol defines the Spanning Tree protocol?

    a. IEEE 802.5

    b. IEEE 802.3

Table A.6 Common Vendors' MAC Addresses

FIRST THREE BYTES	VENDOR
00000C	Cisco
0000A2	Bay Networks
0080D3	Shiva
00AA00	Intel
02608C	3COM
080007	Apple
080009	Hewlett-Packard
080020	Sun
08005A	IBM

   c. IEEE 802.11

   d. IEEE 802.1D

     Answer: d

     The 802.1D spanning tree protocol is an Ethernet link-management protocol that provides link redundancy while preventing routing loops. Since only one active path can exist for an Ethernet network to route properly, the STP algorithm calculates and manages the best loop-free path through the network. Answer a, IEEE 802.5, specifies a token-passing ring access method for LANs. Answer b, IEEE 802.3, specifies an Ethernet bus topology using Carrier Sense Multiple Access Control/Carrier Detect (CSMA/CD). Answer c, IEEE 802.11, is the IEEE standard that specifies 1 Mbps and 2 Mbps wireless connectivity in the 2.4 MHz ISM (Industrial, Scientific, Medical) band. Source: *Designing Network Security* by Merike Kaeo (Cisco Press, 1999).

4. Which choice below is NOT one of the legal IP address ranges specified by RFC1976 and reserved by the Internet Assigned Numbers Authority (IANA) for nonroutable private addresses?

   a. 10.0.0.0 - 10.255.255.255

   b. 127.0.0.0 - 127.0.255.255

   c. 172.16.0.0 - 172.31.255.255

   d. 192.168.0.0 - 192.168.255.255

     Answer: b

The other three address ranges can be used for Network Address Translation (NAT). While NAT is, in itself, not a very effective security measure, a large network can benefit from using NAT with Dynamic Host Configuration Protocol (DHCP) to help prevent certain internal routing information from being exposed. The address 127.0.0.1 is called the "loopback" address. Source: *Designing Network Security* by Merike Kaeo (Cisco Press, 1999).

5. Which statement is correct about ISDN Basic Rate Interface?

   a. It offers 23 B channels and 1 D channel.

   b. It offers 2 B channels and 1 D channel.

   c. It offers 30 B channels and 1 D channel.

   d. It offers 1 B channel and 2 D channels.

   Answer: b

   Integrated Services Digital Network (ISDN) Basic Rate Interface (BRI) offers two B channels which carry user data at 64 Kbps each, and one control and signaling D channel operating at 16 Kbps. Answer a describes ISDN Primary Rate Interface (PRI) for North America and Japan, with 23 B channels at 64 Kbps and one 64 Kbps D channel, for a total throughput of 1.544 Mbps. Answer c describes ISDN PRI for Europe, Australia, and other parts of the world, with 30 64 Kbps B channels and one D channel, for a total throughput of 2.048 Mbps. Answer d is a distracter. Source: *Internetworking Technologies Handbook, Second Edition* (Cisco Press, 1998).

6. In the DoD reference model, which layer conforms to the OSI transport layer?

   a. Process/Application Layer

   b. Host-to-Host Layer

   c. Internet Layer

   d. Network Access Layer

   Answer: b

   In the DoD reference model, the Host-to-Host layer parallels the function of the OSI's transport layer. This layer contains the Transmission Control Protocol (TCP), and the User Datagram Protocol (UDP). Answer a, the DoD Process/Application layer, corresponds to the OSI's top three layers, the Application, Presentation, and Session layers. Answer c, the DoD Internet layer, corresponds to the OSI's Network layer, and answer d, the DoD Network Access Layer, is the equivalent of the Data Link and Physical layers of the OSI model. Source: *MCSE:TCP/IP Study Guide* by Todd Lammle, Monica Lammle, and John

Chellis (Sybex, 1997) and *Handbook of Information Security Management 1999* by Micki Krause and Harold F. Tipton (Auerbach, 1999).

7. What is the Network Layer of the OSI reference model primarily responsible for?

   a. Internetwork packet routing

   b. LAN bridging

   c. SMTP Gateway services

   d. Signal regeneration and repeating

   Answer: a

   Although many routers can perform most of the functions above, the OSI Network layer is primarily responsible for routing. Answer b, bridging, is a Data Link Layer function. Answer c, gateways, most commonly function at the higher layers. Answer d, signal regeneration and repeating, is primarily a Physical layer function. Source: *CCNA Study Guide* by Todd Lammle, Donald Porter, and James Chellis (Sybex, 1999).

8. Which IEEE protocol defines wireless transmission in the 5 GHz band with data rates up to 54 Mbps?

   a. IEEE 802.11a

   b. IEEE 802.11b

   c. IEEE 802.11g

   d. IEEE 802.15

   Answer: a

   IEEE 802.11a specifies high-speed wireless connectivity in the 5 GHz band using Orthogonal Frequency Division Multiplexing with data rates up to 54 Mbps. Answer b, IEEE 802.11b, specifies high-speed wireless connectivity in the 2.4 GHz ISM band up to 11 Mbps. Answer c, IEEE 802.11g, is a proposed standard that offers wireless transmission over relatively short distances at speeds from 20 Mbps up to 54 Mbps and operates in the 2.4 GHz range (and is therefore expected to be backward-compatible with existing 802.11b-based networks). Answer d, IEEE 802.15, defines Wireless Personal Area Networks (WPAN), such as Bluetooth, in the 2.4-2.5 GHz band. Source: IEEE Wireless Working Groups (grouper.ieee.org).

9. Which category of UTP wiring is rated for 100BaseT Ethernet networks?

   a. Category 1

   b. Category 2

   c. Category 3

   d. Category 4

   e. Category 5

Answer: e

Category 5 unshielded twisted-pair (UTP) wire is rated for transmissions of up to 100 Mbps and can be used in 100BaseT Ethernet networks. It is the most commonly installed type of UTP at this time. See Table A.7. Answer a, category 1 twisted-pair wire was used for early analog telephone communications and is not suitable for data. Answer b, category 2 twisted-pair wire, was used in AS/400 and IBM 3270 networks. Derived from IBM Type 3 cable specification. Answer c, category 3 twisted-pair wire, is rated for 10 Mbps and was used in 802.3 10Base-T Ethernet networks, and 4 Mbps Token Ring networks. Answer d, category 4 twisted-pair wire, is rated for 16 Mbps and is used in 4/16 Mbps Token Ring LANs. Source: The Electrical Industry Alliance (EIA/TIA-568).

10. Which choice below is the earliest and the most commonly found Interior Gateway Protocol?

   a. RIP
   b. OSPF
   c. IGRP
   d. EAP

   Answer: a

   The Routing Information Protocol (RIP) bases its routing path on the distance (number of hops) to the destination. RIP maintains optimum routing paths by sending out routing update messages if the network topology changes. For example, if a router finds that a particular link is faulty, it will update its routing table, then send a copy of the modified table to each of its neighbors. Answer b, the Open Shortest Path First (OSPF) is a link-state hierarchical routing algorithm intended as a successor to RIP. It features least-cost routing, multipath routing, and load balancing. Answer c, the Internet Gateway Routing Protocol (IGRP) is a Cisco protocol that uses a composite metric as its

Table A.7 UTP Categories of Performance

UTP CAT	RATED PERFORMANCE IN MHZ	COMMON APPLICATIONS
Cat1	Under 1 MHz	Analog voice, ISDN BRI
Cat2	1 MHz	IBM 3270, AS/400, Apple LocalTalk
Cat3	16 MHz	10BaseT, 4 Mbps Token Ring
Cat4	20 MHz	16 Mbps Token Ring
Cat5	100 MHz	10/100BaseT

routing metric, including bandwidth, delay, reliability, loading, and maximum transmission unit. Answer d, the Extensible Authentication Protocol (EAP), is a general protocol for PPP authentication that supports multiple remote authentication mechanisms. Source: *Introduction to Cisco Router Configuration* edited by Laura Chappell (Cisco Press, 1999).

11. The data transmission method in which data is sent continuously and doesn't use either an internal clocking source or start/stop bits for timing is known as:

   a. Asynchronous

   b. Synchronous

   c. Isochronous

   d. Pleisiochronous

    Answer: c

    Isochronous data is synchronous data transmitting without a clocking source, with the bits sent continuously and no start or stop bits. All bits are of equal importance and are anticipated to occur at regular time intervals. Answer a, asynchronous, is a data transmission method using a start bit at the beginning of the data value, and a stop bit at the end of the value. Answer b, synchronous, is a message-framed transmission method that uses clocking pulses to match the speed of the data transmission. Answer d, pleisiochronous, is a transmission method that uses more than one timing source, sometimes running at different speeds. This method may require master and slave clock devices. Source: *Communications Systems and Networks* by Ray Horak (M&T Books, 2000).

12. Which level of RAID is commonly referred to as "disk mirroring"?

   a. RAID 0

   b. RAID 1

   c. RAID 3

   d. RAID 5

    Answer: b

    Redundant Array of Inexpensive Disks (RAID) is a method of enhancing hard disk fault tolerance, which can improve performance (see Table A.8). RAID 1 maintains a complete copy of all data by duplicating each hard drive. Performance can suffer in some implementations of RAID 1, and twice as many drives are required. Novell developed a type of disk mirroring called disk duplexing, which uses

Table A.8   Commonly Used RAID Types

RAID LEVEL	DESCRIPTION
RAID 0	Multiple Drive Striping
RAID 1	Disk Mirroring
RAID 3	Single Parity Drive
RAID 5	Distributed Parity Information

multiple disk controller cards increasing both performance and reliability. Answer a, RAID 0, gives some performance gains by striping
the data across multiple drives, but reduces fault tolerance, as the
failure of any single drive disables the whole volume. Answer c,
RAID 3, uses a dedicated error-correction disk called a parity drive,
and stripes the data across the other data drives. Answer RAID 5,
uses all disks in the array for both data and error correction, increasing both storage capacity and performance.

13. Which network attack below would NOT be considered a Denial of
Service attack?

    a. Ping of Death

    b. SMURF

    c. Brute Force

    d. TCP SYN

    Answer: c

    A brute force attack is an attempt to use all combinations of key
    patterns to decipher a message. The other three attacks are com-
    monly used to create a Denial of Service (DoS). Answer a, Ping of
    Death, exploits ICMP by sending an illegal ECHO packet of >65K
    octets of data, which can cause an overflow of system variables and
    lead to a system crash. Answer b, SMURF, is a type of attack using
    spoofed ICMP ECHO requests to broadcast addresses, which the
    routers attempt to propagate, congesting the network. Three partici-
    pants are required for a SMURF attack: the attacker, the amplifying
    network, and the victim. Answer d, a TCP SYN flood attack, gener-
    ates phony TCP SYN packets from random IP addresses at a rapid
    rate to fill up the connection queue and stop the system from accept-
    ing legitimate users. Source: *Hacking Exposed* by Stuart McClure, Joel
    Scambray, and George Kurtz (Osborne, 1999).

14. Which choice below is NOT an element of IPSec?
    a. Authentication Header
    b. Layer Two Tunneling Protocol
    c. Security Association
    d. Encapsulating Security Payload

    Answer: b

    The Layer Two Tunneling Protocol (L2TP) is a layer two tunneling protocol that allows a host to establish a virtual connection. Although L2TP, an enhancement to Layer Two Forwarding Protocol (L2F) and supporting some features of Point to Point Tunneling Protocol (PPTP), may coexist with IPSec, it is not natively an IPSec component. Answer a, the Authentication Header (AH), is an authenticating protocol that uses a hash signature in the packet header to validate the integrity of the packet data and the authenticity of the sender. Answer c, the Security Association (SA), is a component of the IPSec architecture that contains the information the IPSec device needs to process incoming and outbound IPSec packets. IPSec devices embed a value called the Security Parameter Index (SPI) in the header to associate a datagram with its SA, and store SAs in a Security Association Database (SAD). Answer d, the Encapsulating Security Payload (ESP), is an authenticating and encrypting protocol that provides integrity, source authentication, and confidentiality services. Source: *Implementing IPSec* by Elizabeth Kaufman and Andrew Newman (Wiley, 1999).

15. Which statement below is NOT true about the difference between cut-through and store-and-forward switching?
    a. A store-and-forward switch reads the whole packet and checks its validity before sending it to the next destination.
    b. Both methods operate at layer two of the OSI reference model.
    c. A cut-through switch reads only the header on the incoming data packet.
    d. A cut-through switch introduces more latency than a store-and-forward switch.

    Answer: d

    A cut-through switch provides less latency than a store-and-forward switch, as it forwards the frame before it has received the complete frame. However, cut-through switches may also forward defective or empty packets. Source: *Virtual LANs* by Mariana Smith (McGraw-Hill, 1998).

16. Which statement is NOT true about the SOCKS protocol?

    a. It is sometimes referred to as an application-level proxy.

    b. It uses an ESP for authentication and encryption.

    c. It operates in the transport layer of the OSI model.

    d. Network applications need to be SOCKS-ified to operate.

    > The correct answer is b. The Encapsulating Security Payload, (ESP) is a component of IPSec. Socket Security (SOCKS) is a transport layer, secure networking proxy protocol. SOCKS replaces the standard network systems calls with its own calls. These calls open connections to a SOCKS proxy server for client authentication, transparently to the user. Common network utilities, like TELNET or FTP, need to be SOCKS-ified, or have their network calls altered to recognize SOCKS proxy calls. Source: *Designing Network Security* by Merike Kaeo (Cisco Press, 1999).

17. Which choice below does NOT relate to analog dial-up hacking?

    a. War Dialing

    b. War Walking

    c. Demon Dialing

    d. ToneLoc

    > *Answer:* b

    > War Walking (or War Driving) refers to scanning for 802.11-based wireless network information, by either driving or walking with a laptop, a wireless adapter in promiscuous mode, some type of scanning software such as NetStumbler or AiroPeek, and a Global Positioning System (GPS). Answer a, War Dialing, is a method used to hack into computers by using a software program to automatically call a large pool of telephone numbers to search for those that have a modem attached. Answer c, Demon Dialing, similar to War Dialing, is a tool used to attack one modem using brute force to guess the password and gain access. Answer d, ToneLoc, was one of the first war-dialing tools used by "phone phreakers." Sources: *Hacking Exposed* by Stuart McClure, Joel Scambray, and George Kurtz (Osborne, 1999) and "War Driving by the Bay" by Kevin Poulsen, The Register, April 13, 2001.

18. Which choice below is NOT a way to get Windows NT passwords?

    a. Obtain the backup SAM from the repair directory.

    b. Boot the NT server with a floppy containing an alternate operating system.

c. Obtain root access to the /etc/passwd file.

d. Use pwdump2 to dump the password hashes directly from the registry.

Answer: c

The /etc/passwd file is a Unix system file. The NT Security Accounts Manager, SAM, contains the usernames and encrypted passwords of all local (and domain, if the server is a domain controller) users. The SAM uses an older, weaker LanManager hash that can be broken easily by tools like L0phtcrack. Physical access to the NT server and the rdisks must be controlled. The "Sam._" file in the repair directory must be deleted after creation of an rdisk. Pwdump and pwdump2 are utilities that allow someone with Administrator rights to target the Local Security Authority Subsystem, isass.exe, from a remote system. Source: *Hacking Exposed* by Stuart McClure, Joel Scambray, and George Kurtz (Osborne, 1999).

19. A "back door" into a network refers to what?

a. Socially engineering passwords from a subject

b. Mechanisms created by hackers to gain network access at a later time

c. Undocumented instructions used by programmers to debug applications

d. Monitoring programs implemented on dummy applications to lure intruders

Answer: b

Back doors are very hard to trace, as an intruder will often create several avenues into a network to be exploited later. The only real way to be sure these avenues are closed after an attack is to restore the operating system from the original media, apply the patches, and restore all data and applications. Answer a, social engineering, is a technique used to manipulate users into revealing information like passwords. Answer c refers to a "trap door," which are undocumented hooks into an application to assist programmers with debugging. Although intended innocently, these can be exploited by intruders. Answer d is a "honey pot" or "padded cell." A honey pot uses a dummy server with bogus applications as a decoy for intruders. Source: *Fighting Computer Crime* by Donn B. Parker (Wiley, 1998).

20. Which protocol below does NOT pertain to e-mail?

a. SMTP

b. POP

   c. CHAP

   d. IMAP

     Answer: c

     The Challenge Handshake Authentication Protocol (CHAP) is used at the startup of a remote link to verify the identity of a remote node. Answer a, the Simple Mail Transfer Protocol (RFCs 821 and 1869), is used by a server to deliver e-mail over the Internet. Answer b, the Post Office Protocol (RFC 1939), enables users to read their email by downloading it from a remote server on to their local computer. Answer d, the Internet Message Access Protocol (RFC 2060), allows users to read their e-mail on a remote server, without downloading the mail locally. Source: *Handbook of Computer Crime Investigation* Edited by Eoghan Casey (Academic Press, 2002).

21. The IP address, 178.22.90.1, is considered to be in which class of address?

   a. Class A

   b. Class B

   c. Class C

   d. Class D

     Answer: b

     The class A address range is 1.0.0.0 to 126.255.255.255. The class B address range is 128.0.0.0 to 191.255.255.255. The class C address range is from 192.0.0.0 to 223.255.255.255. The class D address range is 244.0.0.0 to 239.255.255.255, and is used for multicast packets. Sources: *Designing Network Security* by Merike Kaeo (Cisco Press, 1999) and *CCNA Study Guide* by Todd Lammle, Donald Porter, and James Chellis (Sybex, 1999).

22. What type of firewall architecture employs two network cards and a single screening router?

   a. A screened-host firewall

   b. A dual-homed host firewall

   c. A screened-subnet firewall

   d. An application-level proxy server

     Answer: a

     Like a dual-homed host, a screened-host firewall uses two network cards to connect to the trusted and untrusted networks, but adds a screening router between the host and the untrusted network. Answer b, dual-homed host, has two NICs but not necessarily a screening router. Answer c, screened-subnet firewall, uses two NICs also, but has two screening routers with the host

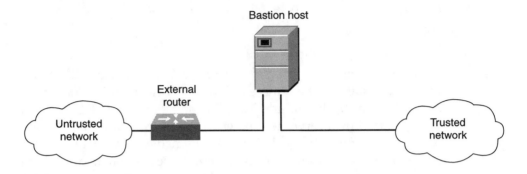

Figure A.1   Screened-host firewall.

acting as a proxy server on its own network segment. One screening router controls traffic local to the network while the second monitors and controls incoming and outgoing Internet traffic, Answer d, application-level proxy, is unrelated to this question. Source: *Hacker Proof* by Lars Klander (Jamsa Press, 1997).

Figure A.1 shows a Screened-host firewall.

23. What is one of the most common drawbacks to using a dual-homed host firewall?

   a. The examination of the packet at the Network layer introduces latency.

   b. The examination of the packet at the Application layer introduces latency.

   c. The ACLs must be manually maintained on the host.

   d. Internal routing may accidentally become enabled.

   Answer: d

   A dual-homed host uses two NICs to attach to two separate networks, commonly a trusted network and an untrusted network. It's important that the internal routing function of the host be disabled to create an application-layer chokepoint and filter packets. Many systems come with routing enabled by default, such as IP forwarding, which makes the firewall useless. The other answers are distracters. Source: *Hacker Proof* by Lars Klander (Jamsa Press, 1997).

24. Which firewall type below uses a dynamic state table to inspect the content of packets?

   a. A packet-filtering firewall

   b. An application-level firewall

c. A circuit-level firewall

d. A stateful-inspection firewall

> *Answer:* d
>
> A stateful-inspection firewall intercepts incoming packets at the Network level, then uses an Inspection Engine to extract state-related information from upper layers. It maintains the information in a dynamic state table and evaluates subsequent connection attempts. Answer a, packet-filtering firewall, is the simplest type of firewall commonly implemented on routers. It operates at the Network layer and offers good performance but is the least secure. Answer b, application-level firewall or application-layer gateway, is more secure because it examines the packet at the application layer, but at the expense of performance. Answer c, circuit-level firewall, is similar to the application-level firewall in that it functions as a proxy server, but differs in that special proxy application software is not needed. Sources: *Hacker Proof* by Lars Klander (Jamsa Press, 1997) and Checkpoint Firewall-1 Stateful Inspection Technology (www.checkpoint.com).

25. Which attack type below does NOT exploit TCP vulnerabilities?

a. Sequence Number attack

b. SYN attack

c. Ping of Death

d. land.c attack

> *Answer:* c
>
> The Ping of Death exploits the fragmentation vulnerability of large ICMP ECHO request packets by sending an illegal packet with more than 65K of data, creating a buffer overflow. Answer a is a TCP sequence number attack, which exploits the nonrandom predictable pattern of TCP connection sequence numbers to spoof a session. Answer b, a TCP SYN attack, is a DoS attack that exploits the TCP three-way handshake. The attacker rapidly generates randomly sourced SYN packets filling the target's connection queue before the connection can timeout. Answer d, land.c attack, is also a DoS attack that exploits TCP SYN packets. The attacker sends a packet that gives both the source and destination as the target's address, and uses the same source and destination port. Sources: *Designing Network Security* by Merike Kaeo (Cisco Press, 1999) and *Mastering Network Security* by Chris Brenton (Sybex, 1999).

26. Which utility below can create a server-spoofing attack?

a. DNS poisoning

b. C2MYAZZ

c. Snort

d. BO2K

> *Answer:* b
>
> C2MYAZZ is a utility that enables server spoofing to implement a session highjacking or man-in-the-middle exploit. It intercepts a client LANMAN authentication logon and obtains the session's logon credentials and password combination, transparently to the user. Answer a, DNS poisoning, is also known as cache poisoning. It is the process of distributing incorrect IP address information for a specific host with the intent to divert traffic from its true destination. Answer c, Snort, is a utility used for network sniffing. Network sniffing is the process of gathering traffic from a network by capturing the data as it passes and storing it to analyze later. Answer d, Back Orifice 2000 (BO2K), is an application-level Trojan Horse used to give an attacker backdoor network access. Source: *Security Complete*, edited by Mark Lierley (Sybex, 2001).

27. Which LAN topology below is MOST vulnerable to a single point of failure?

   a. Ethernet Bus

   b. Physical Star

   c. FDDI

   d. Logical Ring

   > *Answer:* a
   >
   > Ethernet bus topology was the first commercially viable network topology, and consists of all workstations connected to a single coaxial cable. Since the cable must be properly terminated on both ends, a break in the cable stops all communications on the bus. Answer b, the physical star topology acts like a logical bus, but provides better fault tolerance, as a cable break only disconnects the workstation or hub directly affected. Answer d, logical ring topology, is used by Token Ring and FDDI and is highly resilient. Token Ring employs a beacon frame, which, in case of a cable break, initiates auto reconfiguration and attempts to reroute the network around the failed mode. Also, the Token Ring active monitor station performs ring maintenance functions, like removing continuously circulating frames from the ring. FDDI employs a second ring to provide redundancy. Sources: *Virtual LANs* by Mariana Smith (McGraw-Hill, 1998) and *Internetworking Technologies Handbook, Second Edition* (Cisco Press, 1998).

28. Which choice below does NOT accurately describe the difference between multi-mode and single-mode fiber optic cabling?

    a. Multi-mode fiber propagates light waves through many paths, single-mode fiber propagates a single light ray only.

    b. Multi-mode fiber has a longer allowable maximum transmission distance than single-mode fiber.

    c. Single-mode fiber has a longer allowable maximum transmission distance than multi-mode fiber.

    d. Both types have a longer allowable maximum transmission distance than UTP Cat 5.

    Answer: b

    Multi-mode fiber has a shorter allowable maximum transmission distance than single-mode fiber (2km vs. 10km). Multi-mode transmits the light through several different paths in the cable, whereas single-mode uses one light path, making single mode perform better. However, multi-mode is less expensive to install and is used more often in short-to-medium haul networks. Category 5 unshielded twisted pair (UTP) has a maximum transmission distance of 100 meters. Sources: *Catalyst 5000 Series Installation Guide* (Cisco Systems, 1996) and *Gigabit Ethernet* by Jayant Kadambi, Ian Crayford, and Mohan Kalkunte (Prentice Hall PTR, 1998).

29. Which statement below is correct regarding VLANs?

    a. A VLAN restricts flooding to only those ports included in the VLAN.

    b. A VLAN is a network segmented physically, not logically.

    c. A VLAN is less secure when implemented in conjunction with private port switching.

    d. A "closed" VLAN configuration is the least secure VLAN configuration.

    Answer: a

    A virtual local area network (VLAN) allows ports on the same or different switches to be grouped so that traffic is confined to members of that group only, and restricts broadcast, unicast, and multicast traffic. Answer b is incorrect, because a VLAN is segmented logically, rather than physically. Answer c is incorrect. When a VLAN is implemented with private port, or single-user, switching, it provides fairly stringent security because broadcast vulnerabilities are minimized. Answer d is incorrect, as a "closed" VLAN authenticates a user to an access control list on a central authentication server, where they are assigned authorization parameters to determine their level of network access. Sources: "Catalyst 5000 Series Installation Guide" (Cisco Systems) and *Virtual LANs* by Mariana Smith (McGraw-Hill, 1998).

30. Which choice below denotes a packet-switched connectionless wide area network (WAN) technology?

    a. X.25

    b. Frame Relay

    c. SMDS

    d. ATM

    Answer: c

    Switched Multimegabit Data Service (SMDS) is a high-speed, connectionless, packet-switching public network service that extends LAN-like performance to a metropolitan area network (MAN) or a wide area network (WAN). It's generally delivered over a SONET ring with a maximum effective service radius of around 30 miles. Answer a, X.25, defines an interface to the first commercially successful connection-oriented packet-switching network, in which the packets travel over virtual circuits. Answer b, Frame Relay, was a successor to X.25, and offers a connection-oriented packet-switching network. Answer d, Asynchronous Transfer Mode (ATM), was developed from an outgrowth of ISDN standards, and is fast-packet, connection-oriented, cell-switching technology. Source: *Communications Systems and Networks* by Ray Horak (M&T Books, 2000).

31. Which statement below is accurate about the difference between Ethernet II and 802.3 frame formats?

    a. 802.3 uses a "Length" field, whereas Ethernet II uses a "Type" field.

    b. 802.3 uses a "Type" field, whereas Ethernet II uses a "Length" field.

    c. Ethernet II uses a 4-byte FCS field, whereas 802.3 uses an 8-byte Preamble field.

    d. Ethernet II uses an 8-byte Preamble field, whereas 802.3 uses a 4-byte FCS field.

    Answer: a

    802.3 uses a "Length" field which indicates the number of data bytes that are in the data field. Ethernet II uses a "Type" field in the same 2 bytes to identify the message protocol type. Both frame formats use a 8-byte Preamble field at the start of the packet, and a 4-byte Frame Check Sequence (FCS) field at the end of the packet, so

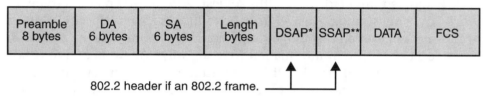

Figure A.2 shows the differences between the Ethernet II and the 802.3 frame formats.

Ethernet_II

Preamble 8 bytes	DA 6 bytes	SA 6 bytes	Type 2 bytes	Data	FCS 4 bytes

802.3_Ethernet

Preamble 8 bytes	DA 6 bytes	SA 6 bytes	Length bytes	DSAP*	SSAP**	DATA	FCS

802.2 header if an 802.2 frame.

Figure A.2 Ethernet II versus 802.3 frame format.

those choices would be incorrect as to a difference in the frame formats. Sources: *Gigabit Ethernet* by Jayant Kadambi, Ian Crayford, and Mohan Kalkunte (Prentice Hall PTR, 1998) and *CCNA Study Guide* by Todd Lammle, Donald Porter, and James Chellis (Sybex, 1999).

Figure A.2 shows the differences between the Ethernet II and the 802.3 frame formats.

32. Which standard below does NOT specify fiber optic cabling as its physical media?

a. 100BaseFX

b. 1000BaseCX

c. 1000BaseLX

d. 1000BaseSX

Answer: b

1000BaseCX refers to 1000Mbps baseband copper cable, using two pairs of 150 ohm balanced cable for CSMA/CD LANs. Answer a, 100BaseFX, specifies a 100 Mbps baseband fiber optic CSMA/CD LAN. Answer c, 1000BaseLX, specifies a 1000Mbps CSMA/CD LAN over long wavelength fiber optics. Answer d, 1000BaseSX, specifies a 1000Mbps CSMA/CD LAN over short wavelength fiber optics. Answers b, c, and d are defined in IEEE 802.3z. Source: *Gigabit Ethernet* by Jayant Kadambi, Ian Crayford, and Mohan Kalkunte (Prentice Hall PTR, 1998).

33. Which type of routing below commonly broadcasts its routing table information to all other routers every minute?
    a. Static Routing
    b. Distance Vector Routing
    c. Link State Routing
    d. Dynamic Control Protocol Routing

    Answer: b

    Distance vector routing uses the routing information protocol (RIP) to maintain a dynamic table of routing information that is updated regularly. It is the oldest and most common type of dynamic routing. Answer a, static routing, defines a specific route in a configuration file on the router and does not require the routers to exchange route information dynamically. Answer c, link state routers, functions like distance vector routers, but only use first-hand information when building routing tables by maintaining a copy of every other router's Link State Protocol (LSP) frame. This helps to eliminate routing errors and considerably lessens convergence time. Answer d is a distracter. Source: *Mastering Network Security* by Chris Brenton (Sybex, 1999).

34. Which protocol is used to resolve a known IP address to an unknown MAC address?
    a. ARP
    b. RARP
    c. ICMP
    d. TFTP

    Answer: a

    The Address Resolution Protocol (ARP) sends a broadcast asking for the host with a specified IP address to reply with its MAC, or hardware address. This information is kept in the ARP Cache. Answer b, the Reverse Address Resolution Protocol (RARP) is commonly used on diskless machines, when the MAC is known, but not the IP address. It asks a RARP server to provide a valid IP address, which is somewhat the reverse of ARP. Answer c, the Internet Control Message Protocol (ICMP) is a management protocol for IP. Answer d, the Trivial File Transfer Protocol (TFTP), is a stripped-down version of the File Transfer Protocol (FTP). Source: *CCNA Study Guide* by Todd Lammle, Donald Porter, and James Chellis (Sybex, 1999).

35. Which statement accurately describes the difference between 802.11b WLAN ad hoc and infrastructure modes?

    a. The ad hoc mode requires an Access Point to communicate to the wired network.

    b. Wireless nodes can communicate peer-to-peer in the infrastructure mode.

    c. Wireless nodes can communicate peer-to-peer in the ad hoc mode.

    d. Access points are rarely used in 802.11b WLANs.

    Answer: c

    Nodes on an IEEE 802.11b wireless LANs can communicate in one of two modes: ad hoc or infrastructure. In ad hoc mode, the wireless nodes communicate directly with each other, without establishing a connection to an access point on a wired LAN. In infrastructure mode, the wireless nodes communicate to an access point, which operates similarly to a bridge or router and manages traffic between the wireless network and the wired network. Source: *Wireless Security Essentials* by Russell Dean Vines (Wiley, 2002).

    Figure A.3 shows access points attached to a wired LAN to create an Infrastructure Mode 802.11b WLAN.

36. Which type of cabling below is the most common type for recent Ethernet installations?

    a. ThickNet

    b. ThinNet

    c. Twinax

    d. Twisted Pair

    Answer: d

    Category 5 Unshielded Twisted Pair (UTP) is rated for very high data throughput (100 Mbps) at short distances (up to 100 meters), and is the standard cable type for Ethernet installations. Answer a, ThickNet, also known as 10Base5, uses traditional thick coaxial (coax) cable at data rates of up to 10 Mbps. Answer b, ThinNet, uses a thinner gauge coax, and is known as 10Base2. It has a shorter maximum segment distance than ThickNet, but is less expensive to install (also known as CheaperNet). Answer c, Twinax, is like ThinNet, but has two conductors, and was used in IBM Systems 36 and earlier AS/400 installations. Source: *Communications Systems and Networks* by Ray Horak (M&T Books, 2000).

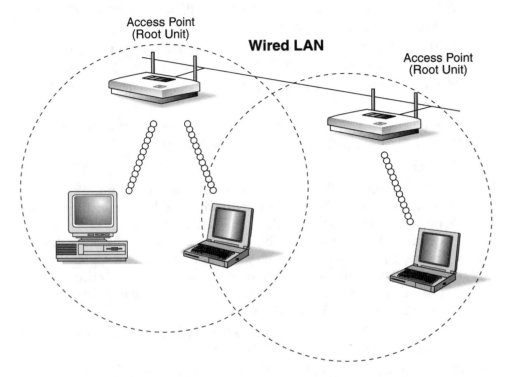

Figure A.3   802.11b infrastructure mode WLAN.

37. Which choice below most accurately describes SSL?

    a. It's a widely used standard of securing e-mail at the Application level.

    b. It gives a user remote access to a command prompt across a secure, encrypted session.

    c. It uses two protocols, the Authentication Header and the Encapsulating Security Payload.

    d. It allows an application to have authenticated, encrypted communications across a network.

    Answer: d

    The Secure Socket Layer (SSL) sits between higher-level application functions and the TCP/IP stack and provides security to applications. It includes a variety of encryption algorithms to secure transmitted data, but the functionality must be integrated into the application. Answer a refers to the Secure/Multipurpose Internet Mail Extension (S/MIME). Most major e-mail clients support

S/MIME today. Answer b describes Secure Shell (SSH). Answer c refers to IPSec. IPSec enables security to be built directly into the TCP/IP stack, without requiring application modification. Source: *Counter Hack* by Ed Skoudis (Prentice Hall PTR, 2002).

38. Which backup method listed below will probably require the backup operator to use the most number of tapes for a complete system restoration, if a different tape is used every night in a five-day rotation?

    a. Full Backup Method
    b. Differential Backup Method
    c. Incremental Backup Method
    d. Ad Hoc Backup Method

    Answer: c

    Most backup methods use the Archive file attribute to determine whether the file should be backed up or not. The backup software determines which files need to be backed up by checking to see if the Archive file attribute has been set, and then resets the Archive bit value to null after the backup procedure. The Incremental Backup Method backs up only files that have been created or modified since the last backup was made, because the Archive file attribute is reset. This can result in the backup operator needing several tapes to do a complete restoration, as every tape with changed files as well as the last full backup tape will need to be restored.

    Answer a, a Full or Complete backup backs up all files in all directories stored on the server regardless of when the last backup was made and whether the files have already been backed up. The Archive file attribute is changed to mark that the files have been backed up, and the tapes or tapes will have all data and applications on it. It's an incorrect answer for this question, however, as it's assumed answers b and c will additionally require differential or incremental tapes.

    Answer b, the Differential Backup Method, backs up only files that have been created or modified since the last backup was made, like an incremental backup. However, the difference between an incremental backup and a differential backup is that the Archive file attribute is not reset after the differential backup is completed, therefore the changed file is backed up every time the differential backup is run. The backup set grows in size until the next full backup as these files continue to be backed up during each subsequent differential backup, until the next complete backup occurs. The advantage of this backup method is that the backup operator should only need the full backup and the one differential backup to restore the system.

Table A.9 shows these three backup methods.

Answer d is a distracter.

Source: http://compreviews.about.com/library/weekly/aa042599. htm and http://www.nwconnection.com/sep.98/techsp98/jobs.html.

39. Which choice below is NOT an element of a fiber optic cable?

   a. Core

   b. BNC

   c. Jacket

   d. Cladding

   Answer: b

   A BNC refers to a Bayonet Neil Concelman RG58 connector for 10Base2. Fiber optic cable has three basic physical elements, the core, the cladding, and the jacket. The core is the innermost transmission medium, which can be glass or plastic. The next outer layer, the cladding is also made of glass or plastic, but has different properties, and helps to reflect the light back into the core. The outermost layer, the jacket, provides protection from heat, moisture, and other environmental elements. Source: *Gigabit Ethernet* by Jayant Kadambi, Ian Crayford, and Mohan Kalkunte (Prentice Hall PTR, 1998).

   Figure A.4 shows a cross-section of a fiber optic cable.

40. Given an IP address of 172.16.0.0, which subnet mask below would allow us to divide the network into the maximum number of subnets with at least 600 host addresses per subnet?

   a. 255.255.224.0

   b. 255.255.240.0

   c. 255.255.248.0

   d. 255.255.252.0

   Answer: d

   The last two octets of this class B address, 252.0, gives us binary: 11111100.00000000. The six subnet bits give us 62 (2^6 -2) subnets, each with 1022 (2^{10} -2) hosts, which allows us to have the maximum number of subnets with almost double the required host addresses. Answer a, 224.0, is 11100000.00000000 binary, which gives us six (2^3 - 2) subnets with 8190 (2^{13} -2) hosts each. Answer b, 240.0, is 11110000.00000000 binary, and gives us 14 (2^4 -2) subnets each with 4094 (2^{12} -2) hosts. Answer c, 248.0, is 11111000.00000000 binary, which creates 30 (2^5 -2) subnets with 2046 (2^{11} -2) hosts. Many books give detailed descriptions of IP subnetting.

Table A.9 Differential versus Incremental Backup Tape Contents

BACKUP METHOD	MONDAY	TUESDAY	WEDNESDAY	THURSDAY	FRIDAY
Differential	Changed File A	Changed Files A & B	Files A, B, & C	Files A, B, C, & D	
Incremental	Changed File A	Changed File B	Changed File C	Changed File D	
Full Backup					All Files

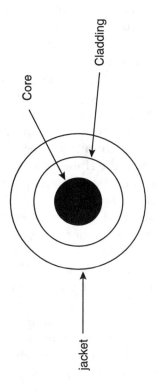

Figure A.4 Fiber optic cable layers.

Chapter 4—Cryptography

1. A cryptographic algorithm is also known as:

   a. A cryptosystem

   b. Cryptanalysis

   c. A cipher

   d. A key

   > *Answer:* c
   >
   > A cipher is a cryptographic transformation that operates on characters or bits. In different words, a cipher is defined as a cryptographic algorithm or mathematical function that operates on characters or bits and implements encryption or decryption. In contrast, a code operates with words, phrases and sentences. In a code, a word may be the encipherment of a sentence or phrase. For example, the word SCARF may be the code for the term BEWARE OF DUTCH TRAITOR IN YOUR MIDST.
   >
   > In answer a, a cryptosystem is a set of transformations from a message space to a ciphertext space. This system includes all cryptovariables (keys), plaintexts and ciphertexts associated with the transformation algorithm. The difference between answers a and c is that answer c, the correct answer, refers to the algorithm alone and answer a refers to the algorithm and all plaintexts, ciphertexts and cryptovariables associated with this algorithm.
   >
   > Answer b, cryptanalysis, refers to being able to "break" the cipher so that the encrypted message can be read. Cryptanalysis may be accomplished by exploiting weaknesses in the cipher or, in some fashion, determining the key. This act of obtaining the plaintext or key from the ciphertext can be used to recover sensitive or classified information and, perhaps, to pass on altered or fake messages in order to deceive the original intended recipient.
   >
   > Answer d, the key or cryptovariable, is used with a particular algorithm to encipher or decipher the plaintext message. By using the key, the algorithm can be publicly known and evaluated for its strength against attack. The key associated with a particular transformation or algorithm can take on many values and the range of all of these possible values is called the *keyspace*. Ideally, an enciphered plaintext message using a specific algorithm will produce a unique ciphertext message for each different key that is used with that algorithm. The situation in which a plaintext message generates identical ciphertext messages using the same transformation algorithm, but

with different cryptovariables, is called *key clustering*. Obviously, this is not a desirable situation, since it effectively reduces the number of keys that have to be tried by an attacker in order to recover the plaintext.

2. Which of the following is NOT an issue with secret key cryptography?

    a. Security of the certification authority.

    b. A networked group of m users with separate keys for each pair of users will require m (m-1)/2 keys.

    c. Secure distribution of the keys.

    d. Compromise of the keys can enable the attacker to impersonate the key owners and, therefore, read and send false messages.

       Answer: a

       The CA is used in public key cryptography, not secret key cryptography. A CA will certify that a public key actually belongs to a specific individual and that the information associated with the individual's key is valid and correct. The CA accomplishes this certification by digitally signing the individual's public key and associated information. The certification professes to another person who wants to send a message to this individual using public key encryption that the public key actually belongs to the intended individual. The Consultation Committee, International Telephone and Telegraph, International Telecommunications Union (CCITT-ITU)/ International Organization for Standardization (ISO) X.509 Authentication framework defines a format for public key certificates. This structure is outlined in Figure A.5.

       Answer b is an important issue in secret key cryptography; therefore it is not the correct answer. If, among a network of m users, each user wants to have secure communications with every other user on the network, then there must be a secret key for each pair of potential users. This concept can be illustrated with five users as shown in Figure A.6. Thus, with five users, the number of independent keys is equal to (5 x 4)/2 or 10 as depicted by the ten connecting lines in Figure A.6.

       The answer c is incorrect since securely distributing the keys to all users is, obviously, a very important requirement.

       Answer d is incorrect since a compromise of the keys can, indeed, enable the attacker to impersonate the key owners and, therefore, read and send false messages.

3. Which of the following is NOT a characteristic of the ElGamal public key cryptosystem?

    a. It can perform encryption.

    b. It can be used to generate digital signatures.

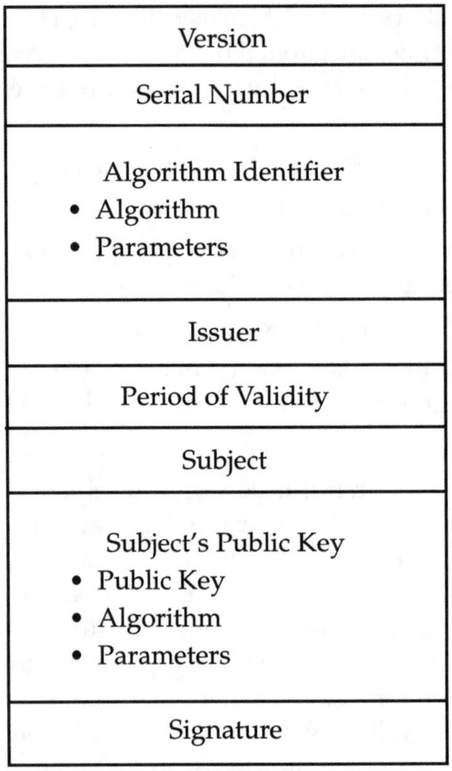

Version
Serial Number
Algorithm Identifier • Algorithm • Parameters
Issuer
Period of Validity
Subject
Subject's Public Key • Public Key • Algorithm • Parameters
Signature

Figure A.5   CCITT-ITU/ ISO X.509 certificate format.

   c. It is based on the discrete logarithm problem.

   d. It can perform encryption, but not digital signatures.

      Answer: d

      The ElGamal public key cryptosystem can perform both encryption and digital signatures based on the discrete logarithm problem. These three characteristics are shown in the examples that follow.

      To generate a key pair in the ElGamal system:

   a. Choose a prime number, p.

   b. Choose two random numbers, g and x (g and x must both be less than p).

   c. Calculate $y = g^x \bmod p$.

   d. The private key is x and the public key is y, g, and p.

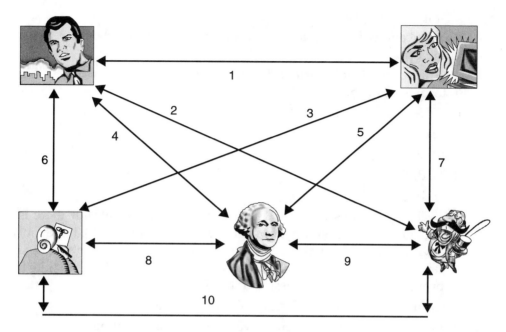

Figure A.6 Networked users requiring independent keys.

To encrypt a message, M, in the ElGamal system:

a. Select a random number, j, such that j is relatively prime to p-1. Recall that two numbers are relatively prime if they have no common factors other than 1.

b. Generate $w = g^j \bmod p$ and $z = y^j M \bmod p$.

c. w and z comprise the ciphertext.

To decrypt the message, M, in the ElGamal system, calculate $M = z/w^x \bmod p$. This can be shown by substituting the values of z and w in the equation as follows:

$M = y^j M \bmod p / g^{jx} \bmod p$

Since $y^j = g^{xj} \bmod p$

$M = (g^{xj} M / g^{jx}) \bmod p$

To sign a message, M, in the ElGamal system:

a. Select a random number, j, such that j is relatively prime to p-1. The value of j must not be disclosed. Generate $w = g^j \bmod p$.

b. Solve for z in the equation $M = (xw + jz) \bmod (p-1)$. The solution to this equation is beyond the scope of this coverage. Suffice to say that an algorithm exists to solve for the variable z.

    c. w and z comprise the signature.

    d. Verification of the signature is accomplished if $g^M \bmod p = y^w w^z \bmod p$.

4. The Transport Layer Security (TLS) 1.0 protocol is based on which Protocol Specification?

    a. SSH-2

    b. SSL-3.0

    c. IPSEC

    d. TCP/IP

       Answer: b

       The differences between TLS and SSL are not great, but there is enough of a difference such that TLS 1.0 and SSL 3.0 are not operationally compatible. If interoperability is desired, there is a capability in TLS that allows it to function as SSL. Question 5 provides additional discussion of the TLS protocol.

5. The primary goal of the TLS Protocol is to provide:

    a. Privacy and authentication between two communicating applications

    b. Privacy and data integrity between two communicating applications

    c. Authentication and data integrity between two communicating applications

    d. Privacy, authentication and data integrity between two communicating applications

       Answer: b

       The TLS Protocol is comprised of the TLS *Record* and *Handshake* Protocols. The TLS Record Protocol is layered on top of a transport protocol such as TCP and provides privacy and reliability to the communications. The privacy is implemented by encryption using symmetric key cryptography such as DES or RC4. The secret key is generated anew for each connection; however, the Record Protocol can be used without encryption. Integrity is provided through the use of a *keyed Message Authentication Code (MAC)* using hash algorithms such as SHA or MD5.

       The TLS Record Protocol is also used to encapsulate a higher-level protocol such as the TLS Handshake Protocol. This Handshake Protocol is used by the server and client to authenticate each other. The authentication can be accomplished using asymmetric key cryptography such as RSA or DSS. The Handshake Protocol also sets up the encryption algorithm and cryptographic keys to enable the application protocol to transmit and receive information.

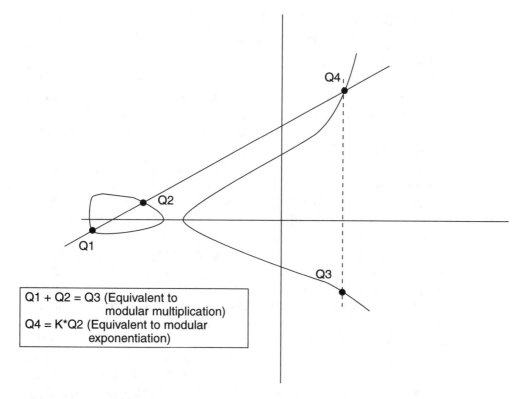

Figure A.7 Graph of the function $y^2 = x^3 + ax + b$.

6. The graph in Figure A.7, which depicts the equation $y^2 = x^3 + ax + b$, denotes the:

   a. Elliptic curve and the elliptic curve discrete logarithm problem

   b. RSA Factoring problem

   c. ElGamal discrete logarithm problem

   d. Knapsack problem

   Answer: a

   The elliptic curve is defined over a finite field comprised of real, complex or rational numbers. The points on an elliptic curve form a Group under addition as shown in Figure A.7. Multiplication (or multiple additions) in an elliptic curve system is equivalent to modular exponentiation; thus, defining a discreet logarithm problem.

7. In communications between two parties, encrypting the hash function of a message with a symmetric key algorithm is equivalent to:

   a. Generating a digital signature

   b. Providing for secrecy of the message

c. Generating a one-way function

d. Generating a keyed Message Authentication Code (MAC)

> *Answer:* d
>
> A MAC is used to authenticate files between users. If the sender and receiver both have the secret key, they are the only ones that can verify the hash function. If a symmetric key algorithm is used to encrypt the one-way hash function, then the one-way hash function becomes a keyed MAC.
>
> Answer a is incorrect because a digital signature between two parties uses an asymmetric key algorithm. If a message is encrypted with the sender's private key, then only the sender's public key can decrypt the message. This proves that the message was sent by the sender since only the sender knows the private key.
>
> In practice, asymmetric key encryption is very slow, especially for long messages. Therefore, a one-way hash of the message is encrypted with the sender's private key instead of encrypting the complete message. Then, the message and the encrypted hash are sent to a second party. The receiver takes the encrypted hash and decrypts it with the sender's public key. Then, the receiver takes the hash of the message, using the same one-way hash algorithm as the sender. The hash generated by the receiver is compared with the decrypted hash sent with the message. If the two hashes are identical, the digital signature is validated. Note that his method also will reveal if the message was changed en route, since the hash calculated by the receiver will, then, be different from the encrypted hash sent along with the message.
>
> Answer b is incorrect since encrypting the hash of the message and sending the message in the clear does nothing to protect the confidentiality of the message. Since the hash function is a one-way function, the message cannot be recovered from its hash.
>
> Answer c is incorrect since encrypting a hash of a message is not a one-way function. If it were, it would be of no use since no one would be able to reverse the process and decrypt it.

8. Which of the following is NOT a characteristic of a cryptographic hash function, H (m), where m denotes the message being hashed by the function H?

a. H (m) is collision free.

b. H (m) is difficult to compute for any given m.

c. The output is of fixed length.

d. H (m) is a one-way function.

Answer: b

For a cryptographic hash function, H (m) is relatively easy to compute for a given m. Answer a is a characteristic of a good cryptographic hash function, in that collision free means that for a given message, M, that produces H (M) = Z, it is computationally infeasible to find another message, M1, such that H (M1) = Z. Answer c is part of the definition of a hash function since it generates a fixed-length result that is independent of the length of the input message. This characteristic is useful for generating digital signatures since the signature can be applied to the fixed-length hash that is uniquely characteristic of the message instead of to the entire message, which is usually much longer than the hash. Answer d relates to answer b in that a one-way function is difficult or impossible to invert. This means that for a hash function H (M) = Z, it is computationally infeasible to reverse the process and find M given the hash Z and the function H.

9. Which one of the following statements BEST describes the operation of the Digital Signature Algorithm (DSA) (National Institute of Standards and Technology, NIST FIPS PUB 186, "Digital Signature Standard," U.S. Department of Commerce, May 1994) at the transmitting end of a communication between two parties?

   a. A message of $< 2^{64}$ bits is input to the DSA, and the resultant message digest of 160 bits is fed into the Secure Hash Algorithm (SHA), which generates the digital signature of the message.

   b. A message of $< 2^{64}$ bits is input to the Secure Hash Algorithm (SHA), and the resultant message digest of 128 bits is fed into the DSA, which generates the digital signature of the message.

   c. A message of $< 2^{64}$ bits is input to the Secure Hash Algorithm (SHA), and the resultant message digest of 160 bits is used as the digital signature of the message.

   d. A message of $< 2^{64}$ bits is input to the Secure Hash Algorithm (SHA), and the resultant message digest of 160 bits is fed into the DSA, which generates the digital signature of the message.

   Answer: d

   Answer d describes the proper sequence of operating on the message and has the correct value of 160 bits for the SHA message digest. At the receiving end, the message is fed into the SHA, and the result is compared to the received message digest to verify the signature. Answer a is incorrect since the order of the DSA and SHA are in reverse sequence from the correct order of their application. Answer b is incorrect since it has the incorrect value of 128 bits for the message digest produced by the SHA. Answer c is incorrect since the message digest has to be fed into the DSA to generate the digital signature of the message.

10. If the application of a hash function results in an m-bit fixed length output, an attack on the hash function that attempts to achieve a collision after 2 m/2 possible trial input values is called a(n):

    a. Adaptive-chosen-plaintext attack

    b. Chosen-ciphertext attack

    c. Birthday attack

    d. Meet-in-the-middle attack

    Answer: c

    This problem is analogous to asking the question "How many people must be in a room for the probability of two people having the same birthday to be equal to 50%?" The answer is 23. Thus, trying $2^{m/2}$ possible trial inputs to a hash function gives a 50% chance of finding two inputs that have the same hash value. Answer a, describes an attack in which the attacker can choose the plaintext to be encrypted and can modify his/her choice based on the results of a previous encryption. Answer b, the chosen-cipher text attack, is where the attacker can select different ciphertexts to be decrypted and has the decrypted plaintext available. This attack is used to determine the key or keys being used. Answer d is an attack against double encryption. This approach shows that for a key length of k bits, a chosen-plaintext attack could find the key after 2^{k+1} trials instead of 2^{2k} attempts. In this attack on double encryption, one encrypts from one end, decrypts from the other and compares the results "in-the-middle."

11. The minimum information necessary on a digital certificate is:

    a. Name, expiration date, digital signature of the certifier

    b. Name, expiration date, public key

    c. Name, serial number, private key

    d. Name, public key, digital signature of the certifier

    Answer: d

    The correct answer is d, where the name of the individual is certified and bound to his/her public key. This certification is validated by the digital signature of the certifying agent. In answer a, the public key is not present to be bound to the person's name. In answer b, the public key and name are present, but there is no digital signature verifying that the public key belongs to the name. Answer c is incorrect on a number of counts. First, the private key is never disclosed to the public and secondly, there is no digital signature.

12. What do the message digest algorithms MD2, MD4 and MD5 have in common?

    a. They all take a message of arbitrary length and produce a message digest of 160-bits.

    b. They all take a message of arbitrary length and produce a message digest of 128-bits.

    c. They are all optimized for 32-bit machines.

    d. They are all used in the Secure Hash Algorithm (SHA).

    Answer: b

    Answer a is obviously, then, incorrect. Answer c is incorrect since MD2 (B.S. Kaliski, "The MD2 Message Digest Algorithm," RFC 1319, April 1992) is targeted for 8-bit machines. It is used in Privacy Enhanced Mail (PEM). MD4 (R.L. Rivest, "The MD4 Message Digest Algorithm," RFC 1186, Oct 1990) and MD5 (R.L. Rivest, "The MD5 Message Digest Algorithm," RFC 1321, April 1992) are designed for 32-bit machines. MD5 is considered more secure than MD4, and MD5 is also used in PEM. Answer d is incorrect since the SHA is a separate algorithm from MD2, MD4, and MD5, but is modeled after MD4. SHA produces a 160-bit message digest.

13. What is the correct sequence which enables an authorized agency to use the Law Enforcement Access Field (LEAF) to decrypt a message sent by using the Clipper Chip? The following designations are used for the respective keys involved—K_f, the family key; K_s, the session key; U, a unique identifier for each Clipper Chip and K_u, the unit key that is unique to each Clipper Chip.

    a. Obtain a court order to acquire the two halves of K_u, the unit key. Recover K_u. Decrypt the LEAF with K_u and then recover Ks, the session key. Use the session key to decrypt the message.

    b. Decrypt the LEAF with the family key, K_f; recover U; obtain a court order to obtain the two halves of K_u; recover K_u; and then recover K_s, the session key. Use the session key to decrypt the message.

    c. Decrypt the LEAF with the family key, K_f; recover U; obtain a court order to obtain K_s, the session key. Use the session key to decrypt the message.

    d. Obtain a court order to acquire the family key, K_f; recover U and K_u; then recover K_s, the session key. Use the session key to decrypt the message.

LEAF FIELD Encrypted with Family Key

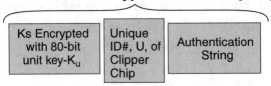

Figure A.8   Leaf field.

Answer: b

The explanation is based on the LEAF as shown in Figure A.8. The message is encrypted with the symmetric session key, K_s. In order to decrypt the message, then, K_s must be recovered. The LEAF contains the session key, but the LEAF is encrypted with the family key, K_f, that is common to all Clipper Chips. The authorized agency has access to K_f and decrypts the LEAF. However, the session key is still encrypted by the 80-bit unit key, K_u, that is unique to each Clipper Chip and is identified by the unique identifier, U. K_u is divided into two halves, and each half is deposited with an escrow agency. The law enforcement agency obtains the two halves of K_u by presenting the escrow agencies with a court order for the key identified by U. The two halves of the key obtained by the court order are XORed together to obtain K_u. Then, K_u is used to recover the session key, K_s, and K_s is used to decrypt the message.

The decryption sequence to obtain K_s can be summarized as:

$$K_f \rightarrow U \rightarrow [1/2K_u \text{ XOR } 1/2 K_u] \rightarrow K_u \rightarrow K_s$$

This is the sequence described in answer b. The sequences described in the other answers are incorrect.

14. What BEST describes the National Security Agency-developed Capstone?

    a. A device for intercepting electromagnetic emissions

    b. The PC Card implementation of the Clipper Chip system

    c. A chip that implements the U.S. Escrowed Encryption Standard

    d. A one-way function for implementation of public key encryption

    Answer: c

    Capstone is a Very Large Scale Integration (VLSI) chip that employs the Escrowed Encryption Standard and incorporates the

Skipjack algorithm, similar to the Clipper Chip. As such, it has a LEAF. Capstone also supports public key exchange and digital signatures. At this time, Capstone products have their LEAF function suppressed and a Certifying Authority provides for key recovery. Answer a is then, obviously, incorrect. For information purposes, though, the U.S. Government program to study and control the interception of electromagnetic emissions that may compromise classified information is called TEMPEST. Answer b is also, obviously, incorrect. However, Capstone was first implemented on a PC card called Fortezza. Answer d is incorrect since Capstone is not a mathematical function, but it incorporates mathematical functions for key exchange, authentication and encryption.

15. Which of the following BEST describes a block cipher?

   a. A symmetric key algorithm that operates on a variable-length block of plaintext and transforms it into a fixed-length block of ciphertext

   b. A symmetric key algorithm that operates on a fixed-length block of plaintext and transforms it into a fixed-length block of ciphertext

   c. An asymmetric key algorithm that operates on a variable-length block of plaintext and transforms it into a fixed-length block of ciphertext

   d. An asymmetric key algorithm that operates on a fixed-length block of plaintext and transforms it into a fixed-length block of ciphertext

   Answer: b

   A block cipher breaks the plaintext into fixed-length blocks, commonly 64-bits, and encrypts the blocks into fixed-length blocks of ciphertext. Another characteristic of the block cipher is that, if the same key is used, a particular plaintext block will be transformed into the same ciphertext block. Examples of block ciphers are DES, Skipjack, IDEA, RC5 and AES. An example of a block cipher in a symmetric key cryptosystem is the Electronic Code Book (ECB) mode of operation. In the ECB mode, a plaintext block is transformed into a ciphertext block as shown in Figure A.9. If the same key is used for each transformation, then a "Code Book" can be compiled for each plaintext block and corresponding ciphertext block.

   Answer a is incorrect since it refers to a variable-length block of plaintext being transformed into a fixed-length block of ciphertext. Recall that this operation has some similarity to a hash function, which takes a message of arbitrary length and converts it into a fixed-length message digest. Answers c and d are incorrect because they involve asymmetric key algorithms, and the block cipher is used with symmetric key algorithms.

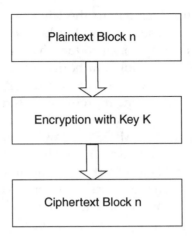

Figure A.9 A ciphertext block.

In other cryptographic modes of operation, such as Cipher Block Chaining (CBC), the result of the encryption of the plaintext block, Pn, is fed into the encryption process of plaintext block Pn+1. Thus, the result of the encryption of one block affects the result of the encryption of the next block in the sequence.

16. An iterated block cipher encrypts by breaking the plaintext block into two halves and, with a subkey, applying a "round" transformation to one of the halves. Then, the output of this transformation is XORed with the remaining half. The round is completed by swapping the two halves. This type of cipher is known as:

    a. RC4

    b. Diffie-Hellman

    c. RC6

    d. Feistel

    Answer: d

    The question stem describes one round of a Feistel cipher. This algorithm was developed by an IBM team led by Horst Feistel. (H. Feistel, "Cryptography and Computer Privacy," *Scientific American*, v.228, n.5, May 1973) The algorithm was called Lucifer and was the basis for the Data Encryption Standard (DES). In answer a, RC4 is a variable key-size stream cipher developed by Ronald Rivest. In this type of cipher, a sequence of bits that are the key is bit-wise XORed with the plaintext. In answer b, Diffie-Hellman describes the first public key algorithm and is based on the difficulty of calculating discrete logarithms in a finite field. (W. Diffie and M.E. Hellman, "New Directions in Cryptography," "*IEEE Transactions on Information Theory,*" v. IT-22, n. 6, Nov 1976). It is used for exchanging keys. RC6, in answer c, is a fast block cipher designed by Rivest, Sidney and Yin. In RC6, the block size, the key size and the number of rounds are variable. The key size can be no larger than 2040 bits. RC6 was one of the five finalists in the Advanced Encryption Standard (AES) competition.

17. A key schedule is:

    a. A list of cryptographic keys to be used at specified dates and times

    b. A method of generating keys by the use of random numbers

    c. A set of subkeys derived from a secret key

    d. Using distributed computing resources to conduct a brute force attack on a symmetric algorithm

    Answer: c

    The subkeys are typically used in iterated block ciphers. In this type of cipher, the plaintext is broken into fixed-length blocks and enciphered in "rounds." In a round, the same transformation is applied using one of the subkeys of the key schedule. (See the answer to question 16.)

18. The Wireless Transport Layer Security (WTLS) Protocol in the Wireless Application Protocol (WAP) stack is based on which Internet Security Protocol?

    a. S-HTTP

    b. TLS

    c. SET

    d. IPSEC

    Answer: b

    TLS is discussed in the answer to question 5. WTLS has to incorporate functionality that is provided for in TLS by TCP in the TCP/IP Protocol suite in that WTLS can operate over UDP. WTLS supports data privacy, authentication and integrity. Because WTLS has to incorporate a large number of handshakes when security is implemented, significant delays may occur. During a WTLS handshake session, WTLS can set up the following security classes:

    Class 1. No certificates

    Class 2. The client does not have a certificate; the server has a certificate

    Class 3. The client and server have certificates

19. The Advanced Encryption Standard (Rijndael) block cipher requirements regarding keys and block sizes have now evolved to which configuration?

    a. Both the key and block sizes can be 128, 192, and 256 bits each.

    b. The key size is 128 bits, and the block size can be 128, 192, or 256 bits.

    c. The block size is 128 bits, and the key can be 128, 192, or 256 bits.

    d. The block size is 128 bits, and the key size is 128 bits.

    Answer: c

    AES is comprised of the three key sizes, 128, 192, and 256 bits with a fixed block size of 128 bits. The Advanced Encryption Standard (AES) was announced on November 26, 2001, as Federal Information Processing Standard Publication (FIPS PUB 197). FIPS PUB 197 states that "This standard may be used by Federal departments and agencies when an agency determines that sensitive (unclassified) information (as defined in P.L. 100-235) requires cryptographic protection. Other FIPS-approved cryptographic algorithms may be used in addition to, or in lieu of, this standard." Depending upon which of the three keys is used, the standard may be referred to as "AES-128," "AES-192" or "AES-256."

    The number of rounds used in the Rijndael cipher is a function of the key size as follows:

    256-bit key → 14 rounds

    192-bit key → 12 rounds

    128-bit key → 10 rounds

    Rijndael has a symmetric and parallel structure that provides for flexibility of implementation and resistance to cryptanalytic attacks. Attacks on Rijndael would involve the use of differential and linear cryptanalysis.

20. The Wireless Transport Layer Security Protocol (WTLS) in the Wireless Application Protocol (WAP) stack provides for security:

    a. Between the WAP gateway and the content server

    b. Between the WAP client and the gateway

    c. Between the Internet and the content server

    d. Between the WAP content server and the WAP client

    Answer: b

    Transport Layer Security (TLS) provides for security between the content server on the Internet and the WAP gateway. (Answer a is,

Figure A.10   WAP to WAP gateway to Internet block diagram.

thus, incorrect.) Similarly, WTLS provides security between the WAP mobile device (client software) and the WAP gateway. Since WAP cannot interface directly with the Internet, all WAP information has to be converted to HTTP in the WAP gateway to enable it to exchange information with the Internet content servers. The simple block diagram of Figure A.10 illustrates these concepts.

A vulnerability occurs since data encrypted with wireless protocols has to be decrypted in the WAP gateway and then re-encrypted with the Internet protocols. This process is reversed when data flows from the Internet content servers to the WAP client. Thus, the information is vulnerable while it is in the decrypted state on the WAP gateway. This condition is known as the WAP Gap. In order to address this issue, the WAP Forum has put forth specifications that will reduce this vulnerability and, thus, support e-commerce applications. These specifications are defined in WAP 1.2 as WMLScript Crypto Library and the WAP Identity Module (WIM). The WMLScript Crypto Library supports end-to-end security by providing for cryptographic functions to be initiated on the WAP client from the Internet content server. These functions include digital signatures originating with the WAP client and encryption and decryption of data. The WIM is a tamper-resistant device, such as a smart card, that cooperates with WTLS and provides cryptographic operations during the handshake phase.

The WAP Forum is also considering another alternative to providing the end-to-end encryption for WAP. This alternative, described in WAP specification 1.3, is the use of a client proxy server that communicates authentication and authorization information to the wireless network server.

Answer c is incorrect since the content server is on the Internet side of the communication and answer d assumes a direct interface between the content server and the client without going through the necessary Internet and wireless protocols.

21. What is a protocol that adds digital signatures and encryption to Internet MIME (Multipurpose Internet Mail Extensions)?

    a. IPSEC

    b. PGP

    c. S/MIME

    d. SET/MIME

    Answer: c

    The MIME protocol specifies a structure for the body of an email message. MIME supports a number of formats in the email body, including graphic, enhanced text and audio, but does not provide security services for these messages. S/MIME defines such services for MIME as digital signatures and encryption based on a standard syntax. Answer a is incorrect since IPSEC is not an email protocol but is a standard that provides encryption, access control, nonrepudiation, and authentication of messages over IP. It is designed to be functionally compatible with IPv6. Answer b is incorrect because PGP, Pretty Good Privacy, brings security to email through the use of a symmetric cipher, such as IDEA, to encipher the message. RSA is used for symmetric key exchange and for digital signatures. PGP is not an augmentation of MIME. RFC 2440 permits other algorithms to be used in PGP. In order of preference, they are ElGamal and RSA for key distribution; triple DES, IDEA and CAST5 for encryption of messages; DSA and RSA for digital signatures and SHA-1 or MD5 for generating hashes of the messages. Answer d is incorrect because there is no such protocol. There is a protocol called SET for Secure Electronic Transaction. It was developed by Visa and MasterCard to secure electronic bankcard transactions. SET requests authorization for payment and requires certificates binding a person's public key to their identity.

22. Digital cash refers to the electronic transfer of funds from one party to another. When digital cash is referred to as anonymous or identified, it means that:

    a. Anonymous—the identity of the cash holder is not known; Identified—the identity of the cash holder is known

    b. Anonymous—the identity of merchant is withheld; Identified—the identity of the merchant is not withheld

    c. Anonymous—the identity of the bank is withheld; Identified—the identity of the bank is not withheld

    d. Anonymous—the identity of the cash holder is not known; Identified—the identity of the merchant is known

Answer: a

Anonymous implementations of digital cash do not identify the cash holder and use blind signature schemes; identified implementations use conventional digital signatures to identify the cash holder. In looking at these two approaches, anonymous schemes are analogous to cash since cash does not allow tracing of the person who made the cash payment while identified approaches are the analog of credit or debit card transactions.

23. Which of the following is NOT a key recovery method?

    a. A message is encrypted with a session key and the session key is, in turn, encrypted with the public key of a trustee agent. The encrypted session key is sent along with the encrypted message. The trustee, when authorized, can then decrypt the message by recovering the session key with the trustee's private key.

    b. A message is encrypted with a session key. The session key, in turn, is broken into parts and each part is encrypted with the public key of a different trustee agent. The encrypted parts of the session key are sent along with the encrypted message. The trustees, when authorized, can then decrypt their portion of the session key and provide their respective parts of the session key to a central agent. The central agent can then decrypt the message by reconstructing the session key from the individual components.

    c. A secret key or a private key is broken into a number of parts and each part is deposited with a trustee agent. The agents can then provide their parts of the key to a central authority, when presented with appropriate authorization. The key can then be reconstructed and used to decrypt messages encrypted with that key.

    d. A message is encrypted with a session key and the session key is, in turn, encrypted with the private key of a trustee agent. The encrypted session key is sent along with the encrypted message. The trustee, when authorized, can then decrypt the message by recovering the session key with the trustee's public key.

    Answer: d

    Encrypting parts of the session key with the private keys of the trustee agents provides no security for the message since the message can be decrypted by recovering the key components of the session key using the public keys of the respective agents. These public keys are available to anyone. Answers a, b, and c are valid means of recovering keys, since key recovery refers to permitting access to encrypted messages under predefined circumstances. Answers a and b are also called *key encapsulation* since the session key is encapsulated in the public keys of the trustee agents and, therefore, can be decrypted only by these trustee agents with their private keys.

24. Theoretically, quantum computing offers the possibility of factoring the products of large prime numbers and calculating discreet logarithms in polynomial time. These calculations can be accomplished in such a compressed time frame because:

    a. Information can be transformed into quantum light waves that travel through fiber optic channels. Computations can be performed on the associated data by passing the light waves through various types of optical filters and solid-state materials with varying indices of refraction, thus drastically increasing the throughput over conventional computations.

    b. A quantum bit in a quantum computer is actually a linear superposition of both the one and zero states and, therefore, can theoretically represent both values in parallel. This phenomenon allows computation that usually takes exponential time to be accomplished in polynomial time since different values of the binary pattern of the solution can be calculated simultaneously.

    c. A quantum computer takes advantage of quantum tunneling in molecular scale transistors. This mode permits ultra high-speed switching to take place, thus, exponentially increasing the speed of computations.

    d. A quantum computer exploits the time-space relationship that changes as particles approach the speed of light. At that interface, the resistance of conducting materials effectively is zero and exponential speed computations are possible.

    Answer: b

    In digital computers, a bit is in either a one or zero state. In a quantum computer, through linear superposition, a quantum bit can be in both states, essentially simultaneously. Thus, computations consisting of trail evaluations of binary patterns can take place simultaneously in exponential time. The probability of obtaining a correct result is increased through a phenomenon called constructive interference of light while the probability of obtaining an incorrect result is decreased through destructive interference. Answer a describes optical computing that is effective in applying Fourier and other transformations to data to perform high-speed computations. Light representing large volumes of data passing through properly shaped physical objects can be subjected to mathematical transformations and recombined to provide the appropriate results. However, this mode of computation is not defined as quantum computing. Answers c and d are diversionary answers that do not describe quantum computing.

25. Which of the following statements BEST describes the Public Key Cryptography Standards (PKCS)?
    a. A set of public-key cryptography standards that support algorithms such as Diffie-Hellman and RSA as well as algorithm independent standards
    b. A set of public-key cryptography standards that support only "standard" algorithms such as Diffie-Hellman and RSA
    c. A set of public-key cryptography standards that support only algorithm-independent implementations
    d. A set of public-key cryptography standards that support encryption algorithms such as Diffie-Hellman and RSA, but does not address digital signatures

    Answer: a

    PKCS supports algorithm-independent and algorithm-specific implementations as well as digital signatures and certificates. It was developed by a consortium including RSA Laboratories, Apple, DEC, Lotus, Sun, Microsoft and MIT. At this writing, there are 15 PKCS standards. Examples of these standards are:

    PKCS #1. Defines mechanisms for encrypting and signing data using the RSA public-key system

    PKCS #3. Defines the Diffie-Hellman key agreement protocol

    PKCS #10. Describes a syntax for certification requests

    PKCS #15. Defines a standard format for cryptographic credentials stored on cryptographic tokens

26. An interface to a library of software functions that provide security and cryptography services is called:
    a. A security application programming interface (SAPI)
    b. An assurance application programming interface (AAPI)
    c. A cryptographic application programming interface (CAPI)
    d. A confidentiality, integrity and availability application programming interface (CIAAPI)

    Answer: c

    CAPI is designed for software developers to call functions from the library and, thus, make it easier to implement security services. An example of a CAPI is the Generic Security Service API (GSS-API.) The GSS-API provides data confidentiality, authentication, and data integrity services and supports the use of both public and secret key mechanisms. The GSS-API is described in the Internet Proposed Standard RFC 2078. The other answers are made-up distracters.

27. The British Standard 7799/ISO Standard 17799 discusses cryptographic policies. It states, "An organization should develop a policy on its use of cryptographic controls for protection of its information . . . . When developing a policy, the following should be considered:" (Which of the following items would most likely NOT be listed?)

   a. The management approach toward the use of cryptographic controls across the organization

   b. The approach to key management, including methods to deal with the recovery of encrypted information in the case of lost, compromised or damaged keys

   c. Roles and responsibilities

   d. The encryption schemes to be used

   Answer: d

   A policy is a general statement of management's intent, and therefore, a policy would not specify the encryption scheme to be used. Answers a, b, and c are appropriate for a cryptographic policy. The general standards document is BSI ISO/IEC 17799:2000,BS 7799-I: 2000, *Information technology-Code of practice for information security management*, British Standards Institution, London, UK. The standard is intended to "provide a comprehensive set of controls comprising best practices in information security." ISO refers to the International Organization for Standardization and IEC is the International Electrotechnical Commission. These two entities form the system for worldwide standardization.

   The main chapter headings of the standard are:

   - Security Policy
   - Organizational Security
   - Asset Classification and Control
   - Personnel Security
   - Physical and Environmental Security
   - Communications and Operations Management
   - Access Control
   - Systems Development and Maintenance
   - Business Continuity Management
   - Compliance

28. The Number Field Sieve (NFS) is a:

    a. General purpose factoring algorithm that can be used to factor large numbers

    b. General purpose algorithm to calculate discreet logarithms

    c. General purpose algorithm used for brute force attacks on secret key cryptosystems

    d. General purpose hash algorithm

    Answer: a

    The NFS has been successful in efficiently factoring numbers larger than 115 digits and a version of NFS has successfully factored a 155-digit number. Clearly, factoring is an attack that can be used against the RSA cryptosystem in which the public and private keys are calculated based on the product of two large prime numbers. Answers b, c, and d are distracters.

29. DESX is a variant of DES in which:

    a. Input plaintext is bitwise XORed with 64 bits of additional key material before encryption with DES.

    b. Input plaintext is bitwise XORed with 64 bits of additional key material before encryption with DES, and the output of DES is also bitwise XORed with another 64 bits of key material.

    c. The output of DES is bitwise XORed with 64 bits of key material.

    d. The input plaintext is encrypted X times with the DES algorithm using different keys for each encryption.

    Answer: b

    DESX was developed by Ron Rivest to increase the resistance of DES to brute force key search attacks; however, the resistance of DESX to differential and linear attacks is equivalent to that of DES with independent subkeys.

30. The ANSI X9.52 standard defines a variant of DES encryption with keys k1, k2, and k3 as:

    $$C = E_{k3} [D_{k2} [E_{k1} [M]]]$$

    What is this DES variant?

    a. DESX

    b. Triple DES in the EEE mode

    c. Double DES with an encryption and decryption with different keys

    d. Triple DES in the EDE mode

Answer: d

This version of triple DES performs an encryption (E) of plaintext message M with key k_1, a decryption (D) with key k_2 (essentially, another encryption), and a third encryption with key k_3. Another implementation of DES EDE is accomplished with keys k1 and k2 being independent, but with keys k1 and k3 being identical. This implementation of triple DES is written as:

$C = E_{k1} [D_{k2} [E_{k1} [M]]]$

Answer a is incorrect since, in DESX, input plaintext is bitwise XORed with 64 bits of additional key material before encryption with DES, and the output of DES is also bitwise XORed with another 64 bits of key material. Answer b, DES in the EEE, mode is written as:

$C = E_{k3} [E_{k2} [E_{k1} [M]]]$

where three consecutive encryptions are performed on plaintext message, M, with three independent keys, k1, k2, k3.

Answer c is incorrect since the question contains three encryptions. Implementing two DES encryptions does not provide the additional security anticipated over a single DES encryption because of the meet-in-the-middle attack. Consider a DES cipher with a key size of p. A double encryption will result in an effective key size of 2p and yield the final result R. Thus, one would anticipate that one would have to search a key space of 2^{2p} in an exhaustive search of the keys. However, it can be shown that a search of the key space on the order of 2p is all that is necessary. This search is the same size as required for a single DES encryption. This situation is illustrated as follows:

The sequences shown illustrate the first DES encryption of a plaintext message M with all keys k1 through k2p yielding the intermediate encrypted results C1 through C2p.

$E_{k1} [M] \rightarrow C1$

$E_{k2} [M] \rightarrow C2$

.

.

$E_{k2p} [M] \rightarrow C2p$

If we have available ciphertext R where $R = E_{k2} [E_{k1} [M]]$ for a pair of secret keys k1 and k2, for each key m there is only one key k such that $D_m[R] = E_k[M]$ where D is the decipherment of R back from the second DES encipherment. In other words, there are 2p possible keys that will result in the pair [M,R] and, thus, can be found in a search of order 2p.

31. Using a modulo 26 substitution cipher where the letters A to Z of the alphabet are given a value of 0 to 25, respectively, encrypt the message "OVERLORD BEGINS." Use the key K =NEW and D =3 where D is the number of repeating letters representing the key. The encrypted message is:

    a. BFAEQKEH XRKFAW

    b. BFAEPKEH XRKFAW

    c. BFAEPKEH XRKEAW

    d. BFAERKEH XRKEAW

    Answer: c

    The solution is as follows:

    OVERLORD becomes 14 21 4 17 11 14 17 3

    BEGINS becomes 1 4 6 8 13 18

    The key NEW becomes 13 4 22

    Adding the key repetitively to OVERLORD BEGINS modulo 26 yields 1 5 0 4 15 10 4 7 23 17 10 4 0 22, which translates to BFAEPKEH XRKEAW

32. The algorithm of the 802.11 Wireless LAN Standard that is used to protect transmitted information from disclosure is called:

    a. Wireless Application Environment (WAE)

    b. Wired Equivalency Privacy (WEP)

    c. Wireless Transaction Protocol (WTP)

    d. Wireless Transport Layer Security Protocol (WTLS)

    Answer: b

    WEP is designed to prevent the violation of the confidentiality of data transmitted over the wireless LAN. Another feature of WEP is to prevent unauthorized access to the network. The other answers are protocols in the Wireless Application Protocol, the security of which is discussed in Question 21.

33. The Wired Equivalency Privacy algorithm (WEP) of the 802.11 Wireless LAN Standard uses which of the following to protect the confidentiality of information being transmitted on the LAN?

    a. A secret key that is shared between a mobile station (e.g., a laptop with a wireless Ethernet card) and a base station access point

    b. A public/private key pair that is shared between a mobile station (e.g., a laptop with a wireless Ethernet card) and a base station access point

c. Frequency shift keying (FSK) of the message that is sent between a mobile station (e.g., a laptop with a wireless Ethernet card) and a base station access point

d. A digital signature that is sent between a mobile station (e.g., a laptop with a wireless Ethernet card) and a base station access point

Answer: a

The transmitted packets are encrypted with a secret key and an Integrity Check (IC) field comprised of a CRC-32 check sum that is attached to the message. WEP uses the RC4 variable key-size stream cipher encryption algorithm. RC4 was developed in 1987 by Ron Rivest and operates in output feedback mode. Researchers at the University of California at Berkely (wep@isaac.cs.berkeley.edu) have found that the security of the WEP algorithm can be compromised, particularly with the following attacks:

- Passive attacks to decrypt traffic based on statistical analysis
- Active attack to inject new traffic from unauthorized mobile stations, based on known plaintext
- Active attacks to decrypt traffic, based on tricking the access point
- Dictionary-building attack that, after analysis of about a day's worth of traffic, allows real-time automated decryption of all traffic

The Berkeley researchers have found that these attacks are effective against both the 40-bit and the so-called 128-bit versions of WEP using inexpensive off-the-shelf equipment. These attacks can also be used against networks that use the 802.11b Standard, which is the extension to 802.11 to support higher data rates, but does not change the WEP algorithm.

The weaknesses in WEP and 802.11 are being addressed by the IEEE 802.11i Working Group. WEP will be upgraded to WEP2 with the following proposed changes:

- Modifying the method of creating the initialization vector (IV)
- Modifying the method of creating the encryption key
- Protection against replays
- Protection against IV collision attacks
- Protection against forged packets

In the longer term, it is expected that the Advanced Encryption Standard (AES) will replace the RC4 encryption algorithm currently used in WEP.

34. In a block cipher, diffusion can be accomplished through:
    a. Substitution
    b. XORing
    c. Nonlinear S-boxes
    d. Permutation

    Answer: d

    Diffusion is aimed at obscuring redundancy in the plaintext by spreading the effect of the transformation over the ciphertext. Permutation is also known as *transposition* and operates by rearranging the letters of the plaintext. Answer a, substitution, is used to implement *confusion* in a block cipher. Confusion tries to hide the relationship between the plaintext and the ciphertext. The Caesar cipher is an example of a substitution cipher. Answer b is incorrect since XORing, for example, as used in a stream cipher, implements confusion and not diffusion. Similarly, nonlinear S-boxes implement substitution. In DES, for example, there are eight different S-boxes that each has an input of 6 bits and an output of 4 bits. Thus, nonlinear substitution is effected.

35. The National Computer Security Center (NCSC) is:

    a. A division of the National Institute of Standards and Technology (NIST) that issues standards for cryptographic functions and publishes them as Federal Information Processing Standards (FIPS)

    b. A branch of the National Security Agency (NSA) that initiates research and develops and publishes standards and criteria for trusted information systems

    c. A joint enterprise between the NSA and NIST for developing cryptographic algorithms and standards

    d. An activity within the U.S. Department of Commerce that provides information security awareness training and develops standards for protecting sensitive but unclassified information

    Answer: b

    The NCSC promotes information systems security awareness and technology transfer through many channels, including the annual National Information Systems Security Conference. It was founded in 1981 as the Department of Defense Computer Security Center, and its name was change in 1985 to NCSC. It developed the Trusted Computer Evaluation Program Rainbow series for evaluating commercial products against information system security criteria. All the other answers are, therefore incorrect since they refer to NIST, which is under the U.S. Department of Commerce.

36. A portion of a Vigenère cipher square is given below using five (1, 2, 14, 16, 22) of the possible 26 alphabets. Using the key word bow, which of the following is the encryption of the word "advance" using the Vigenère cipher in Table A.10?

    a. b r r b b y h
    b. b r r b j y f
    c. b r r b b y f
    d. b r r b c y f

    Answer: c

    The Vigenère cipher is a *polyalphabetic* substitution cipher. The key word *bow* indicates which alphabets to use. The letter b indicates the alphabet of row 1, the letter o indicates the alphabet of row 14, and the letter w indicates the alphabet of row 22. To encrypt, arrange the key word, repetitively over the plaintext as shown in Table A.11. Thus, the letter a of the plaintext is transformed into b of alphabet in row 1, the letter d is transformed into r of row 14, the letter v is transformed into r of row 22 and so on.

37. There are two fundamental security protocols in IPSEC. These are the Authentication Header (AH) and the Encapsulating Security Payload (ESP). Which of the following correctly describes the functions of each?

    a. ESP-data encrypting protocol that also validates the integrity of the transmitted data; AH-source authenticating protocol that also validates the integrity of the transmitted data

    b. ESP-data encrypting and source authenticating protocol; AH-source authenticating protocol that also validates the integrity of the transmitted data

    c. ESP-data encrypting and source authenticating protocol that also validates the integrity of the transmitted data; AH-source authenticating protocol

    d. ESP-data encrypting and source authenticating protocol that also validates the integrity of the transmitted data; AH-source authenticating protocol that also validates the integrity of the transmitted data

    Answer: d

    ESP does have a source authentication and integrity capability through the use of a hash algorithm and a secret key. It provides confidentiality by means of secret key cryptography. DES and triple DES secret key block ciphers are supported by IPSEC and other algorithms will also be supported in the future. AH uses a hash algorithm in the packet header to authenticate the sender and validate the integrity of the transmitted data.

Table A.10 Vigenère Cipher

PLAINTEXT	A	B	C	D	E	F	G	H	I	J	K	L	M	N	O	P	Q	R	S	T	U	V	W	X	Y	Z
1	b	c	d	e	f	g	h	i	j	k	l	m	n	o	p	q	r	s	t	u	v	w	x	y	z	a
2	c	d	e	f	g	h	i	j	k	l	m	n	o	p	q	r	s	t	u	v	w	x	y	z	a	b
14	o	p	q	r	s	t	u	v	w	x	y	z	a	b	c	d	e	f	g	h	i	j	k	l	m	n
16	q	r	s	t	u	v	w	x	y	z	a	b	c	d	e	f	g	h	i	j	k	l	m	n	o	p
22	w	x	y	z	a	b	c	d	e	f	g	h	i	j	k	l	m	n	o	p	q	r	s	t	u	v

Table A.11   Encryption of Key Word *bow*

Key word	b	o	w	b	o	w	b
Plaintext	a	d	v	a	n	c	e
Ciphertext	b	r	r	b	b	y	f

38. Which of the following is NOT an advantage of a stream cipher?

   a. The same equipment can be used for encryption and decryption.

   b. It is amenable to hardware implementations that result in higher speeds.

   c. Since encryption takes place bit by bit, there is no error propagation.

   d. The receiver and transmitter must be synchronized.

     Answer: d

     The transmitter and receiver must be synchronized since they must use the same keystream bits for the same bits of the text that are to be enciphered and deciphered. Usually, synchronizing frames must be sent to effect the synchronization and, thus, additional overhead is required for the transmissions. Answer a describes an advantage since stream ciphers commonly use Linear Feedback Shift Registers (LFSRs) to generate the keystream and use XORs to operate on the plaintext input stream. Because of the characteristics of the XOR, the same XOR gates and LFSRs can also decrypt the message. Since LFSRs and XORs are used in a stream cipher to encrypt and decrypt, these components are amenable to hardware implementation, which means higher speeds of operation. Thus, answer b describes an advantage. For answer c, stream ciphers encrypt individual bits with no feedback of the generated ciphertext bits and, therefore, errors do not propagate.

39. Which of the following is NOT a property of a public key cryptosystem? (Let P represent the private key, Q represent the public key and M the plaintext message.)

   a. $Q[P(M)] = M$

   b. $P[Q(M)] = M$

   c. It is computationally infeasible to derive P from Q.

   d. P and Q are difficult to generate from a particular key value.

     Answer: d

     Answer d refers to the initial computation wherein the private and public keys are computed. The computation in this direction is relatively straightforward. Answers a and b state the true property of public key cryptography which is that a plaintext message encrypted with the private key can be decrypted by the public key and vice versa. Answer c states that it is computationally infeasible to derive the private key from the public key. Obviously, this is a critical property of public key cryptography.

40. A form of digital signature where the signer is not privy to the content of the message is called a:

    a. Zero knowledge proof

    b. Blind signature

    c. Masked signature

    d. Encrypted signature

    Answer: b

    A blind signature algorithm for the message M uses a blinding factor, f; a modulus m; the private key, s, of the signer and the public key, q, of the signer. The sender, who generates f and knows q, presents the message to the signer in the form:

    Mf^q (mod m)

    Thus, the message is not in a form readable by the signer since the signer does not know f. The signer signs Mf^q (mod m) with his/her private key, returning

    $(Mf^q)^s$ (mod m)

    This factor can be reduced to fM^s (mod m) since s and q are inverses of each other. The sender then divides fM^s (mod m) by the blinding factor, f, to obtain

    M^s (mod m)

    M^s (mod m) is, therefore, the message, M, signed with the private key, s, of the signer.

    Answer a refers to a zero knowledge proof. In general, a zero knowledge proof involves a person, A, trying to prove that he/she knows something, S, to another person, B, without revealing S or anything about S. Answers c and d are distracters.

41. The following compilation represents what facet of cryptanalysis?

A	8.2	J	0.2	S	6.3
B	1.5	K	0.8	T	9.1
C	2.8	L	4.0	U	2.8
D	4.3	M	2.4	V	1.0
E	12.7	N	6.7	W	2.4
F	2.2	O	7.5	X	0.2
G	2.0	P	1.9	Y	2.0
H	6.1	Q	0.1	Z	0.1
I	7.0	R	6.0		

a. Period analysis

b. Frequency analysis

c. Cilly analysis

d. Cartouche analysis

Answer: b

The compilation is from a study by H. Becker and F. Piper that was originally published in *Cipher Systems: The Protection of Communication*. The listing shows the relative frequency in percent of the appearance of the letters of the English alphabet in large numbers of passages taken from newspapers and novels. Thus, in a substitution cipher, an analysis of the frequency of appearance of certain letters may give clues to the actual letter before transformation. Note that the letters E, A, and T have relatively high percentages of appearance in English text.

Answer a refers to a cryptanalysis that is looking for sequences that repeat themselves and for the spacing between repetitions. This approach is used to break the Vigenère cipher. Answer c is a reference to a cilly, which was a three-character message key used in the German Enigma machine.

In answer d, a cartouche is a set of hieroglyphs surrounded by a loop. A cartouche referring to King Ptolemy was found on the Rosetta Stone.

Chapter 5—Security Architecture and Models

1. When microcomputers were first developed, the instruction fetch time was much longer than the instruction execution time because of the relatively slow speed of memory accesses. This situation led to the design of the:

   a. Reduced Instruction Set Computer (RISC)

   b. Complex Instruction Set Computer (CISC)

   c. Superscalar processor

   d. Very-Long-Instruction-Word (VLIW) processor

   Answer: b

   The logic was that since it took a long time to fetch an instruction from memory relative to the time required to execute that instruction in the CPU, then the number of instructions required to implement a program should be reduced. This reasoning naturally resulted in densely coded instructions with more decode and execution cycles in the processor. This situation was ameliorated by *pipelining* the instructions wherein the decode and execution cycles of one instruction would be overlapped in time with the fetch cycle of the next instruction. Answer a, *RISC*, evolved when packaging and memory technology advanced to the point where there was not much difference in memory access times and processor execution times. Thus, the objective of the RISC architecture was to reduce the number of cycles required to execute an instruction. Accordingly, this increased the number of instructions in the average program by approximately 30%, but it reduced the number of cycles per instruction on the average by a factor of four. Essentially, the RISC architecture uses simpler instructions but makes use of other features such as optimizing compilers to reduce the number of instructions required and large numbers of general purpose registers in the processor and data caches. The *superscalar processor*, answer c, allows concurrent execution of instructions in the same pipelined stage. A *scalar processor* is defined as a processor that executes one instruction at a time. The term superscalar denotes multiple, concurrent operations performed on scalar values as opposed to *vectors* or *arrays* that are used as objects of computation in *array processors*. For answer d, the *very-long-instruction-word (VLIW)* processor, multiple, concurrent operations are performed in a single instruction. Because multiple operations are performed in one instruction rather than using multiple instructions, the number of instructions is reduced relative to those in a scalar processor. However, for this approach to be feasible, the operations in each VLIW instruction must be independent of each other.

2. The main objective of the Java Security Model (JSM) is to:

   a. Protect the user from hostile, network mobile code
   b. Protect a web server from hostile, client code
   c. Protect the local client from user-input hostile code
   d. Provide accountability for events

   Answer: a

   When a user accesses a Web page through a browser, class files for an applet are downloaded automatically, even from untrusted sources. To counter this possible threat, Java provides a customizable *sandbox* to which the applets' execution is confined. This sandbox provides such protections as preventing reading and writing to a local disk, prohibiting the creation of a new process, prevention of making a network connection to a new host and preventing the loading of a new dynamic library and directly calling a native method. The sandbox security features are designed into the *Java Virtual Machine (JVM)*. These features are implemented through array bounds checking, structured memory access, type-safe reference cast checking to ensure that casting to an object of a different type is valid, and checking for null references and automatic garbage collection. These checks are designed to limit memory accesses to safe, structured operations. Answers b, c, and d are distracters.

3. Which of the following would NOT be a component of a general enterprise security architecture model for an organization?

   a. Information and resources to ensure the appropriate level of risk management
   b. Consideration of all the items that comprise information security, including distributed systems, software, hardware, communications systems, and networks
   c. A systematic and unified approach for evaluating the organization's information systems security infrastructure and defining approaches to implementation and deployment of information security controls
   d. IT system auditing

   Answer: d

   The auditing component of the IT system should be independent and distinct from the information system security architecture for a system. In answer a, the resources to support intelligent risk management decisions include technical expertise, applicable evaluation processes, refinement of business objectives, and delivery plans. Answer b promotes an enterprise-wide view of information system security issues. For answer c, the intent is to show that a comprehensive security architecture model includes all phases involved in information system security including planning, design, integrating, testing, and production.

4. In a multilevel security system (MLS), the Pump is:

   a. A two-way information flow device

   b. A one-way information flow device

   c. Compartmented Mode Workstation (CMW)

   d. A device that implements role-based access control

   Answer: b

   The *Pump* (M.H. Kang, I.S. Moskowitz, "A Pump for Rapid, Reliable, Secure Communications," *The 1st ACM Conference on Computer and Communications Security*, Fairfax, VA, 1993) was developed at the U.S. Naval Research Laboratory (NRL). It permits information flow in one direction only, from a lower level of security classification or sensitivity to a higher level. It is a convenient approach to multilevel security in that it can be used to put together systems with different security levels. Answer a is a distracter. Answer c, the *CMW*, refers to windows-based workstations that require users to work with information at different classification levels. Thus, users may work with multiple windows with different classification levels on their workstations. When data is attempted to be moved from one window to another, mandatory access control policies are enforced. This prevents information of a higher classification from being deposited to a location of lower classification. Answer d, *role-based access control*, is an access control mechanism and is now being considered for mandatory access control based on users' roles in their organizations.

5. The Bell-LaPadula model addresses which one of the following items?

   a. Covert channels

   b. The creation and destruction of subjects and objects

   c. Information flow from high to low

   d. Definition of a secure state transition

   Answer: c

   Information flow from high to low is addressed by the * *-property* of the Bell–LaPadula model, which states that a subject cannot write data from a higher level of classification to a lower level of classification. This property is also known as the *confinement property* or the *no write down* property. In answer a, *covert channels* are not addressed by the model. The Bell-LaPadula model deals with information flow through normal channels and does not address the covert passing of information through unintended paths. The creation and destruction of subjects and objects, answer b, is not addressed by the model. Answer d refers to the fact that the model discusses a secure transition from one secure state to another, but it never provides a definition of a secure transition.

6. In order to recognize the practical aspects of multilevel security in which, for example, an unclassified paragraph in a Secret document has to be moved to an Unclassified document, the Bell-LaPadula model introduces the concept of a:

   a. Simple security property
   b. Secure exchange
   c. Data flow
   d. Trusted subject

   Answer: d

   The model permits a *trusted subject* to violate the *-property but to comply with the intent of the *-property. Thus, a person who is a trusted subject could move unclassified data from a classified document to an unclassified document without violating the intent of the *-property. Another example would be for a trusted subject to downgrade the classification of material when it has been determined that the downgrade would not harm national or organizational security and would not violate the intent of the *-property. The *simple security property (ss-property)*, answer a, *states* that a subject cleared for one classification cannot read data from a higher classification. This property is also known as the *no read up* property. Answers b and c are distracters.

7. In a refinement of the Bell–LaPadula model, the *strong tranquility property* states that:

   a. Objects never change their security level.
   b. Objects never change their security level in a way that would violate the system security policy.
   c. Objects can change their security level in an unconstrained fashion.
   d. Subjects can read up.

   Answer: a

Answer b is known as the *weak tranquility property*. Answers c and d are distracters.

8. As an analog of confidentiality labels, integrity labels in the Biba model are assigned according to which of the following rules?

   a. Objects are assigned integrity labels identical to the corresponding confidentiality labels.

   b. Objects are assigned integrity labels according to their trustworthiness; subjects are assigned classes according to the harm that would be done if the data were modified improperly.

   c. Subjects are assigned classes according to their trustworthiness; objects are assigned integrity labels according to the harm that would be done if the data were modified improperly.

   d. Integrity labels are assigned according to the harm that would occur from unauthorized disclosure of the information.

   Answer: c

   As subjects in the world of confidentiality are assigned clearances related to their trustworthiness, subjects in the Biba model are assigned to integrity classes that are indicative of their trustworthiness. Also, in the context of confidentiality, objects are assigned classifications related to the amount of harm that would be caused by unauthorized disclosure of the object. Similarly, in the integrity model, objects are assigned to classes related to the amount of harm that would be caused by the improper modification of the object. Answer a is incorrect since integrity properties and confidentiality properties are opposites. For example, in the Bell-LaPadula model, there is no prohibition against a subject at one classification reading information from a lower level of confidentiality. However, when maintenance of the integrity of data is the objective, reading of information from a lower level of integrity by a subject at a higher level of integrity risks contaminating data at the higher level of integrity. Thus, the simple and * -properties in the Biba model are complements of the corresponding properties in the Bell-LaPadula model. Recall that the *Simple Integrity Property* states that a subject at one level of integrity is not permitted to observe (read) an object of a lower integrity (*no read down*). Also, the **- Integrity Property* states that an object at one level of integrity is not permitted to modify (write to) an object of a higher level of integrity (*no write up*). Answer b is incorrect since the words "object" and "subject" are interchanged. In answer d, unauthorized disclosure refers to confidentiality and not to integrity.

9. The Clark-Wilson Integrity Model (D. Clark, D. Wilson, "A Comparison of Commercial and Military Computer Security Policies," *Proceedings of the 1987 IEEE Computer Society Symposium on Research in Security and Privacy, Los Alamitos, CA, IEEE Computer Society Press, 1987*) focuses on what two concepts?

   a. Separation of duty and well-formed transactions

   b. Least privilege and well-formed transactions

   c. Capability lists and domains

   d. Well-formed transactions and denial of service

   Answer: a

   The Clark-Wilson Model is a model focused on the needs of the commercial world and is based on the theory that integrity is more important than confidentiality for commercial organizations. Further, the model incorporates the commercial concepts of separation of duty and well-formed transactions. The *well-formed transaction* of the model is implemented by the *transformation procedure (TP.)* A TP is defined in the model as the mechanism for transforming the set of *constrained data items (CDIs)* from one valid state of integrity to another valid state of integrity. The Clark-Wilson Model defines rules for separation of duty that denote the relations between a user, TPs, and the CDIs that can be operated upon by those TPs. The model talks about the *access triple* that is the user, the program that is permitted to operate on the data, and the data. Answers b, c, and d are distracters.

10. The model that addresses the situation wherein one group is not affected by another group using specific commands is called the:

    a. Information flow model

    b. Non-interference model

    c. Composition model

    d. Clark-Wilson model

    Answer: b

    In the *non-interference model*, security policy assertions are defined in the abstract. The process of moving from the abstract to developing conditions that can be applied to the transition functions that operate on the objects is called *unwinding*. Answer a refers to the *information flow model* in which information is categorized into classes, and rules define how information can flow between the classes. The model can be defined as [O, P, S, T] where O is the set of objects, P is the flow policy, S represents the valid states, and T represents the state transitions. The flow policy is usually implemented as a lattice structure. The *composition model*, answer c, investigates the resultant security properties when subsystems are combined. Answer d, the Clark-Wilson model, is discussed in question 9.

11. The secure path between a user and the Trusted Computing Base (TCB) is called:

    a. Trusted distribution

    b. Trusted path

    c. Trusted facility management

    d. The security perimeter

    Answer: b

    Answer a, *trusted distribution*, ensures that valid and secure versions of software have been received correctly. *Trusted facility management*, answer c, is concerned with the proper operation of trusted facilities as well as system administration and configuration. Answer d, the *security perimeter,* is the boundary that separates the TCB from the remainder of the system. Recall that the *TCB* is the totality of protection mechanisms within a computer system that are trusted to enforce a security policy.

12. The Common Criteria terminology for the degree of examination of the product to be tested is:

    a. Target of Evaluation (TOE)

    b. Protection Profile (PP)

    c. Functionality (F)

    d. Evaluation Assurance Level (EAL)

    Answer: d

    The *Evaluation Assurance Levels* range from EA1 (functional testing) to EA7 (detailed testing and formal design verification). The *Target of Evaluation (TOE)*, answer a, refers to the product to be tested. Answer b, *Protection Profile (PP)*, is an implementation-independent specification of the security requirements and protections of a product that could be built. A *Security Target (ST)* is a listing of the security claims for a particular IT security product. Also, the Common Criteria describes an intermediate grouping of security requirement components as a *package*. *Functionality*, answer c, refers to Part 2 of the Common Criteria that contains standard and well-understood functional security requirements for IT systems.

13. A difference between the Information Technology Security Evaluation Criteria (ITSEC) and the Trusted Computer System Evaluation Criteria (TCSEC) is:

    a. TCSEC addresses availability as well as confidentiality

    b. ITSEC addresses confidentiality only

    c. ITSEC addresses integrity and availability as well as confidentiality

    d. TCSEC separates functionality and assurance

    Answer: c

    TCSEC addresses confidentiality only and bundles functionality and assurance. Thus, answers a, b, and d are incorrect. By separating functionality and assurance as in ITSEC, one could specify fewer security functions that have a high level of assurance. This separation carried over into the Common Criteria.

14. Which of the following items BEST describes the standards addressed by Title II, Administrative Simplification, of the Health Insurance Portability and Accountability Act (*U.S. Kennedy-Kassebaum Health Insurance and Portability Accountability Act -HIPAA-Public Law 104-19*)?

    a. Transaction Standards, to include Code Sets; Unique Health Identifiers; Security and Electronic Signatures and Privacy

    b. Transaction Standards, to include Code Sets; Security and Electronic Signatures and Privacy

    c. Unique Health Identifiers; Security and Electronic Signatures and Privacy

    d. Security and Electronic Signatures and Privacy

    Answer: a

    HIPAA was designed to provide for greater access to personal health care information, enable portability of health care insurance, establish strong penalties for health care fraud, and streamline the health care claims process through administrative simplification. To accomplish the latter, Title II of the HIPAA law, Administrative Simplification, requires standardizing the formats for the electronic transmission of health care information. The *transactions and code sets* portion includes standards for submitting claims, enrollment information, premium payments, and others as adopted by HHS. The standard for transactions is the ANSI ASC X12N version 4010 EDI Standard. Standard code sets are required for diagnoses and inpatient services, professional services, dental services (replaces 'D' codes), and drugs (instead of 'J' codes). Also, local codes are not to be used. *Unique health identifiers* are required to identify health care providers, health plans, employers, and individuals. *Security and electronic signatures* are specified to protect health care information. *Pri-*

vacy protections are required to ensure that there is no unauthorized disclosure of individually identifiable health care information. Answers b, c, and d are incorrect since they do not include all four major standards. Additional information can be found at http://aspe.hhs.gov/adminsimp.

15. Which one of the following is generally NOT considered a covered entity under Title II, Administrative Simplification, of the HIPAA law?

   a. Health care providers who transmit health information electronically in connection with standard transactions

   b. Health plans

   c. Employers

   d. Health care clearinghouses

   Answer: c

   Employers are not specifically covered under HIPAA. HIPAA applies to health care providers that transmit health care information in electronic form, health care clearinghouses, and health plans. However, some employers may be covered under the Gramm-Leach-Bliley Act. The *Gramm-Leach-Bliley (GLB) Act* was enacted on November 12, 1999, to remove Depression era restrictions on banks that limited certain business activities, mergers, and affiliations. It repeals the restrictions on banks affiliating with securities firms contained in sections 20 and 32 of the Glass-Steagall Act. GLB became effective on November 13, 2001. GLB also requires health plans and insurers to protect member and subscriber data in electronic and other formats. These health plans and insurers will fall under new state laws and regulations that are being passed to implement GLB, since GLB explicitly assigns enforcement of the health plan and insurer regulations to state insurance authorities (15 U.S.C. §6805). Some of the privacy and security requirements of Gramm-Leach-Bliley are similar to those of HIPAA. Most states required that health plans and insurers comply with the GLB requirements by July 1, 2001, and financial institutions were required to be in full compliance with Gramm-Leach-Bliley by this date. Answers a, b, and d are incorrect since they are covered by the HIPAA regulations.

16. The principles of Notice, Choice, Access, Security, and Enforcement refer to which of the following?

   a. Authorization

   b. Privacy

   c. Nonrepudiaton

   d. Authentication

   Answer: b

These items are *privacy* principles. *Notice* refers to the collection, use, and disclosure of *personally identifiable information (PII)*. *Choice* is the choice to opt out or opt in regarding the disclosure of PII to third parties; *Access* is access by consumers to their PII to permit review and correction of information. *Security* is the obligation to protect PII from unauthorized disclosure. *Enforcement* is the enforcement of applicable privacy policies and obligations. The other answers are distracters.

17. What is the simple security property of which one of the following models is described as:

"A user has access to a client company's information, c, if and only if for all other information, o, that the user can read, either $x(c) \neq z(o)$ or $x(c) = x(o)$, where $x(c)$ is the client's company and $z(o)$ is the competitors of $x(c)$."

 a. Biba

 b. Lattice

 c. Bell-LaPadula

 d. Chinese wall

 Answer: d

This model, (D.C. Brewer and M.J. Nash, "Chinese Wall Model," *Proceedings of the 1989 IEEE Computer Society Symposium on Security and Privacy*, 1989), defines rules that prevent conflicts of interest in organizations that may have access to information from companies that are competitors of each other. Essentially, the model states that a user working on one account cannot work on a competitor's account for a designated period of time. Answer a, the *Biba model*, is an integrity model that is an analog of the *Bell-LaPadula confidentiality model* of answer c. Answer b, the *lattice*, refers to the general information flow model where security levels are represented by a lattice structure. The model defines a transitive ordering relation, $\leq$, on security classes. Thus, for security classes X, Y, and Z, the ordering relation $X \leq Y \leq Z$ describes the situation where Z is the highest security class and X is the lowest security class, and there is an ordering among the three classes.

18. The two categories of the policy of *separation of duty* are:

 a. Span of control and functional separation

 b. Inference control and functional separation

 c. Dual control and functional separation

 d. Dual control and aggregation control

 Answer: c

Dual control requires that two or more subjects act together simultaneously to authorize an operation. A common example is the requirement that two individuals turn their keys simultaneously in two physically separated areas to arm a weapon. Functional separation implies a sequential approval process such as requiring the approval of a manager to send a check generated by a subordinate. Answer a is incorrect. Span of control refers to the number of subordinates that can be optimally managed by a superior. Answer b is incorrect. Inference control is implementing protections that prevent the inference of information not authorized to a user from information that is authorized to be accessed by a user. Answer d is incorrect, but aggregation refers to the acquisition of large numbers of data items to obtain information that would not be available by analyzing a small number of the data items.

19. In the National Information Assurance Certification and Accreditation Process (NIACAP), a *type accreditation* performs which one of the following functions?

    a. Evaluates a major application or general support system

    b. Verifies the evolving or modified system's compliance with the information agreed on in the System Security Authorization Agreement (SSAA)

    c. Evaluates an application or system that is distributed to a number of different locations

    d. Evaluates the applications and systems at a specific, self-contained location

    Answer: c

    Answer a is the NIACAP *system accreditation.* Answer b is the Phase 2 or *Verification phase* of the Defense Information Technology Security Certification and Accreditation Process (DITSCAP). The objective is to use the SSAA to establish an evolving yet binding agreement on the level of security required before the system development begins or changes to a system are made. After accreditation, the SSAA becomes the baseline security configuration document. Answer d is the NIACAP *site accreditation.*

20. Which of the following processes establish the minimum national standards for certifying and accrediting national security systems?

    a. CIAP

    b. DITSCAP

    c. NIACAP

    d. Defense audit

Answer: c

The NIACAP provides a standard set of activities, general tasks, and a management structure to certify and accredit systems that will maintain the information assurance and security posture of a system or site. The NIACAP is designed to certify that the information system meets documented accreditation requirements and will continue to maintain the accredited security posture throughout the system life cycle. Answer a, CIAP, is being developed for the evaluation of critical commercial systems and uses the NIACAP methodology. DITSCAP, answer b, establishes for the defense entities a standard process, set of activities, general task descriptions, and a management structure to certify and accredit IT systems that will maintain the required security posture. The process is designed to certify that the IT system meets the accreditation requirements and that the system will maintain the accredited security posture throughout the system life cycle. The four phases to the DITSCAP are Definition, Verification, Validation, and Post Accreditation. Answer d is a distracter.

21. Which of the following terms is NOT associated with a Read Only Memory (ROM)?

    a. Flash memory

    b. Field Programmable Gate Array (FPGA)

    c. Static RAM (SRAM)

    d. Firmware

    Answer: c

    Static Random Access Memory (SRAM) is *volatile* and, therefore, loses its data if power is removed from the system. Conversely, a ROM is *nonvolatile* in that it does not lose its content when power is removed. *Flash memories,* answer a, are a type of electrically programmable ROM. Answer b, *FPGA,* is a type of Programmable Logic Device (PLD) that is programmed by blowing fuse connections on the chip or using an antifuse that makes a connection when a high voltage is applied to the junction. For answer d, *firmware* is a program that is stored on ROMs.

22. Serial data transmission in which information can be transmitted in two directions, but only one direction at a time, is called:

    a. Simplex

    b. Half-duplex

    c. Synchronized

    d. Full-duplex

    Answer: b

The time required to switch transmission directions in a half-duplex line is called the *turnaround time*. Answer a, *simplex*, refers to communication that takes place in one direction only. Answer c is a distracter. Full-duplex, answer d, can transmit and receive information in both directions simultaneously. The transmissions can be asynchronous or synchronous. In asynchronous transmission, a start bit is used to indicate the beginning of transmission. The start bit is followed by data bits and, then, by one or two stop bits to indicate the end of the transmission. Since start and stop bits are sent with every unit of data, the actual data transmission rate is lower since these "overhead" bits are used for synchronization and do not carry information. In this mode, data is sent only when it is available and the data is not transmitted continuously. In synchronous transmission, the transmitter and receiver have synchronized clocks and the data is sent in a continuous stream. The clocks are synchronized by using transitions in the data and, therefore, start and stop bits are not required for each unit of data sent.

23. The ANSI ASC X12 (American National Standards Institute Accredited Standards Committee X12) Standard version 4010 applies to which one of the following HIPAA categories?

   a. Privacy
   b. Code sets
   c. Transactions
   d. Security

   Answer: c

   The transactions addressed by HIPAA are:

   ■ Health claims or similar encounter information
   ■ Health care payment and remittance advice
   ■ Coordination of Benefits
   ■ Health claim status
   ■ Enrollment and disenrollment in a health plan
   ■ Eligibility for a health plan
   ■ Health plan premium payments
   ■ Referral certification and authorization

   The HIPAA EDI transaction standards to address these HIPAA transactions include the following:

   ■ Health care claims or coordination of benefits
   ■ Retail drug NCPCP (National Council for Prescription Drug Programs) v. 32
   ■ Dental claim ASC X12N 837: dental

- Professional claim ASC X12N 837: professional
- Institutional claim ASC X12N 837: institutional
- Payment and remittance advice ASC X12N 835
- Health claim status ASC X12N 276/277
- Plan enrollment ASC X12 834
- Plan eligibility ASC X12 270/271
- Plan premium payments ASC X12 820
- Referral certification ASC X12 N 278

The American National Standards Institute was founded in 1917 and is the only source of American Standards. The ANSI Accredited Standards Committee X12 was chartered in 1979 and is responsible for cross-industry standards for electronic documents. The HIPAA privacy standards, answer a, were finalized in April, 2001, and implementation must be accomplished by April 14, 2003. The privacy rule covers individually identifiable health care information transmitted, stored in electronic or paper form, or communicated orally. Protected health information (PHI) may not be disclosed unless disclosure is approved by the individual, permitted by the legislation, required for treatment, part of health care operations, required by law, or necessary for payment. PHI is defined as individually identifiable health information that is transmitted by electronic media, maintained in any medium described in the definition of electronic media under HIPAA, or is transmitted or maintained in any other form or medium. Answer b, code sets, refers to the codes that are used to fill in the data elements of the HIPAA transaction standards. Examples of these codes are:

- ICD-9-CM (vols. 1 and 2) International Classification of Diseases, 9th Ed., Clinical Modification—Diseases, injuries, impairments, other health related problems, their manifestations, and causes of injury, disease, impairment, or other health-related problems

- CPT (Current Procedural Terminology, 4th Ed. [CPT-4]), CDT (Code on Dental Procedures and Nomenclature, 2nd Ed. [CDT-2]) or ICD-9-CM (vol. 3)—Procedures or other actions taken to prevent, diagnose, treat, or manage diseases, injuries, and impairments

- NDC (National Drug Codes)—drugs

- HCPCS (Health Care Financing Administration Common Procedure Coding System)

- Other health-related services, other substances, equipment, supplies, or other items used in health care services

The proposed HIPAA Security Rule, answer d, mandates the protection of the confidentiality, integrity, and availability of protected health information (PHI) through:

- Administrative procedures
- Physical safeguards
- Technical services and mechanisms

The rule also addresses electronic signatures, but the final rule will depend on industry progress on reaching a standard. In addition, the proposed security rule requires the appointment of a security officer.

24. A 1999 law that addresses privacy issues related to health care, insurance and finance and that will be implemented by the states is:

   a. Gramm-Leach-Bliley (GLB)

   b. Kennedy-Kassebaum

   c. Medical Action Bill

   d. Insurance Reform Act

   Answer: a

   See the answers to Question 15 for a discussion of GLB. Answer b refers to the HIPAA legislation (*U.S. Kennedy-Kassebaum Health Insurance and Portability Accountability Act—HIPAA-Public Law 104-19*). Answers c and d are distracters.

25. The Platform for Privacy Preferences (P3P) was developed by the World Wide Web Consortium (W3C) for what purpose?

   a. To implement public key cryptography for transactions

   b. To evaluate a client's privacy practices

   c. To monitor users

   d. To implement privacy practices on Web sites

   Answer: d

   As of this writing, the latest W3C working draft of P3P is *P3P 1.0, 28 January, 2002* (www.w3.org/TR). An excerpt of the W3C P3P Specification states "P3P enables Web sites to express their privacy practices in a standard format that can be retrieved automatically and interpreted easily by user agents. P3P user agents will allow users to be informed of site practices (in both machine- and human-readable formats) and to automate decision-making based on these practices when appropriate. Thus users need not read the privacy policies at every site they visit."

   With P3, an organization can post its privacy policy in machine-readable form (XML) on its Web site. This policy statement includes:

- Who has access to collected information
- The type of information collected
- How the information is used
- The legal entity making the privacy statement

P3P also supports user agents that allow a user to configure a P3P-enabled Web browser with the user's privacy preferences. Then, when the user attempts to access a Web site, the user agent compares the user's stated preferences with the privacy policy in machine-readable form at the Web site. Access will be granted if the preferences match the policy. Otherwise, either access to the Web site will be blocked or a pop-up window will appear notifying the user that he/she must change their privacy preferences. Usually, this means that the user has to lower his/her privacy threshold. Answers a, b, and c are distracters.

26. What process is used to accomplish high-speed data transfer between a peripheral device and computer memory, bypassing the Central Processing Unit (CPU)?

    a. Direct memory access

    b. Interrupt processing

    c. Transfer under program control

    d. Direct access control

    Answer: a

    With DMA, a DMA controller essentially takes control of the memory busses and manages the data transfer directly. Answer b, interrupt processing, involves an external signal interrupting the "normal" CPU program flow. This interrupt causes the CPU to halt processing and "jump" to another program that services the interrupt. When the interrupt has been serviced, the CPU returns to continue executing the original program. Program control transfer, answer c, is accomplished by the processor executing input/output (I/O) instructions. Answer d is a distracter.

27. An associative memory operates in which one of the following ways?

    a. Uses indirect addressing only

    b. Searches for values in memory exceeding a specified value

    c. Searches for a specific data value in memory

    d. Returns values stored in a memory address location specified in the CPU address register

    Answer: c

    Answer a refers to an addressing mode used in computers where the address location that is specified in the program instruction contains the address of the final desired location. Answer b is a distracter and answer d is the description of the direct or absolute addressing mode.

28. The following concerns usually apply to what type of architecture?
    - Desktop systems can contain sensitive information that may be at risk of being exposed.
    - Users may generally lack security awareness.
    - Modems present a vulnerability to dial-in attacks.
    - Lack of proper backup may exist.
    a. Distributed
    b. Centralized
    c. Open system
    d. Symmetric

    Answer: a

    Additional concerns associated with distributed systems include:

    - A desktop PC or workstation can provide an avenue of access into critical information systems of an organization.
    - Downloading data from the Internet increases the risk of infecting corporate systems with a malicious code or an unintentional modification of the databases.
    - A desktop system and its associated disks may not be protected from physical intrusion or theft.

    For answer b, a *centralized* system, all the characteristics cited do not apply to a central host with no PCs or workstations with large amounts of memory attached. Also, the vulnerability presented by a modem attached to a PC or workstation would not exist. An *open system* or architecture, answer c, is comprised of vendor-independent subsystems that have published specifications and interfaces in order to permit operations with the products of other suppliers. One advantage of an open system is that it is subject to review and evaluation by independent parties. Answer d is a distracter.

29. The definition "A relatively small amount (when compared to primary memory) of very high speed RAM, which holds the instructions and data from primary memory, that has a high probability of being accessed during the currently executing portion of a program" refers to what category of computer memory?
    a. Secondary
    b. Real
    c. Cache
    d. Virtual

Answer: c

Cache logic attempts to predict which instructions and data in main (primary) memory will be used by a currently executing program. It then moves these items to the higher speed cache in anticipation of the CPU requiring these programs and data. Properly designed caches can significantly reduce the apparent main memory access time and thus increase the speed of program execution. Answer a, *secondary memory*, is a slower memory (such as a magnetic disk) that provides non-volatile storage. *Real or primary memory*, answer b, is directly addressable by the CPU and is used for the storage of instructions and data associated with the program that is being executed. This memory is usually high-speed, Random Access Memory (RAM). Answer d, *virtual memory*, uses secondary memory in conjunction with primary memory to present the CPU with a larger, apparent address space of the real memory locations.

30. The organization that "establishes a collaborative partnership of computer incident response, security and law enforcement professionals who work together to handle computer security incidents and to provide both proactive and reactive security services for the U.S. Federal government" is called:

   a. CERT®/CC
   b. Center for Infrastructure Protection
   c. Federal CIO Council
   d. Federal Computer Incident Response Center

   Answer: d

   To again quote the FedCIRC charter, "FedCIRC provides assistance and guidance in incident response and provides a centralized approach to incident handling across agency boundaries." Specifically, the mission of FedCIRC is to:

   ■ Provide civil agencies with technical information, tools, methods, assistance, and guidance
   ■ Be proactive and provide liaison activities and analytical support
   ■ Encourage the development of quality products and services through collaborative relationships with Federal civil agencies, the Department of Defense, academia, and private industry
   ■ Promote the highest security profile for government information technology (IT) resources
   ■ Promote incident response and handling procedural awareness with the federal government

   Answer a, the CERT Coordination Center (CERT/CC), is a unit of the Carnegie Mellon University Software Engineering Institute (SEI).

SEI is a Federally funded R&D Center. CERT's mission is to alert the Internet community to vulnerabilities and attacks and to conduct research and training in the areas of computer security, including incident response. Answer b is a distracter and answer c, the Federal Chief Information Officers' Council, is the sponsor of FedCIRC.

Chapter 6—Operations Security

1. Which book of the Rainbow series addresses the Trusted Network Interpretation (TNI)?

   a. Red Book

   b. Orange Book

   c. Green Book

   d. Purple Book

   Answer: a

   The Red Book is one book of the Rainbow Series, a six-foot-tall stack of books on evaluating "Trusted Computer Systems" according to the National Security Agency. The term "Rainbow Series" comes from the fact that each book is a different color. The Trusted Network Interpretation (TNI) extends the evaluation classes of the Trusted Systems Evaluation Criteria (DOD 5200.28-STD) to trusted network systems and components.

   Answer b, the Orange Book, is the main book of the Rainbow Series and most of the other books elaborate on the information contained in this book. The Orange Book is the DoD Trusted Computer System Evaluation Criteria [DOD 5200.28][1]. Answer c, the Green Book, is CSC-STD-002-85, the DoD Password Management Guidelines. Answer d, the Purple Book, is NCSC-TG-014, Guidelines for Formal Verification Systems. Source: NCSC-TG-005 Trusted Network Interpretation [Red Book] and DoD Trusted Computer System Evaluation Criteria [DOD 5200.28-Orange Book.]

2. Which choice describes the Forest Green Book?

   a. It is a tool that assists vendors in data gathering for certifiers.

   b. It is a Rainbow series book that defines the secure handling of storage media.

   c. It is a Rainbow series book that defines guidelines for implementing access control lists.

   d. It does not exist; there is no "Forest Green Book."

   Answer: b

   The Forest Green book is a Rainbow series book that defines the secure handling of sensitive or classified automated information system memory and secondary storage media, such as degaussers, magnetic tapes, hard disks, floppy disks, and cards. The Forest Green book details procedures for clearing, purging, declassifying, or destroying automated information system (AIS) storage media to prevent data remanence. Data remanence is the residual physical representation of data that has been erased in some way. After storage media is erased there may be some physical characteristics that allow data to be reconstructed.

Answer a is the Blue Book, NCSC-TG-019 Trusted Product Evaluation Questionnaire Version-2. The Blue book is a tool to assist system developers and vendors in gathering data to assist evaluators and certifiers assessing trusted computer systems.

Answer c is the Grey/Silver Book, NCSC-TG-020A, the Trusted UNIX Working Group (TRUSIX) Rationale for Selecting Access Control. The Grey/Silver book defines guidelines for implementing access control lists (ACLs) in the UNIX system. Source: NCSC-TG-025 A Guide to Understanding Data Remanence in Automated Information Systems, NCSC-TG-020A Trusted UNIX Working Group (TRUSIX) Rationale for Selecting Access Control, and NCSC-TG-019 Trusted Product Evaluation Questionnaire Version-2.

3. Which term below BEST describes the concept of "least privilege"?

   a. Each user is granted the lowest clearance required for their tasks.

   b. A formal separation of command, program, and interface functions.

   c. A combination of classification and categories that represents the sensitivity of information.

   d. Active monitoring of facility entry access points.

   Answer: a

   The "least privilege" principle requires that each subject in a system be granted the most restrictive set of privileges (or lowest clearance) needed for the performance of authorized tasks. The application of this principle limits the damage that can result from accident, error, or unauthorized use. Applying this principle may limit the damage resulting from accidents, errors, or unauthorized use of system resources.

   Answer b describes "separation of privilege," which is the separation of functions, namely between the commands, programs, and interfaces implementing those functions, such that malicious or erroneous code in one function is prevented from affecting the code or data of another function.

   Answer c is a security level. A security level is the combination of hierarchical classification and a set of non-hierarchical categories that represents the sensitivity of information.

   Answer d is a distracter. Source: DoD 5200.28-STD—Department of Defense Trusted Computer System Evaluation Criteria.

4. Which general TCSEC security class category describes that mandatory access policies be enforced in the TCB?

   a. A

   b. B

   c. C

   d. D

> *Answer:* b
>
> The Trusted Computer System Evaluation Criteria [Orange Book] defines major hierarchical classes of security by the letters D (least secure) through A (most secure):
>
> **D.** Minimal protection
>
> **C.** Discretionary protection (C1&C2)
>
> **B.** Mandatory protection (B1, B2, B3)
>
> **A.** Verified protection; formal methods (A1)
>
> Source: DoD 5200.28-STD—Department of Defense Trusted Computer System Evaluation Criteria.
>
> Table A.12 shows these TCSEC Security Evaluation Categories.

5. Which statement below is the BEST definition of "need-to-know"?

   a. Need-to-know ensures that no single individual (acting alone) can compromise security controls.

   b. Need-to-know grants each user the lowest clearance required for their tasks.

Table A.12   TCSEC Security Evaluation Categories

CLASS	DESCRIPTION
D:	minimal protection
C:	discretionary protection
C1:	discretionary security protection
C2:	controlled access protection
B:	mandatory protection
B1:	labeled security protection
B2:	structured protection
B3:	security domains
A1:	verified protection

   c. Need-to-know limits the time an operator performs a task.

   d. Need-to-know requires that the operator have the minimum knowledge of the system necessary to perform his task.

   Answer: d

   The concept of "need-to-know" means that, in addition to whatever specific object or role rights a user may have on the system, the user has also the minimum amount of information necessary to perform his job function. Answer a is "separation of duties," assigning parts of tasks to different personnel. Answer b is "least privilege," the user has the minimum security level required to perform his job function. Answer c is "rotation of duties," wherein the amount of time an operator is assigned a security-sensitive task is limited before being moved to a different task with a different security classification.

6. Place the four systems security modes of operation in order, from the most secure to the least:

   _____ a. Dedicated Mode

   _____ b. Multilevel Mode

   _____ c. Compartmented Mode

   _____ d. System High Mode

   Answer: a, d, c, and b

   The "mode of operation" is a description of the conditions under which an AIS functions, based on the sensitivity of data processed and the clearance levels and authorizations of the users. Four modes of operation are defined:

   Dedicated Mode. An AIS is operating in the dedicated mode when each user with direct or indirect individual access to the AIS, its peripherals, remote terminals, or remote hosts has all of the following:

   a. A valid personnel clearance for all information on the system

   b. Formal access approval for, and has signed nondisclosure agreements for all the information stored and/or processed (including all compartments, subcompartments, and/or special access programs)

   c. A valid need-to-know for all information contained within the system

   System-High Mode. An AIS is operating in the system-high mode when each user with direct or indirect access to the AIS, its peripherals, remote terminals, or remote hosts has all of the following:

a. A valid personnel clearance for all information on the AIS

b. Formal access approval for, and has signed nondisclosure agreements for all the information stored and/or processed (including all compartments, subcompartments, and/or special access programs)

c. A valid need-to-know for some of the information contained within the AIS

Compartmented Mode. An AIS is operating in the compartmented mode when each user with direct or indirect access to the AIS, its peripherals, remote terminals, or remote hosts has all of the following:

a. A valid personnel clearance for the most restricted information processed in the AIS

b. Formal access approval for, and has signed nondisclosure agreements for that information to which he/she is to have access

c. A valid need-to-know for that information to which he/she is to have access

Multilevel Mode. An AIS is operating in the multilevel mode when all the following statements are satisfied concerning the users with direct or indirect access to the AIS, its peripherals, remote terminals, or remote hosts:

a. Some do not have a valid personnel clearance for all the information processed in the AIS.

b. All have the proper clearance and have the appropriate formal access approval for that information to which he/she is to have access.

c. All have a valid need-to-know for that information to which they are to have access.

Source: DoD 5200.28-STD—Department of Defense Trusted Computer System Evaluation Criteria.

7. Which media control below is the BEST choice to prevent data remanence on magnetic tapes or floppy disks?

a. Overwriting the media with new application data

b. Degaussing the media

c. Applying a concentration of hydriodic acid (55% to 58% solution) to the gamma ferric oxide disk surface

d. Making sure the disk is re-circulated as quickly as possible to prevent object reuse

Answer: b

Degaussing is recommended as the best method for purging most magnetic media. Degaussing is a process whereby the magnetic media is erased, i.e., returned to its initial virgin state. Erasure via degaussing may be accomplished in two ways:

- In AC erasure, the media is degaussed by applying an alternating field that is reduced in amplitude over time from an initial high value (i.e., AC-powered)

- In DC erasure, the media is saturated by applying a unidirectional field (i.e., DC-powered or by employing a permanent magnet)

Another point about degaussing: Degaussed magnetic hard drives will generally require restoration of factory-installed timing tracks, so data purging is recommended. Also, physical destruction of CDROM or WORM media is required.

Answer a is not recommended because the application may not completely overwrite the old data properly, and strict configuration controls must be in place on both the operating system and the software itself. Also, bad sectors on the media may not permit the software to overwrite old data properly. To satisfy the DoD clearing requirement, it is sufficient to write any character to all data locations in question (purging).

To purge the media, the DoD requires overwriting with a pattern, then its complement, and finally with another pattern; e.g., overwrite first with 0011 0101, followed by 1100 1010, then 1001 0111. The number of times an overwrite must be accomplished depends on the storage media, sometimes on its sensitivity, and sometimes on differing DoD component requirements, but seven times is often recommended.

Answer c is a rarely used method of media destruction, and acid solutions should be used in a well-ventilated area only by qualified personnel.

Answer d is wrong. Source: NCSC-TG-025 A Guide to Understanding Data Remanence in Automated Information Systems.

8. Which choice below is the BEST description of an audit trail?

   a. Audit trails are used to detect penetration of a computer system and to reveal usage that identifies misuse.

   b. An audit trail is a device that permits simultaneous data processing of two or more security levels without risk of compromise.

   c. An audit trail mediates all access to objects within the network by subjects within the network.

   d. Audit trails are used to prevent access to sensitive systems by unauthorized personnel.

   Answer: a

An audit trail is a set of records that collectively provide documentary evidence of processing used to aid in tracing from original transactions forward to related records and reports, and/or backward from records and reports to their component source transactions. Audit trails may be limited to specific events or may encompass all of the activities on a system.

User audit trails can usually log:

- All commands directly initiated by the user
- All identification and authentication attempts
- Files and resources accessed

It is most useful if options and parameters are also recorded from commands. It is much more useful to know that a user tried to delete a log file (e.g., to hide unauthorized actions) than to know the user merely issued the delete command, possibly for a personal data file.

Answer b is a description of a multilevel device. A multilevel device is a device that is used in a manner that permits it to process data of two or more security levels simultaneously without risk of compromise. To accomplish this, sensitivity labels are normally stored on the same physical medium and in the same form (i.e., machine-readable or human-readable) as the data being processed.

Answer c refers to a network reference monitor, an access control concept that refers to an abstract machine that mediates all access to objects within the network by subjects within the network.

Answer d is incorrect, because audit trails are detective, and answer d describes a preventative process, access control. Source: NCSC-TG-001 A Guide to Understanding Audit in Trusted Systems and DoD 5200.28-STD—Department of Defense Trusted Computer System Evaluation Criteria.

9. Which TCSEC security class category below specifies "trusted recovery" controls?

    a. C2

    b. B1

    c. B2

    d. B3

    Answer: d

    TCSEC security categories B3 and A1 require the implementation of trusted recovery. Trusted recovery is the procedures and/or mechanisms provided to assure that, after an ADP system failure or other discontinuity, recovery without a protection compromise is obtained. A system failure represents a serious security risk because security controls may be bypassed when the system is not functioning normally. Trusted recovery has two primary activities: preparing for a system failure (backup) and recovering the system.

Source: DoD 5200.28-STD—Department of Defense Trusted Computer System Evaluation Criteria.

10. Which choice does NOT describe an element of configuration management?

    a. Configuration management involves information capture and version control.

    b. Configuration management reports the status of change processing.

    c. Configuration management is the decomposition process of a verification system into Configuration Items (CIs).

    d. Configuration management documents the functional and physical characteristics of each configuration item.

      Answer: c

      Configuration management is a discipline applying technical and administrative direction to:

      ■ Identify and document the functional and physical characteristics of each configuration item for the system

      ■ Manage all changes to these characteristics

      ■ Record and report the status of change processing and implementation

      Configuration management involves process monitoring, version control, information capture, quality control, bookkeeping, and an organizational framework to support these activities. The configuration being managed is the verification system plus all tools and documentation related to the configuration process.

      Answer c is the description of an element of Configuration Identification.

      Source: *NCSC-TG-014-89, Guidelines for Formal Verification Systems* [Purple Book].

11. Which choice below does NOT accurately describe a task of the Configuration Control Board?

    a. The CCB should meet periodically to discuss configuration status accounting reports.

    b. The CCB is responsible for documenting the status of configuration control activities.

c. The CCB is responsible for assuring that changes made do not jeopardize the soundness of the verification system.

d. The CCB assures that the changes made are approved, tested, documented, and implemented correctly.

Answer: b

All analytical and design tasks are conducted under the direction of the vendor's corporate entity called the Configuration Control Board (CCB). The CCB is headed by a chairperson who is responsible for assuring that changes made do not jeopardize the soundness of the verification system and assures that the changes made are approved, tested, documented, and implemented correctly.

The members of the CCB should interact periodically, either through formal meetings or other available means, to discuss configuration management topics such as proposed changes, configuration status accounting reports, and other topics that may be of interest to the different areas of the system development. These interactions should be held to keep the entire system team updated on all advancements or alterations in the verification system.

Answer b describes configuration accounting. Configuration accounting documents the status of configuration control activities and, in general, provides the information needed to manage a configuration effectively. The configuration accounting reports are reviewed by the CCB. Source: *NCSC-TG-014-89, Guidelines for Formal Verification Systems.*

12. Which choice below is NOT a security goal of an audit mechanism?

a. Deter perpetrators' attempts to bypass the system protection mechanisms

b. Review employee production output records

c. Review patterns of access to individual objects

d. Discover when a user assumes a functionality with privileges greater than his own

Answer: b

The audit mechanism of a computer system has five important security goals:

1. The audit mechanism must "allow the review of patterns of access to individual objects, access histories of specific processes

and individuals, and the use of the various protection mechanisms supported by the system and their effectiveness.[2]"

2. Allow discovery of both users' and outsiders' repeated attempts to bypass the protection mechanisms.

3. Allow discovery of any use of privileges that may occur when a user assumes a functionality with privileges greater than his or her own, i.e., programmer to administrator. In this case, there may be no bypass of security controls, but nevertheless, a violation is made possible.

4. Act as a deterrent against perpetrators' habitual attempts to bypass the system protection mechanisms. However, to act as a deterrent, the perpetrator must be aware of the audit mechanism's existence and its active use to detect any attempts to bypass system protection mechanisms.

5. Supply "an additional form of user assurance that attempts to bypass the protection mechanisms that are recorded and discovered."[3] Even if the attempt to bypass the protection mechanism is successful, the audit trail will still provide assurance by its ability to aid in assessing the damage done by the violation, thus improving the system's ability to control the damage.

Answer b is a distracter.

Source: NCSC-TG-001 A Guide to Understanding Audit in Trusted Systems [Tan Book], and Gligor, Virgil D., "Guidelines for Trusted Facility Management and Audit," University of Maryland, 1985.

13. Which choice below is NOT a common element of user account administration?

   a. Periodically verifying the legitimacy of current accounts and access authorizations

   b. Authorizing the request for a user's system account

   c. Tracking users and their respective access authorizations

   d. Establishing, issuing, and closing user accounts

   Answer: b

   For proper separation of duties, the function of user account establishment and maintenance should be separated from the function of initiating and authorizing the creation of the account. User account management focuses on identification, authentication, and access authorizations. This is augmented by the process of auditing and otherwise periodically verifying the legitimacy of current accounts and access authorizations. Also, there are considerations involved in the timely modification or removal of access and associated issues for employees who are reassigned, promoted, or terminated, or who retire.

Source: *National Institute of Standards and Technology, An Introduction to Computer Security: The NIST Handbook Special Publication 800-12.*

14. Which element of Configuration Management listed below involves the use of Configuration Items (CIs)?

    a. Configuration Accounting

    b. Configuration Audit

    c. Configuration Control

    d. Configuration Identification

       Answer: d

       Configuration management entails decomposing the verification system into identifiable, understandable, manageable, trackable units known as Configuration Items (CIs). A CI is a uniquely identifiable subset of the system that represents the smallest portion to be subject to independent configuration control procedures. The decomposition process of a verification system into CIs is called configuration identification. CIs can vary widely in size, type, and complexity. Although there are no hard-and-fast rules for decomposition, the granularity of CIs can have great practical importance. A favorable strategy is to designate relatively large CIs for elements that are not expected to change over the life of the system, and small CIs for elements likely to change more frequently.

       Answer a, configuration accounting, documents the status of configuration control activities and in general provides the information needed to manage a configuration effectively. It allows managers to trace system changes and establish the history of any developmental problems and associated fixes.

       Answer b, configuration audit, is the quality assurance component of configuration management. It involves periodic checks to determine the consistency and completeness of accounting information and to verify that all configuration management policies are being followed.

       Answer c, configuration control, is a means of assuring that system changes are approved before being implemented, only the proposed and approved changes are implemented, and the implementation is complete and accurate.

    Source: *NCSC-TG-014-89, Guidelines for Formal Verification Systems.*

15. Which standard defines the International Standard for the Common Criteria?

    a. IS15408

    b. BS7799

    c. DoD 5200.28-STD

    d. CSC-STD-002-85

    Answer: a

    ISO/IEC 15408-1 is the International Standards version of the Common Criteria. The ISO approved and published the CC text as the new International Standard (IS) 15408 on December 1, 1999[4]. As of this writing the Common Criteria version is 2.1.

    Answer b is the Code of Practice for Information Security Management (BS7799) developed by the British Standards Institute. The BS7799 standard effectively comes in two parts:

    ■ ISO/IEC 17799:2000 (Part 1) is the standard code of practice and can be regarded as a comprehensive catalogue of recommended security policy.

    ■ BS7799-2:1999 (Part 2) is a standard specification for an Information Security Management System (ISMS). An ISMS is the means by which Senior Management monitors and controls their security, minimizing the residual business risk and ensuring that security continues to fulfill corporate, customer, and legal requirements.[5]

    Answer c is the Orange Book, the DoD Trusted Computer System Evaluation Criteria.

    Answer d is the Green Book, the DoD Password Management Guidelines.

    Source: The Common Criteria Project.

16. Which statement below is NOT correct about reviewing user accounts?

    a. User account reviews cannot be conducted by outside auditors.

    b. User account reviews can examine conformity with the concept of least privilege.

    c. User account reviews may be conducted on a system-wide basis.

    d. User account reviews may be conducted on an application-by-application basis.

    Answer: a

    It is necessary to regularly review user accounts on a system. Such reviews may examine the levels of access each individual has, conformity with the concept of least privilege, whether all accounts are still active, whether management authorizations are up-to-date, or whether required training has been completed, for example. These reviews can be conducted on at least two levels: on an application-by-application basis or on a systemwide basis. Both kinds of reviews can be conducted by, among others, in-house systems personnel (a self-audit), the organization's internal audit staff, or external auditors.

Source: *National Institute of Standards and Technology, An Introduction to Computer Security: The NIST Handbook Special Publication 800-12.*

17. Which statement below MOST accurately describes configuration control?

    a. The decomposition process of a verification system into CIs

    b. Assuring that only the proposed and approved system changes are implemented

    c. Tracking the status of current changes as they move through the configuration control process

    d. Verifying that all configuration management policies are being followed

    > *Answer:* b

    > Configuration control is a means of assuring that system changes are approved before being implemented, only the proposed and approved changes are implemented, and the implementation is complete and accurate. This involves strict procedures for proposing, monitoring, and approving system changes and their implementation. Configuration control entails central direction of the change process by personnel who coordinate analytical tasks, approve system changes, review the implementation of changes, and supervise other tasks such as documentation.

    > Answer a is configuration identification. The decomposition process of a verification system into Configuration Items (CIs) is called configuration identification. A CI is a uniquely identifiable subset of the system that represents the smallest portion to be subject to independent configuration control procedures.

    > Answer c is configuration accounting. Configuration accounting documents the status of configuration control activities and, in general, provides the information needed to manage a configuration effectively. It allows managers to trace system changes and establish the history of any developmental problems and associated fixes. Configuration accounting also tracks the status of current changes as they move through the configuration control process. Configuration accounting establishes the granularity of recorded information and thus shapes the accuracy and usefulness of the audit function.

Answer d is configuration audit. Configuration audit is the quality assurance component of configuration management. It involves periodic checks to determine the consistency and completeness of accounting information and to verify that all configuration management policies are being followed. A vendor's configuration management program must be able to sustain a complete configuration audit by an NCSC review team.

Source: NCSC-TG-014, Guidelines for Formal Verification Systems.

18. Which term below MOST accurately describes the Trusted Computing Base (TCB)?

    a. A computer that controls all access to objects by subjects

    b. A piece of information that represents the security level of an object

    c. Formal proofs used to demonstrate the consistency between a system's specification and a security model

    d. The totality of protection mechanisms within a computer system

    Answer: d

    The Trusted Computing Base (TCB)—The totality of protection mechanisms within a computer system, including hardware, firmware, and software, the combination of which is responsible for enforcing a security policy. A TCB consists of one or more components that together enforce a unified security policy over a product or system. The ability of a trusted computing base to correctly enforce a security policy depends solely on the mechanisms within the TCB and on the correct input by system administrative personnel of parameters (e.g., a user's clearance) related to the security policy.

    Answer a describes the reference monitor concept. The reference monitor is an access control concept that refers to an abstract machine that mediates all accesses to objects by subjects. The Security Kernel consists of the hardware, firmware, and software elements of a Trusted Computing Base (or Network Trusted Computing Base partition) that implement the reference monitor concept. It must mediate all accesses, be protected from modification, and be verifiable as correct.

    Answer b refers to a sensitivity label. A sensitivity label is a piece of information that represents the extra security level of an object and describes the sensitivity (e.g., classification) of the data in the object. Sensitivity labels are used by the TCB as the basis for mandatory access control decisions.

    Answer c describes formal verification. This is the process of using formal proofs to demonstrate the consistency (design verification) between a formal specification of a system and a formal security policy model or (implementation verification) between the formal specification and its program implementation. Source: DoD 5200.28-STD— Department of Defense Trusted Computer System Evaluation Criteria

19. Which choice below would NOT be considered a benefit of employing incident-handling capability?

   a. An individual acting alone would not be able to subvert a security process or control.

   b. It enhances internal communications and the readiness of the organization to respond to incidents.

   c. It assists an organization in preventing damage from future incidents.

   d. Security training personnel would have a better understanding of users' knowledge of security issues.

   Answer: a

   The primary benefits of employing an incident-handling capability are containing and repairing damage from incidents and preventing future damage. Additional benefits related to establishing an incident-handling capability are:

   Enhancement of the risk assessment process. An incident-handling capability will allow organizations to collect threat data that may be useful in their risk assessment and safeguard selection processes (e.g., in designing new systems). Statistics on the numbers and types of incidents in the organization can be used in the risk-assessment process as an indication of vulnerabilities and threats.

   Enhancement of internal communications and the readiness of the organization to respond to any type of incident, not just computer security incidents. Internal communications will be improved, management will be better organized to receive communications, and contacts within public affairs, legal staff, law enforcement, and other groups will have been pre-established.

   Security training personnel will have a better understanding of users' knowledge of security issues. Trainers can use actual incidents to vividly illustrate the importance of computer security. Training that is based on current threats and controls recommended by incident-handling staff provides users with information more specifically directed to their current needs, thereby reducing the risks to the organization from incidents.

Answer a is a benefit of employing "separation of duties" controls.

Source: *National Institute of Standards and Technology, An Introduction to Computer Security: The NIST Handbook Special Publication 800-12.*

20. Which statement below is accurate about Evaluation Assurance Levels (EALs) in the Common Criteria (CC)?

    a. A security level equal to the security level of the objects to which the subject has both read and write access

    b. A statement of intent to counter specified threats

    c. Requirements that specify the security behavior of an IT product or system

    d. Predefined packages of assurance components that make up security confidence rating scale

    Answer: d

    An Evaluation Assurance Level (EAL) is one of seven increasingly rigorous packages of assurance requirements from CC Part 3. Each numbered package represents a point on the CC's predefined assurance scale. An EAL can be considered a level of confidence in the security functions of an IT product or system. The EALs have been developed with the goal of preserving the concepts of assurance drawn from the source criteria, such as the Trusted Computer System Evaluation Criteria (TCSEC), Information Technology Security Evaluation Criteria (ITSEC), or Canadian Trusted Computer Evaluation Criteria (CTCPEC), so that results of previous evaluations remain relevant. EAL levels 2–7 are generally equivalent to the assurance portions of the TCSEC C2-A1 scale, although exact TCSEC mappings do not exist.

    Answer a is the definition of Subject Security Level. A subject's security level is equal to the security level of the objects to which it has both read and write access. A subject's security level must always be dominated by the clearance of the user with which the subject is associated.

    Answer b describes a Security Objective, which is a statement of intent to counter specified threats and/or satisfy specified organizational security policies and assumptions.

    Answer c describes Security Functional Requirements. These are requirements, preferably from CC Part 2, that when taken together specify the security behavior of an IT product or system.

    Source: CC Project and DoD 5200.28-STD.

21. Which choice below is the BEST description of operational assurance?

    a. Operational assurance is the process of examining audit logs to reveal usage that identifies misuse.

    b. Operational assurance has the benefit of containing and repairing damage from incidents.

c. Operational assurance is the process of reviewing an operational system to see that security controls are functioning correctly.

d. Operational assurance is the process of performing pre-employment background screening.

Answer: c

Operational assurance is the process of reviewing an operational system to see that security controls, both automated and manual, are functioning correctly and effectively. Operational assurance addresses whether the system's technical features are being bypassed or have vulnerabilities and whether required procedures are being followed.

To maintain operational assurance, organizations use two basic methods: system audits and monitoring. A system audit is a one-time or periodic event to evaluate security. Monitoring refers to an ongoing activity that examines either the system or the users.

Answer a is a description of an audit trail review. Answer b is a description of a benefit of incident handling. The main benefits of proper incident handling are containing and repairing damage from incidents, and preventing future damage. Answer d describes a personnel control.

Source: *National Institute of Standards and Technology, An Introduction to Computer Security: The NIST Handbook Special Publication 800-12.*

22. Which choice below MOST accurately describes a Covert Storage Channel?

a. A process that manipulates observable system resources in a way that affects response time

b. An information transfer path within a system

c. A communication channel that allows a process to transfer information in a manner that violates the system's security policy

d. An information transfer that involves the direct or indirect writing of a storage location by one process and the direct or indirect reading of the storage location by another process

Answer: d

A covert storage channel typically involves a finite resource (e.g., sectors on a disk) that is shared by two subjects at different security levels. One way to think of the difference between covert timing channels and covert storage channels is that covert timing channels are essentially memoryless, whereas covert storage channels are not. With a timing channel, the information transmitted from the sender must be sensed by the receiver immediately, or it will be lost. However, an error code indicating a full disk which is exploited to create a storage channel may stay constant for an indefinite amount of time, so a receiving process is not as constrained by time.

Answer a is a partial description of a covert timing channel. A covert timing channel is a covert channel in which one process signals information to another by modulating its own use of system resources (e.g., CPU time) in such a way that this manipulation affects the real response time observed by the second process.

Answer b is a generic definition of a channel. A channel may also refer to the mechanism by which the path is effected.

Answer c is a higher-level definition of a covert channel. While a covert storage channel fits this definition generically, answer d is the proper specific definition.

Source: DoD 5200.28-STD—Department of Defense Trusted Computer System Evaluation Criteria and NCSC-TG-030, A Guide To Understanding Covert Channel Analysis of Trusted Systems [Light Pink Book].

23. Which choice below is the BEST description of a Protection Profile (PP), as defined by the Common Criteria (CC)?

a. A statement of security claims for a particular IT security product

b. A reusable definition of product security requirements

c. An intermediate combination of security requirement components

d. The IT product or system to be evaluated

   Answer: b

   The Common Criteria (CC) is used in two ways:

- As a standardized way to describe security requirements for IT products and systems

- As a sound technical basis for evaluating the security features of these products and systems

The CC defines three useful constructs for building IT security requirements: the Protection Profile (PP), the Security Target (ST), and the Package. The PP is an implementation-independent statement of security needs for a set of IT security products. The PP contains a set of security requirements and is intended to be a reusable definition of product security requirements that are known to be useful and effective. A PP gives consumers a means of referring to a specific set of security needs and communicating them to manufacturers and helps future product evaluation against those needs.

Answer a defines the Security Target (ST). The ST is a statement of security claims for a particular IT security product or system. The ST parallels the structure of the PP, though it has additional elements that include product-specific detailed information. An ST is the basis for agreement among all parties as to what security the product or system offers, and therefore the basis for its security evaluation.

Answer c describes the Package. The Package is an intermediate combination of security requirements components. The package permits the expression of a set of either functional or assurance requirements that meet some particular need, expressed as a set of security objectives.

Answer d describes the Target of Evaluation (TOE). The TOE is an IT product or system to be evaluated, the security characteristics of which are described in specific terms by a corresponding ST, or in more general terms by a PP. This evaluation consists of rigorous analysis and testing performed by an accredited, independent laboratory. The scope of a TOE evaluation is set by the Evaluation Assurance Level (EAL) and other requirements specified in the ST. Part of this process is an evaluation of the ST itself, to ensure that it is correct, complete, and internally consistent and can be used as the baseline for the TOE evaluation.

Source: Common Criteria Project.

24. Which choice below is NOT one of the four major aspects of configuration management?
    a. Configuration status accounting
    b. Configuration product evaluation
    c. Configuration auditing
    d. Configuration identification

    Answer: b

    The four major aspects of configuration management are:

    ■ Configuration identification
    ■ Configuration control
    ■ Configuration status accounting
    ■ Configuration auditing

    These aspects are described earlier in this chapter. Answer b is a distracter. Source: *NCSC-TG-014-89, Guidelines for Formal Verification Systems* [Purple Book].

25. Which choice below MOST accurately describes "partitioned security mode"?
    a. All personnel have the clearance and formal access approval.
    b. All personnel have the clearance but not necessarily formal access approval.

c. The only state in which certain privileged instructions may be executed.

d. A system containing information accessed by personnel with different security clearances.

Answer: b

A partitioned security mode is a mode of operation wherein all personnel have the clearance but not necessarily formal access approval and need-to-know for all information contained in the system.

Answer a is a compartmented security mode. A compartmented security mode is a mode of operation wherein all personnel have a valid personnel clearance, formal access approval and signed nondisclosure agreements, and valid need-to-know for that information to which he/she is to have access.

Answer c is executive state. Executive state is one of several states in which a system may operate and the only one in which certain privileged instructions may be executed. Such instructions cannot be executed when the system is operating in other (e.g., user) states. Synonymous with supervisor state.

Answer d is multilevel secure. Multilevel secure is a class of system containing information with different sensitivities that simultaneously permits access by users with different security clearances and needs-to-know, but prevents users from obtaining access to information for which they lack authorization.

Source: DoD 5200.28-STD—Department of Defense Trusted Computer System Evaluation Criteria.

26. Which choice below is NOT an example of a media control?

a. Sanitizing the media before disposition

b. Printing to a printer in a secured room

c. Physically protecting copies of backup media

d. Conducting background checks on individuals

Answer: d

Answer d is a personnel control. Most support and operations staff have special access to the system. Some organizations conduct background checks on individuals filling these positions to screen out possibly untrustworthy individuals.

Answer a: The process of removing information from media before disposition is called sanitization. Three techniques are commonly used for media sanitization: overwriting, degaussing, and destruction.

Answer b: It may be necessary to actually output data to the media in a secure location, such as printing to a printer in a locked room instead of to a general-purpose printer in a common area.

Answer c: Physical protection of copies of backup media stored offsite should be accorded a level of protection equivalent to media containing the same information stored onsite.

Source: *National Institute of Standards and Technology, An Introduction to Computer Security: The NIST Handbook Special Publication 800-12.*

27. Which statement below is the BEST example of "separation of duties"?

    a. An activity that checks on the system, its users, or the environment.

    b. Getting users to divulge their passwords.

    c. One person initiates a request for a payment and another authorizes that same payment.

    d. A data entry clerk may not have access to run database analysis reports.

    Answer: c

    Separation of duties refers to dividing roles and responsibilities so that a single individual cannot subvert a critical process. In financial systems, no single individual should normally be given the authority to issue checks. Checks and balances need to be designed into both the process as well as the specific, individual positions of personnel who will implement the process.

    Answer a describes system monitoring.

    Answer b is "social engineering," a method of subverting system controls by getting users or administrators to divulge information about systems, including their passwords.

    Answer d describes "least privilege." Least privilege refers to the security objective of granting users only those accesses they need to perform their official duties. Least privilege does not mean that all users will have extremely little functional access; some employees will have significant access if it is required for their position. It is important to make certain that the implementation of least privilege does not interfere with the ability to have personnel substitute for each other without undue delay. Without careful planning, access control can interfere with contingency plans.

    Source: *National Institute of Standards and Technology, An Introduction to Computer Security: The NIST Handbook Special Publication 800-12.*

28. Which minimum TCSEC security class category specifies "trusted distribution" controls?

    a. C2

    b. B2

c. B3

d. A1

Answer: d

Trusted distribution is defined by the Orange Book as a requirement of A1 TCB assurance. Trusted distribution includes procedures to ensure that all of the TCB configuration items, such as the TCB software, firmware, hardware, and updates, distributed to a customer site arrive exactly as intended by the vendor without any alterations.

Any alteration to the TCB at any time during the system life cycle could result in a violation of the system security policy. Assurance that the system security policy is correctly implemented and operational throughout the system life cycle is provided by different TCSEC requirements. At TCSEC class Al, trusted distribution, in conjunction with configuration management, provides assurance that the TCB software, firmware, and hardware, both original and updates, are received by a customer site exactly as specified by the vendor's master copy. Trusted distribution also ensures that TCB copies sent from other than legitimate parties are detected. Source: NCSC-TG-008 A Guide to Understanding Trusted Distribution in Trusted Systems [Lavender Book].

29. Which statement is accurate about "trusted facility management"?

a. The role of a security administrator shall be identified and auditable in C2 systems and above.

b. The role of a security administrator shall be identified and auditable in B2 systems and above.

c. The TCB shall support separate operator and administrator functions for C2 systems and above.

d. The TCB shall support separate operator and administrator functions for B2 systems and above.

Answer: d

Trusted Facility Management has two different requirements, one for B2 systems and another for B3 systems. The B2 requirements state: the TCB shall support separate operator and administrator functions. The B3 requirements are as follows: The functions performed in the role of a security administrator shall be identified. System administrative personnel shall only be able to perform security administrator functions after taking a distinct auditable action to assume the security administrator role on the system. Non-security functions that can be performed in the security administration role shall be limited strictly to those essential to performing the security role effectively.[6]

Source: NCSC-TG-O15, Guide To Understanding Trusted Facility Management [Brown Book].

30. Which statement below is accurate about the concept of Object Reuse?

   a. Object reuse protects against physical attacks on the storage medium.

   b. Object reuse ensures that users do not obtain residual information from system resources.

   c. Object reuse applies to removable media only.

   d. Object reuse controls the granting of access rights to objects.

   Answer: b

   Object reuse mechanisms ensure system resources are allocated and reassigned among authorized users in a way that prevents the leak of sensitive information, and ensure that the authorized user of the system does not obtain residual information from system resources. Object reuse is defined as "The reassignment to some subject of a storage medium (e.g., page frame, disk sector, magnetic tape) that contained one or more objects. To be securely reassigned, no residual data can be available to the new subject through standard system mechanisms."[7] The object reuse requirement of the TCSEC is intended to assure that system resources, in particular storage media, are allocated and reassigned among system users in a manner which prevents the disclosure of sensitive information.

   Answer a is incorrect. Object reuse does not necessarily protect against physical attacks on the storage medium. Answer c is also incorrect, as object reuse applies to all primary and secondary storage media, such as removable media, fixed media, real and virtual main memory (including registers), and cache memory. Answer d refers to authorization, the granting of access rights to a user, program, or process. Source: NCSC-TG-018, A Guide To Understanding Object Reuse in Trusted Systems [Light Blue Book].

Chapter 7—Applications and Systems Development

1. The definition "the science and art of specifying, designing, implementing and evolving programs, documentation and operating procedures whereby computers can be made useful to man" is that of:

   a. Structured analysis/structured design (SA/SD)

   b. Software engineering

   c. An object-oriented system

   d. Functional programming

   Answer: b

   This definition of software engineering is a combination of popular definitions of engineering and software. One definition of engineering is "the application of science and mathematics to the design and construction of artifacts which are useful to man." A definition of software is that it "consists of the programs, documentation and operating procedures by which computers can be made useful to man." Answer a, SA/SD, deals with developing specifications that are abstractions of the problem to be solved and not tied to any specific programming languages. Thus, SA/SD, through *data flow diagrams (DFDs)*, shows the main processing entities and the data flow between them without any connection to a specific programming language implementation. An *object-oriented system*, answer c, is a group of independent *objects* that can be requested to perform certain operations or exhibit specific behaviors. These objects cooperate to provide the system's required functionality. The objects have an *identity* and can be created as the program executes (*dynamic lifetime*). To provide the desired characteristics of object-oriented systems, the objects are *encapsulated*, i.e., they can only be accessed through messages sent to them to request performance of their defined operations. The object can be viewed as a "black box" whose internal details are hidden from outside observation and cannot normally be modified. Objects also exhibit the *substitution* property, which means that objects providing compatible operations can be substituted for each other. In summary, an object-oriented system contains objects that exhibit the following properties:

   ■ Identity—each object has a name that is used to designate that object.

   ■ Encapsulation—an object can only be accessed through messages to perform its defined operations.

- Substitution—objects that perform compatible operations can be substituted for each other.
- Dynamic lifetimes—objects can be created as the program executes.

Answer d, functional programming, uses only mathematical functions to perform computations and solve problems. This approach is based on the assumption that any algorithm can be described as a mathematical function. Functional languages have the characteristics that:

- They support functions and allow them to be manipulated by being passed as arguments and stored in data structures.
- Functional abstraction is the only method of procedural abstraction.

2. In software engineering, the term *verification* is defined as:

   a. To establish the truth of correspondence between a software product and its specification

   b. A complete, validated specification of the required functions, interfaces, and performance for the software product

   c. To establish the fitness or worth of a software product for its operational mission

   d. A complete, verified specification of the overall hardware-software architecture, control structure, and data structure for the product

   Answer: a

   In the Waterfall model (W.W. Royce, "Managing the Development of Large Software Systems: Concepts and Techniques," *Proceedings, WESCON*, August 1970), answer b defines the term *requirements*. Similarly, answer c, defines the term *validation*, and answer d is the definition of *product design*. In summary, the steps of the Waterfall model are:

   - System feasibility
   - Software plans and requirements
   - Product design
   - Detailed design
   - Code
   - Integration
   - Implementation
   - Operations and maintenance

   In this model, each phase finishes with a verification and validation (V&V) task that is designed to eliminate as many problems as possible in the results of that phase.

3. The discipline of identifying the components of a continually evolving system for the purposes of controlling changes to those components and maintaining integrity and traceability throughout the life cycle is called:

   a. Change control

   b. Request control

   c. Release control

   d. Configuration management

   Answer: d

   This is demonstrated in *Configuration management of computer-based systems*, British Standards Institution, 1984. Answers a, b, and c are components of the maintenance activity of software life cycle models. In general, one can look at the maintenance phase as the progression from request control, to change control, to release control. Answer b, *request control*, is involved with the users' requests for changes to the software. *Change control*, answer a, involves the analysis and understanding of the existing code, and the design of changes, and corresponding test procedures. Answer c, *release control*, involves deciding which requests are to be implemented in the new release, performing the changes and conducting testing.

4. The basic version of the Construction Cost Model (COCOMO), which proposes quantitative, life-cycle relationships, performs what function?

   a. Estimates software development effort based on user function categories

   b. Estimates software development effort and cost as a function of the size of the software product in source instructions

   c. Estimates software development effort and cost as a function of the size of the software product in source instructions modified by manpower buildup and productivity factors

   d. Estimates software development effort and cost as a function of the size of the software product in source instructions modified by hardware and input functions

   Answer: b

   The Basic COCOMO Model (B.W. Boehm, *Software Engineering Economics*, Prentice-Hall, Englewood Cliffs, New Jersey, 1981) proposes the following equations:

   "The number of man-months (MM) required to develop the most common type of software product, in terms of the number of thousands of delivered source instructions (KDSI) in the software product"

   $$MM = 2.4 \, (KDSI)^{1.05}$$

"The development schedule (TDEV) in months"

$\text{TDEV} = 2.5(\text{MM})^{0.38}$

In addition, Boehm has developed an intermediate COCOMO Model that also takes into account hardware constraints, personnel quality, use of modern tools, and other attributes and their aggregate impact on overall project costs. A detailed COCOMO Model, by Boehm, accounts for the effects of the additional factors used in the intermediate model on the costs of individual project phases.

Answer b describes a *function point measurement model* that does not require the user to estimate the number of delivered source instructions. The software development effort is determined using the following five user functions:

- External input types
- External output types
- Logical internal file types
- External interface file types
- External inquiry types

These functions are tallied and weighted according to complexity and used to determine the software development effort.

Answer c describes the Rayleigh curve applied to software development cost and effort estimation. A prominent model using this approach is the Software Life Cycle Model (SLIM) estimating method. In this method, estimates based on the number of lines of source code are modified by the following two factors:

- The manpower buildup index (MBI), which estimates the rate of buildup of staff on the project
- A productivity factor (PF), which is based on the technology used

Answer d is a distracter.

5. A refinement to the basic Waterfall Model that states that software should be developed in increments of functional capability is called:

a. Functional refinement

b. Functional development

c. Incremental refinement

d. Incremental development

Answer: d

The advantages of *incremental development* include the ease of testing increments of functional capability and the opportunity to incorporate user experience into a successively refined product. Answers a, b, and c are distracters.

6. The Spiral Model of the software development process (B.W. Boehm, "A Spiral Model of Software Development and Enhancement," *IEEE Computer*, May, 1988) uses the following metric relative to the spiral:

   a. The radial dimension represents the cost of each phase

   b. The radial dimension represents progress made in completing each cycle

   c. The angular dimension represents cumulative cost

   d. The radial dimension represents cumulative cost

   Answer: d

   The radial dimension represents cumulative cost and the angular dimension represents progress made in completing each cycle of the spiral. The spiral model is actually a meta-model for software development processes. A summary of the stages in the spiral is as follows:

   - The spiral begins in the top, left-hand quadrant by determining the objectives of the portion of the product being developed, the alternative means of implementing this portion of the product, and the constraints imposed on the application of the alternatives.

   - Next, the risks of the alternatives are evaluated based on the objectives and constraints. Following this step, the relative balances of the perceived risks are determined.

   - The spiral then proceeds to the lower right-hand quadrant where the development phases of the projects begin. A major review completes each cycle and then the process begins anew for succeeding phases of the project. Typical succeeding phases are software product design, integration and test plan development, additional risk analyses, operational prototype, detailed design, code, unit test, acceptance test, and implementation.

   Answers a, b, and c are distracters.

7. In the Capability Maturity Model (CMM) for software, the definition "describes the range of expected results that can be achieved by following a software process" is that of:

   a. Structured analysis/structured design (SA/SD)

   b. Software process capability

   c. Software process performance

   d. Software process maturity

   Answer: b

   A *software process* is a set of activities, methods, and practices that are used to develop and maintain software and associated products. *Software process capability* is a means of predicting the outcome of the next software project conducted by an organization. Answer c, *software process performance,* is the result achieved by following a software process. Thus, software capability is aimed at expected results while software performance is focused on results that have been achieved. *Software process maturity,* answer d, is the extent to which a software process is:

- Defined
- Managed
- Measured
- Controlled
- Effective

Software process maturity, then, provides for the potential for growth in capability of an organization. An immature organization develops software in a crisis mode, usually exceeds budgets and time schedules, and software processes are developed in an ad hoc fashion during the project. In a mature organization, the software process is effectively communicated to staff, the required processes are documented and consistent, software quality is evaluated, and roles and responsibilities are understood for the project.

Answer a is a distracter, but is discussed in question 1.

8. Which of the following is NOT a Software CMM maturity level?

a. Initial

b. Repeatable

c. Behavioral

d. Managed

Answer: c

The word behavioral is a distracter. The five software process maturity levels are:

- Initial—the software process is ad hoc and most processes are undefined.
- Repeatable—fundamental project management processes are in place.
- Defined—the software process for both management and engineering functions is documented, standardized, and integrated into the organization.
- Managed—the software process and product quality are measured, understood, and controlled.
- Optimizing—continuous process improvement is being performed.

9. The main differences between a *software process assessment* and a *software capability evaluation* are:

   a. Software process assessments determine the state of an
   organization's current software process and are used to gain support
   from within the organization for a software process improvement
   program; software capability evaluations are used to identify
   contractors who are qualified to develop software or to monitor the
   state of the software process in a current software project.

   b. Software capability evaluations determine the state of an
   organization's current software process and are used to gain support
   from within the organization for a software process improvement
   program; software process assessments are used to identify
   contractors who are qualified to develop software or to monitor the
   state of the software process in a current software project.

   c. Software process assessments are used to develop a risk profile for
   source selection; software capability evaluations are used to develop
   an action plan for continuous process improvement.

   d. Software process assessments and software capability evaluations are
   essentially identical, and there are no major differences between the two.

   Answer: a

   The correct answer is a. Answers b, c, and d are distracters. If, in
   answer c, the terms "software process assessments" and "software capability evaluations" were interchanged, that result would also be correct.
   It would then read, "Software capability evaluations are used to develop
   a risk profile for source selection; software process assessments are used
   to develop an action plan for continuous process improvement."

10. Which of the following is NOT a common term in object-oriented
    systems?

    a. Behavior

    b. Message

    c. Method

    d. Function

    Answer: d

    Answer a, *behavior*, is a characteristic of an object. The object is
    defined as a collection of operations that, when selected, reveal or
    manipulate the state of the object. Thus, consecutive invocations of
    an object may result in different behaviors, based on the last
    operations selected. Answer b, *message*, is a request sent to an object
    to carry out a particular operation. A *method*, answer c, is the code
    that describes what the object will do when sent a message.

11. In object-oriented programming, when all the methods of one class are passed on to a subclass, this is called:

    a. Forward chaining

    b. Inheritance

    c. Multiple Inheritance

    d. Delegation

    Answer: b

    In *inheritance*, all the methods of one class, called a superclass, are inherited by a subclass. Thus, all messages understood by the superclass are understood by the subclass. In other words, the subclass inherits the behavior of the superclass. Answer a is a distracter and describes data-driven reasoning used in expert systems. *Multiple inheritance*, answer c, describes the situation where a subclass inherits the behavior of multiple superclasses. Answer d, delegation, is an alternative to inheritance in an object-oriented system. With *delegation*, if an object does not have a method to satisfy a request it has received, it can delegate the request to another object.

12. Which of the following languages is NOT an object-oriented language?

    a. Smalltalk

    b. Simula 67

    c. Lisp

    d. C++

    Answer: c

    Lisp, for list processing, is a functional language that processes symbolic expressions rather than numbers. It is used in the artificial intelligence field. The languages cited in answers a, b, and d are object-oriented languages.

13. Which of the following items is NOT a component of a knowledge-based system (KBS)?

    a. Knowledge base

    b. Procedural code

    c. Inference Engine

    d. Interface between the user and the system

    Answer: b

    Procedural code in a *procedural language* implies sequential execution of instructions based on the von Neumann architecture of a CPU, Memory, and Input/Output device. Variables are part of the sets of instructions used to solve a particular problem and, thus, the data are not separate from the statements. Such languages have control statements such as *goto, if...then...else* and so on. The program execution is iterative and corresponds to a sequence of state changes in a state machine. Answer a, *knowledge base*, refers to the rules and facts of the particular problem domain. *The inference engine,* answer c, takes the inputs to the KBS and uses the knowledge base to infer new facts and to solve the problem. Answer d refers to the interface between the user and the system through which the data are entered, displayed, and output.

14. In an expert system, the process of beginning with a possible solution and using the knowledge in the knowledge base to justify the solution based on the raw input data is called:

    a. Dynamic reasoning

    b. Forward chaining

    c. Backward chaining

    d. A blackboard solution

    Answer: c

    Backward chaining is generally used when there are a large number of possible solutions relative to the number of inputs. Answer a is a distracter. Answer b, *forward chaining,* is the reasoning approach that can be used when there is a small number of solutions relative to the number of inputs. The input data is used to reason "forward" to prove that one of the possible solutions in a small solution set is the correct one. The *blackboard,* answer d, is an expert system reasoning methodology in which a solution is generated by the use of a virtual "blackboard" wherein information or potential solutions are placed on the blackboard by a plurality of individuals or expert knowledge sources. As more information is placed on the blackboard in an iterative process, a solution is generated.

15. An off-the-shelf software package that implements an inference engine, a mechanism for entering knowledge, a user interface, and a system to provide explanations of the reasoning used to generate a solution is called:

    a. An expert system shell

    b. A knowledge base

    c. A neural network

    d. A knowledge acquisition system

    Answer: a

An *expert system shell* provides the fundamental building blocks of an expert system and supports the entering of domain knowledge. Thus, for an application that is not complex and does not require the custom development of the components of an expert system, an expert system shell is a useful tool that will save development time. A knowledge base, answer b, is a component of an expert system and is described in Question 13. A *neural network* is another type of artificial intelligence system that uses the neurons of the brain as a model and solves problems using nonlinear pattern-matching techniques and "learning" approaches. A *knowledge acquisition system*, answer d, refers to the means of identifying and acquiring the knowledge to be entered into the knowledge base. In simple terms, it is trying to determine how an expert thinks when developing a solution to a problem.

16. What key professional or professionals are required to develop an expert system?

    a. Knowledge engineer and object designer

    b. Knowledge engineer and domain expert

    c. Domain expert

    d. Domain expert and object designer

    Answer: b

    The *knowledge engineer* usually has a computer-related and expert system background, but does not have the knowledge of the specific discipline or domain being addressed by the expert system. For example, the expert system being developed may be a medical diagnostic system requiring input from diagnostic specialists and other types of physicians. These individuals are the *domain experts*. It is the job of the knowledge engineer to elicit the critical knowledge from the domain expert and incorporate it into the expert system knowledge base. The term "object designer" in the answers is a distracter.

17. An expert system that has rules of the form "If w is low and x is high then y is intermediate," where w and x are input variables and y is the output variable, is called a:

    a. Neural network

    b. Realistic expert system

    c. Boolean expert system

    d. Fuzzy expert system

    Answer: d

    A fuzzy expert system is an expert system that uses fuzzy membership functions and rules, instead of Boolean logic, to reason about data. Thus, fuzzy variables can have an approximate range of values instead of the binary True or False used in conventional expert systems. When it is desired to convert the fuzzy output to a single value, *defuzzification* is used. One approach to defuzzification is the CENTROID method. With this method, a value of the output variable is computed by finding the variable value of the center of gravity of the membership function for the fuzzy output value. Answers a and b are distracters, and answer c is incorrect since it refers to Boolean values of one or zero.

18. What is a "subject-oriented, integrated, time-variant, non-volatile collection of data in support of management's decision-making process"?

   a. Data mart

   b. Data warehouse

   c. Data model

   d. Data architecture

   Answer: b

   This definition of a data warehouse is that of Bill Inmon, a pioneer in the field. To create a *data warehouse*, data is taken from an operational database, redundancies are removed, and the data is "cleaned up" in general. This activity is referred to as *normalizing* the data. Then the data is placed into a relational database and can be analyzed using On-Line Analytical Processing (OLAP) and statistical modeling tools. The data warehouse can be used as a *Decision Support System (DSS)*, for example, by performing a time series analysis of the data. The data in the data warehouse must be maintained to ensure that it is timely and valid. The term *data scrubbing* refers to maintenance of the data warehouse by deleting information that is unreliable or no longer relevant. A *data mart*, answer a, is a database that is comprised of data or relations that have been extracted from the data warehouse. Information in the data mart is usually of interest to a particular group of people. For example, a data mart may be developed for all health care-related data. Answers c and d are distracters, although a *data model*, in this context, sometimes refers to the result of analyzing relationships among enterprise-wide data items. Another perspective on data models is discussed in the answers to Question 21.

19. The process of analyzing large data sets in a data warehouse to find non-obvious patterns is called:

   a. Data mining

   b. Data scanning

   c. Data administration

   d. Derived data

Answer: a

For example, mining of consumer-related data may show a correlation between the number of children under four years old in a household and the fathers' preferences in aftershave lotion. Answer b is a distracter. *Data administration,* answer c, describes the degree of management's dedication to the data warehouse concept. Answer d, *derived data,* is data that is obtained through the processing of raw data.

20. The equation $Z = f\left[\sum w_n i_n\right]$, where Z is the output, w_n are weighting functions, and i_n is a set of inputs describes:

a. An expert system

b. A knowledge-based system

c. An artificial neural network (ANN)

d. A knowledge acquisition system

Answer: c

The equation defines a *single layer ANN* as shown in Figure A.11. Each input, i_n, is multiplied by a weight, w_n, and these products are fed into a summation transfer function, $\sum$, that generates an output, Z. Most neural networks have multiple layers of summation and weighting functions, whose interconnections can also be changed.

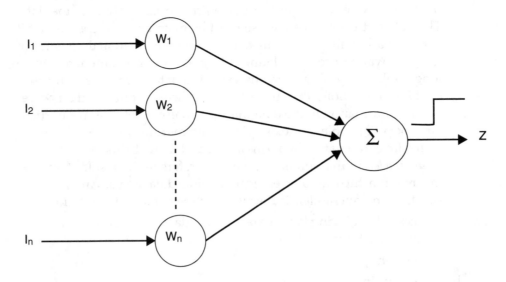

Figure A.11   A single layer artificial neural network.

There are a number of different learning paradigms for neural networks, including *reinforcement* learning and *back propagation*. In reinforcement learning a training set of inputs is provided to the ANN along with a measure of how close the network is coming to a solution. Then, the weights and connections are readjusted. In back propagation, information is fed back inside the neural network from the output and is used by the ANN to make weight and connection adjustments. Answers a and b are distracters that describe systems that use knowledge-based rules of experts to solve problems using an inferencing mechanism. A *knowledge acquisition system*, answer d, refers to the means of identifying and acquiring the knowledge to be entered into the knowledge base of an expert system.

21. A database that comprises tools to support the analysis, design, and development of software and support good software engineering practices is called a:

    a. Data model

    b. Database management system (DBMS)

    c. Data dictionary

    d. Data type dictionary

    Answer: c

    Computer Aided Software Engineering (CASE) tools and an *Integrated Project Support Environment (IPSE)* are terms used to describe similar software engineering support environments. Answer a, *data model*, "is a basic system of constructs used in describing reality," (Kent, W., *Data and Reality*, North Holland, 1978). A *DBMS*, answer b, is a system that supports the creation, use, and administration of a database system. Answer d, a *data type dictionary*, refers to a collection of items on which certain operations, such as insert, delete, and search, are to be performed. This arrangement of items is in contrast to a *priority queue*, in which the collection of items is arranged in order of priority and the relevant operations to be performed are insert, find-max, and delete-max.

22. Another type of artificial intelligence technology involves genetic algorithms. Genetic algorithms are part of the general class known as:

    a. Neural networks

    b. Suboptimal computing

    c. Evolutionary computing

    d. Biological computing

    Answer: c

Evolutionary computing uses the Darwinian principles of survival of the fittest, mutation, and the adaptation of successive generations of populations to their environment. The *genetic algorithm* implements this process through iteration of generations of a constant-size population of items or individuals. Each individual is characterized by a finite string of symbols called *genomes*. The genomes are used to represent possible solutions to a problem in a fixed search space. For example, if the fixed population of the first generation of individuals consists of random binary numbers, and the problem is to find the minimum binary number that can be represented by an individual, each binary number is assigned a *fitness value* based on the individual's binary number value. The smaller the binary number represented by a *parent* individual, the higher level of fitness that is assigned to it. Through cross breeding among the numbers (known as *crossover*), mutations of the numbers, and pairing of numbers with high fitness ratings, the smallest value that can be represented by the number of bits in the binary number will emerge in later generations. Answer a, neural networks, is incorrect and has been discussed extensively in previous questions in this chapter. Answer b is a distracter and answer d, biological computing, refers to computation performed by using certain characteristics of living organisms.

23. The Object Request Architecture (ORA) is a high-level framework for a distributed environment. It consists of four components. Which of the following items is NOT one of those components?

   a. Object Request Brokers (ORBs)

   b. Object Services

   c. Application Objects

   d. Application Services

   Answer: d

   Answers a, b, and c plus *Common Facilities* comprise the ORA. The ORA is a product of the *Object Management Group (OMG)*, which is a nonprofit consortium in Framingham, Massachusetts that was put together in 1989 to promote the use of object technology in distributed computing systems (www.omg.org). In answer a, the *ORB* is the fundamental building block of ORA and manages the communications between the ORA entities. The purpose of the ORB is to support the interaction of objects in heterogeneous, distributed environments. The objects may be on different types of computing platforms. Answer b, *Object Services*, supports the ORB in creating and tracking objects as well as performing access control functions. *Application Objects*, answer c, and *Common Facilities* support the end user and use the system services to perform their functions.

24. A standard that uses the Object Request Broker (ORB) to implement exchanges among objects in a heterogeneous, distributed environment is called:

    a. The Object Management Group (OMG) Object Model

    b. A Common Object Request Broker Architecture (CORBA)

    c. Open Architecture

    d. An Interface Definition Language (IDL)

    > *Answer:* b

    > In answer a, the *OMG Object Model* provides standard means for describing the externally visible characteristics of objects. Answer c is a distracter. *IDL*, answer d, is a standard interface language that is used by clients to request services from objects.

25. Another model that allows two software components to communicate with each other independent of their platforms' operating systems and languages of implementation is:

    a. Common Object Model (COM)

    b. Sandbox

    c. Basic Object Model (BOM)

    d. Spiral Model

    > *Answer:* a

    > As in the object-oriented paradigm, COM works with encapsulated objects. Communications with a COM object are through an *interface contract* between an object and its clients that defines the functions that are available in the object and the behavior of the object when the functions are called. Answer b, a *sandbox*, is an access control-based protection mechanism. It is commonly applied to restrict the access rights of mobile code that is downloaded from a Web site as an applet. The code is set up to run in a "sandbox" that blocks its access to the local workstation's hard disk, thus preventing the code from malicious activity. The sandbox is usually interpreted by a virtual machine such as the Java Virtual Machine. Answer c is a distracter and answer d refers to the software development life cycle model as discussed in Question 6.

26. A distributed object model that has similarities to the Common Object Request Broker Architecture (CORBA) is:

    a. Distributed Component Object Model (DCOM)

    b. The Chinese Wall Model

    c. Inference Model

    d. Distributed Data Model

Answer: a

DCOM is the distributed version of COM that supports remote objects as if the objects reside in the client's address space. A COM client can access a COM object through the use of a pointer to one of the object's interfaces and, then, invoking methods through that pointer. As discussed in Question 24, CORBA is a distributed object framework developed by the Object Management Group. Answer b, the *Chinese Wall Model* (D.C. Brewer & M.J. Nash, "Chinese Wall Model," *Proceedings of the 1989 IEEE Computer Society Symposium on Security and Privacy*, pp. 215-228, 1989), uses internal rules to "compartmentalize" areas in which individuals may work to prevent disclosure of proprietary information and to avoid conflicts of interest. The Chinese Wall model also incorporates the principle of separation of duty. Answers c and d are distracters.

27. Which of the following is NOT a characteristic of a client in the client/server model?

    a. Extensive user interface

    b. May be diskless

    c. Data entry screens

    d. Systems backup and database protection

    Answer: d

    In the client/server model, the server is the data storage resource and is responsible for data backups and protection/maintenance of the database. Answer b refers to a diskless workstation or PC at the client side. By not providing local data storage capabilities at the client side, security is increased since the data is less vulnerable at a protected server location. Also, because the client is the user's path into the network, the client must have extensive, user friendly interfaces such as described in answers a and c.

28. A client/server implementation approach in which any platform may act as a client or server or both is called:

    a. Simple file transfer

    b. Peer-to-peer

    c. Application Programming Interface (API)

    d. Graphical User Interface (GUI)

    Answer: b

    In answer a, a workstation or PC uses terminal emulation software and a client application program to receive data from a host machine. For answer c, an API defines how the client and server appear to each other and supports the exchange of information without either entity knowing the details of a particular resource that is accessed using the API. One example is the Generalized Security Application Programming Interface (GSAPI) that applications can use to access security services. Answer d, the GUI approach, is similar to the API implementation and employs a user interface such as SQL to access a server database.

29. Which of the following is NOT a characteristic of a distributed data processing (DDP) approach?

    a. Consists of multiple processing locations that can provide alternatives for computing in the event of a site becoming inoperative.

    b. Distances from user to processing resource are transparent to the user.

    c. Security is enhanced because of networked systems.

    d. Data stored at multiple, geographically separate locations is easily available to the user.

    Answer: c

    Security is more of a concern in distributed systems since there are vulnerabilities associated with the network and the many locations from which unauthorized access to the computing resources can occur. Answers a, b, and d are characteristics of a DDP architecture.

30. A database management system (DBMS) is useful in situations where:

    a. Rapid development of applications is required and preprogrammed functions can be used to provide those applications along with other support features such as security, error recovery, and access control.

    b. Data are processed infrequently and results are not urgently needed.

    c. Large amounts of data are to be processed in time-critical situations.

    d. The operations to be performed on the data are modified infrequently and the operations are relatively straightforward.

    Answer: a

    A DBMS is called for when the required skilled programming resources are not available, information to be stored and accessed is common to many organizational business units, the processing requirements change frequently and timely responses are required for queries on the data.

Chapter 8—Business Continuity Planning—Disaster Recovery Planning

1. Which choice below is the MOST accurate description of a warm site?

   a. A backup processing facility with adequate electrical wiring and air conditioning, but no hardware or software installed

   b. A backup processing facility with most hardware and software installed, which can be operational within a matter of days

   c. A backup processing facility with all hardware and software installed and 100% compatible with the original site, operational within hours

   d. A mobile trailer with portable generators and air conditioning

   Answer: b

   The three most common types of remote off-site backup processing facilities are hot sites, warm sites, and cold sites. They are primarily differentiated by how much preparation is devoted to the site, and therefore how quickly the site can be used as an alternate processing site. Answer c is an example of a "cold" site, which is a designated computer operations room with HVAC, that may have few or no computing systems installed and therefore would require a substantial effort to install the hardware and software required to begin alternate processing. This type of site is rarely useful in an actual emergency.

   Answer b, a "warm" site, is a backup processing facility with most hardware and software installed, which would need a minor effort to be up and running as an alternate processing center. It may use cheaper or older equipment and create a degradation in processing performance, but would be able to handle the most important processing tasks. A "hot" site, answer c, has all the required hardware and software installed to begin alternate processing either immediately or within an acceptably short time frame. This site would be 100% compatible with the original site and would only need an upgrade of the most current data to duplicate operations. Source: *The International Handbook of Computer Security* by Jae K. Shim, Anique A. Qureshi, and Joel G. Siegel (The Glenlake Publishing Co. Ltd, 2000), and "NFPA 1600 Standard on Disaster/Emergency Management and Business Continuity," National Fire Protection Association, 2000 edition.

   Table A.13 shows a common scheme to classify the recovery time frame needs of each business function.

Table A.13 Recovery Time Frame Classification Scheme

RATING CLASS	RECOVERY TIMEFRAME NEEDED
AAA	Immediate recovery needed; no downtime allowed.
AA	Full functional recovery required within four hours.
A	Same business day recovery required.
B	Up to 24 hours downtime acceptable.
C	24 to 72 hours downtime acceptable.
D	Greater than 72 hours downtime acceptable.

2. Which choice below is NOT an accurate description or element of remote sensing technology?

    a. Photographic, radar, infrared, or multi-spectral imagery from manned or unmanned aircraft

    b. Photographic, radar, infrared, or multi-spectral imagery from land-based tracking stations

    c. Photographic, radar, infrared, or multi-spectral imagery from geostationary or orbiting satellites

    d. RS intelligence may be integrated into geographic information systems (GIS) to produce map-based products

    Answer: b

    Remote sensing is the acquisition of information via aerial or satellite sensors. The most critical category of information to capture immediately following a disaster is accurate and timely intelligence about the scope, extent, and impact of the event. Intelligent and effective decisions hinge on the credible characterization of the situation. If the disaster is extensive enough, it may cause serious damage to the telephone or wireless infrastructure and ground communications may be unusable to accurately assess the situation. Remote sensing systems can provide a highly effective alternative means of gathering intelligence about the event. Answer a describes remote sensing using aerial-derived information. Answer c describes satellite-derived remote sensing. Answer d describes a common use of the remote sensing data. Source: "Remote Sensing in Federal Disaster Areas, Standard Operating Procedures," FEMA 9321.1-PR, June 1999

3. Which disaster recovery/emergency management plan testing type below is considered the most cost-effective and efficient way to identify areas of overlap in the plan before conducting more demanding training exercises?

a. Full-scale exercise

b. Walk-through drill

c. Table-top exercise test

d. Evacuation drill

Answer: c

In a table-top exercise, members of the emergency management group meet in a conference room setting to discuss their responsibilities and how they would react to emergency scenarios. Disaster recovery/emergency management plan testing scenarios have several levels, and can be called different things. The primary hierarchy of disaster/emergency testing plan types is shown below.

Checklist review. Plan is distributed and reviewed by business units for its thoroughness and effectiveness.

Table-top exercise or structured walk-through test. Members of the emergency management group meet in a conference room setting to discuss their responsibilities and how they would react to emergency scenarios by stepping through the plan.

Walk-through drill or simulation test. The emergency management group and response teams actually perform their emergency response functions by walking through the test, without actually initiating recovery procedures. More thorough than the table-top exercise.

Functional drills. Test specific functions such as medical response, emergency notifications, warning and communications procedures, and equipment, although not necessarily all at once. Also includes evacuation drills, where personnel walk the evacuation route to a designated area where procedures for accounting for the personnel are tested.

Parallel test or full-scale exercise. A real-life emergency situation is simulated as closely as possible. Involves all of the participants that would be responding to the real emergency, including community and external organizations. The test may involve ceasing some real production processing.

Source: "Emergency Management Guide for Business and Industry," Federal Emergency Management Agency, August 1998 and *Computer Security Basics*, by Deborah Russell and G.T. Gangemi, Sr. (O'Reilly, 1992).

4. Which task below would normally be considered a BCP task, rather than a DRP task?

   a. Life safety processes

   b. Project scoping

   c. Restoration procedures

   d. Recovery procedures

   Answer: b

   Although many processes in making business continuity plans are similar to processes in creating disaster recovery plans, several differences exist. Business continuity planning processes that are unique to BCP could include:

   ■ Project scoping and assigning roles

   ■ Creating business impact and vulnerability assessments

   ■ Choosing alternate processing sites

   whereas unique disaster recovery/emergency management processes could include:

   ■ Implementing relocation procedures to the alternate site

   ■ Plan testing and training

   ■ Recovering data

   ■ Salvaging damaged equipment

   Source: "CISSP Examination Textbooks, Volume One: Theory," by S. Rao Vallabhaneni, SRV Professional Publications first edition 2000 and "Handbook of Information Security Management," by Micki Krause and Harold F. Tipton, Auerback, 1999 edition.

5. Which choice below is NOT a role or responsibility of the person designated to manage the contingency planning process?

   a. Providing direction to senior management

   b. Providing stress reduction programs to employees after an event

   c. Ensuring the identification of all critical business functions

   d. Integrating the planning process across business units

   Answer: b

   Contingency planners have many roles and responsibilities when planning business continuity, disaster recovery, emergency management, or business resumption processes. In addition to answers a, c, and d, above, some of these roles and responsibilities can include:

   ■ Ensuring executive management compliance with the contingency plan program

- Providing periodic management reports and status
- Coordinating and integrating the activation of emergency response organizations

Answer b, providing stress reduction programs to employees after an event, is a responsibility of the human resources area. Source: *Contingency Planning and Management*, "Contingency Planning 101," by Kelley Goggins, March 1999.

6. Which choice below is NOT an emergency management procedure directly related to financial decision making?

   a. Establishing accounting procedures to track the costs of emergencies

   b. Establishing procedures for the continuance of payroll

   c. Establishing critical incident stress procedures

   d. Establishing program procurement procedures

   Answer: c

   Answers a, b, and d are all examples of emergency management procedures which must be established by the financial department to ensure that fiscal decisions are executed in accordance with authority levels and accounting practices. Answer c is an example of a procedure that should be developed by the human resources department. The quality of employee morale and well-being can include psychological needs as well as physical needs, and the role of the human resources department is critical in monitoring and managing immediate, short-term, and long-term employee stress. Source: "NFPA 1600 Standard on Disaster/Emergency Management and Business Continuity," National Fire Protection Association, 2000 edition.

7. Which choice below is NOT considered an appropriate role for senior management in the business continuity and disaster recovery process?

   a. Delegate recovery roles

   b. Publicly praise successes

   c. Closely control media and analyst communications

   d. Assess the adequacy of information security during the disaster recovery

   Answer: d

   The tactical assessment of information security is a role of information management or technology management, not senior management. In addition to the elements of answers a, b, and c above, senior management has many very important roles in the process of disaster recovery, including:

■ Remaining visible to employees and stakeholders

■ Directing, managing, and monitoring the recovery

■ Rationally amending business plans and projections

■ Clearly communicating new roles and responsibilities

Senior management must resist the temptation to participate hands-on in the recovery effort, as these efforts should be delegated. Information or technology management has more tactical roles to play, such as:

■ Identifying and prioritizing mission-critical applications

■ Continuously reassessing the recovery site's stability

■ Recovering and constructing all critical data

Source: "Business Recovery Checklist," KPMG LLP 2001.

8. Which choice below is NOT considered a potential hazard resulting from natural events?

a. Earthquake/land shift

b. Forest fire

c. Arson

d. Urban fire

Answer: c

According to the NFPA, arson is an example of a potential hazard caused by a human event. Fires, in themselves, are considered natural events, like forest fires, range fires, urban or city fires, unless arson is thought to be the source of the blaze. Of the three categories of potential hazards (natural, technological, and human), human events could include:

■ General strikes

■ Terrorism

■ Sabotage

■ Mass hysteria

■ Civil unrest

Source: "NFPA 1600 Standard on Disaster/Emergency Management and Business Continuity," National Fire Protection Association, 2000 edition.

9. Which choice below represents the most important first step in creating a business resumption plan?

a. Performing a risk analysis

b. Obtaining senior management support

c. Analyzing the business impact

d. Planning recovery strategies

Answer: b

The business resumption, or business continuity plan, must have total, highly visible senior management support. Senior management must agree on the scope of the project, delegate resources for the success of the project, and support the timeline and training efforts. Source: *Contingency Planning and Management*, "Contingency Planning 101," by Kelley Goggins, March 1999.

10. Which choice below would NOT be a valid reason for testing the disaster recovery plan?

a. Testing provides the contingency planner with recent documentation.

b. Testing verifies the accuracy of the recovery procedures.

c. Testing prepares the personnel to properly execute their emergency duties.

d. Testing identifies deficiencies within the recovery procedures.

Answer: a

Answers b, c, and d are all excellent reasons for testing a disaster recovery plan. Until a disaster recovery plan has been tested thoroughly, no plan can be considered complete. Since the functionality of the plan directly determines the ability of an organization to survive a business interrupting event, testing is the only way to have some degree of confidence that the plan will work. Answer a is a distracter. Source: *The International Handbook of Computer Security*, by Jae K. Shim, Anique A. Qureshi, and Joel G. Siegel (The Glenlake Publishing Co. Ltd, 2000).

11. Which choice below is NOT a commonly accepted definition for a disaster?

a. An occurrence that is outside the normal computing function

b. An occurrence or imminent threat to the entity of widespread or severe damage, injury, loss of life, or loss of property

c. An emergency that is beyond the normal response resources of the entity

d. A suddenly occurring event that has a long-term negative impact on social life

Answer: a

The disaster/emergency management and business continuity community consists of many different types of entities, such as governmental (federal, state, and local), nongovernmental (business and industry), and individuals. Each entity has its own focus and its own definition of a disaster. Answers b, c, and d are examples of these various definitions of disasters.

■ A very common definition of a disaster is "a suddenly occurring or unstoppable developing event that":

■ Claims loss of life, suffering, loss of valuables, or damage to the environment.

■ Overwhelms local resources or efforts.

■ Has a long-term impact on social or natural life that is always negative in the beginning.

Source: "NFPA 1600 Standard on Disaster/Emergency Management and Business Continuity," National Fire Protection Association, 2000 edition.

12. Which choice below is NOT considered an appropriate role for Financial Management in the business continuity and disaster recovery process?

a. Tracking the recovery costs

b. Monitoring employee morale and guarding against employee burnout

c. Formally notifying insurers of claims

d. Reassessing cash flow projections

Answer: b

Monitoring employee morale and guarding against employee burnout during a disaster recovery event is the proper role of human resources. Other emergency recovery tasks associated with human resources could include:

■ Providing appropriate retraining

■ Monitoring productivity of personnel

■ Providing employees and family with counseling and support

In addition to answers a, c, and d above, during an emergency, the financial area is responsible for:

■ Re-establishing accounting processes, such as payroll, benefits, and accounts payable

■ Re-establishing transaction controls and approval limits

Source: "Business Recovery Checklist," KPMG LLP 2001, and *Contingency Planning and Management*, "Contingency Planning 101," by Kelley Goggins, March 1999.

13. Which choice below most accurately describes a business continuity program?

    a. Ongoing process to ensure that the necessary steps are taken to identify the impact of potential losses and maintain viable recovery

    b. A program that implements the mission, vision, and strategic goals of the organization

    c. A determination of the effects of a disaster on human, physical, economic, and natural resources

    d. A standard that allows for rapid recovery during system interruption and data loss

    Answer: a

    A business continuity program is an ongoing process supported by senior management and funded to ensure that the necessary steps are taken to identify the impact of potential losses, maintain viable recovery strategies and recovery plans, and ensure continuity of services through personnel training, plan testing, and maintenance. Answer b describes a disaster/emergency management program. A disaster/emergency management program, like a disaster recovery program, is a program that implements the mission, vision, and strategic goals and objectives as well as the management framework of the program and organization. Answer c describes a damage assessment. A damage assessment is an appraisal or determination of the effects of a disaster on human, physical, economic, and natural resources. Answer d is a distracter. Source: "NFPA 1600 Standard on Disaster/Emergency Management and Business Continuity," National Fire Protection Association, 2000 edition.

14. What is the responsibility of the contingency planner regarding LAN backup and recovery if the LAN is part of a building server environment?

    a. Getting a copy of the recovery procedures from the building server administrator

    b. Recovering client/server systems owned and supported by internal staff

    c. Classifying the recovery time frame of the business unit LAN

    d. Identifying essential business functions

    Answer: a

    When any part of the LAN is not hosted internally, and is part of a building server environment, it is the responsibility of the contingency planner to identify the building server administrator, identify for him the recovery time frame required for your business applications, obtain a copy of the recovery procedures, and participate in the validation of the building's server testing. If all or part of the business is not in the building server environment, then the other three choices are also the responsibility of the contingency planner. Source: *Contingency Planning and Management*, "Contingency Planning 101," by Kelley Goggins, March 1999.

15. Which choice below is the correct definition of a Mutual Aid Agreement?

    a. A management-level analysis that identifies the impact of losing an entity's resources

    b. An appraisal or determination of the effects of a disaster on human, physical, economic, and natural resources

    c. A prearranged agreement to render assistance to the parties of the agreement

    d. Activities taken to eliminate or reduce the degree of risk to life and property

    Answer: c

    A mutual aid agreement is used by two or more parties to provide for assistance if one of the parties experiences an emergency. It is expected that the other parties will assist the affected party in various ways, perhaps by making office space available, or computing time or resources, or supplying manpower if needed. While mutual aid agreements may be a very cost-effective solution for disaster recovery, it does not provide for full operations redundancy. An example of a problem with a total reliance on mutual aid would be the event that affects all parties to the agreement, thereby rendering the agreement useless. While they are an effective means to provide some resources to the organization in an emergency, they in themselves are not a replacement for a full disaster recovery plan, including alternate computer processing sites.

    Answer a describes a business continuity plan. Answer b describes a damage assessment, and answer d describes risk mitigation. Source: "NFPA 1600 Standard on Disaster/Emergency Management and Business Continuity," National Fire Protection Association, 2000 edition, and "Emergency Management Guide for Business and Industry," Federal Emergency Management Agency, August 1998.

16. In which order should the following steps be taken to create an emergency management plan?

    ——— a. Implement the plan

    _____ b. Form a planning team

_____ c. Develop a plan

_____ d. Conduct a vulnerability assessment

    Answer: b, d, c, and a

The proper order of steps in the emergency management planning process is:

- Establish a planning team
- Analyze capabilities and hazards
- Develop the plan
- Implement the plan

Source: "Emergency Management Guide for Business and Industry," Federal Emergency Management Agency, August 1998.

17. Place the BRP groups below in their properly tiered organizational structure, from highest to lowest:

——— a. Policy group

——— b. Senior executives

——— c. Emergency response team

——— d. Disaster management team

    Answer: b, a, d, and c

Some organizations with mature business resumption plans (BRPs) employ a tiered structure that mirrors the organization's hierarchy. Senior management is always the highest level of decision-makers in the BRP process, although the policy group also consists of upper-level executives. The policy group approves emergency management decisions involving expenditures, liabilities, and service impacts. The next group, the disaster management team, often consists of department and business unit representatives and makes decisions regarding life safety and disaster recovery efforts. The next group, the emergency response team, supplies tactical response to the disaster, and may consist of members of data processing, user support, or persons with first aid and evacuation responsibilities. Source: *Contingency Planning and Management*, "Business Contingency Planning 201," by Paul H. Rosenthal May, 2000.

18. Which choice below most accurately describes a business impact analysis (BIA)?

a. A program that implements the strategic goals of the organization

b. A management-level analysis that identifies the impact of losing an entity's resources

c. A prearranged agreement between two or more entities to provide assistance

d. Activities designed to return an organization to an acceptable operating condition

Answer: b

A business impact analysis (BIA) measures the effect of resource loss and escalating losses over time in order to provide the entity with reliable data upon which to base decisions on hazard mitigation and continuity planning. A BIA is performed as one step during the creation of a Business Continuity Plan (BCP). A common five-step approach to a BCP could consist of:

- BCP project scope creation
- Business impact assessment
- Recovery strategy development
- Recovery plan development
- Implementation, testing, and maintenance.

Answer a is a definition of a disaster/emergency management program. Answer c describes a mutual aid agreement. Answer d is the definition of a recovery program. Source: "NFPA 1600 Standard on Disaster/Emergency Management and Business Continuity," National Fire Protection Association, 2000 edition and "Handbook of Information Security Management," by Micki Krause and Harold F. Tipton, Auerback, 1999 edition.

19. In which order should the following steps be taken to perform a vulnerability assessment?

_____ a. List potential emergencies

_____ b. Estimate probability

——— c. Assess external and internal resources

——— d. Assess potential impact

Answer: a, b, d, and c

Common steps to performing a vulnerability assessment could be:

1. List potential emergencies, both internally to your facility and externally to the community. Natural, man-made, technological, and human error are all categories of potential emergencies and errors.

2. Estimate the likelihood that each emergency could occur, in a subjective analysis.

TYPE OF EMERGENCY	Probability	Human Impact	Property Impact	Business Impact	Internal Resources	External Resources	Total
	High 5 ←→ Low 1	High Impact 5 ←——→ 1 Low Impact			Weak Resources 5 ←→ 1 Strong Resources		

Figure A.12   Sample vulnerability assessment matrix.

3. Assess the potential impact of the emergency on the organization in the areas of human impact (death or injury), property impact (loss or damage), and business impact (market share or credibility).

4. Assess external and internal resources required to deal with the emergency, and determine if they are located internally or if external capabilities or procedures are required.

Source: "Emergency Management Guide for Business and Industry," Federal Emergency Management Agency, August 1998.

Figure A.12 shows a sample vulnerability matrix. This can be used to create a subjective impact analysis for each type of emergency and its probability. The lower the final number the better, as a high number means a high probability, impact, or lack of remediation resources.

20. According to FEMA, which choice below is NOT a recommended way to purify water after a disaster?

a. Adding 16 drops per gallon of household liquid bleach to the water

b. Boiling from 3 to 5 minutes

c. Adding water treatment tablets to the water

d. Distilling the water for twenty minutes

Answer: c

FEMA recommends that water treatment products sold in camping or surplus stores should not be used, unless the only active ingredient is 5.25 percent hypochlorite. When adding liquid bleach, it should contain 5.25 percent hypochlorite and no other added cleaners or scents. Distilling the water is the most highly recommended method, as it also removes other chemicals and heavy metals, as well as most microbes. Source: *Emergency Water and Food Procedures*, Federal Emergency Management Agency, April, 1997.

21. Which choice below is NOT a recommended step to take when resuming normal operations after an emergency?

a. Re-occupy the damaged building as soon as possible.

b. Account for all damage-related costs.

c. Protect undamaged property.

d. Conduct an investigation.

Answer: a

Re-occupying the site of a disaster or emergency should not be undertaken until a full safety inspection has been done, an investigation into the cause of the emergency has been completed, and all damaged property has been salvaged and restored. During and after an emergency, the safety of personnel must be monitored, any remaining hazards must be assessed, and security must be maintained at the scene. After all safety precautions have been taken, an inventory of damaged and undamaged property must be done to begin salvage and restoration tasks. Also, the site must not be re-occupied until all investigative processes have been completed. Detailed records must be kept of all disaster-related costs and valuations must be made of the effect of the business interruption. Source: "Emergency Management Guide for Business and Industry," Federal Emergency Management Agency, August 1998.

22. In developing an emergency or recovery plan, which choice below would NOT be considered a short-term objective?

a. Priorities for restoration

b. Acceptable downtime before restoration

c. Minimum resources needed to accomplish the restoration

d. The organization's strategic plan

Answer: d

The organization's strategic plan is considered a long-term goal. In developing plans, consideration should be given to both short-term and long-term goals and objectives. Short-term goals can include:

- Vital personnel, systems, operations, and equipment
- Priorities for restoration and mitigation
- Acceptable downtime before restoration to a minimum level of operations
- Minimum resources needed to accomplish the restoration
  Long-term goals and objectives can include:
- The organization's strategic plan
- Management and coordination of activities
- Funding and fiscal management
- Management of volunteer, contractual, and entity resources

Source: "NFPA 1600 Standard on Disaster/Emergency Management and Business Continuity," National Fire Protection Association, 2000 edition.

23. When should security isolation of the incident scene start?
    a. Immediately after the emergency is discovered
    b. As soon as the disaster plan is implemented
    c. After all personnel have been evacuated
    d. When hazardous materials have been discovered at the site

    Answer: a

    Isolation of the incident scene should begin as soon as the emergency has been discovered. Authorized personnel should attempt to secure the scene and control access; however, no one should be placed in physical danger to perform these functions. It's important for life safety that access be controlled immediately at the scene, and only by trained personnel directly involved in the disaster response. Additional injury or exposure to recovery personnel after the initial incident must be tightly controlled. Source: "Emergency Management Guide for Business and Industry," Federal Emergency Management Agency, August, 1998.

24. Place the following backup processing alternatives in order, from the most expensive solution to the least expensive:
    _____ a. Warm site
    _____ b. Hot site
    _____ c. Cold site
    _____ d. Mutual aid agreement

Answer: b, a, c, and d

A mutual aid agreement is likely to be the least expensive of the four, as it doesn't necessarily entail any resource investment. As far as the ability of the alternatives to actually provide redundancy and processing in the event of a business-interrupting incident, the order is exactly the opposite, with mutual aid and cold sites providing the least, and hot sites providing the highest level of processing redundancy assurance. Source: *The International Handbook of Computer Security*, by Jae K. Shim, Anique A. Qureshi, and Joel G. Siegel (The Glenlake Publishing Co. Ltd, 2000).

25. Which choice below is incorrect regarding when a BCP, DRP, or emergency management plan should be evaluated and modified?

    a. Never; once it has been tested it should not be changed.

    b. Annually, in a scheduled review.

    c. After training drills, tests, or exercises.

    d. After an emergency or disaster response.

    Answer: a

    Emergency management plans, business continuity plans, and disaster recovery plans should be regularly reviewed, evaluated, modified, and updated. At a minimum, the plan should be reviewed at an annual audit. It should also be re-evaluated:

    ■ After tests or training exercises, to adjust any discrepancies between the test results and the plan

    ■ After a disaster response or an emergency recovery, as this is an excellent time to amend the parts of the plan that were not effective

    ■ When personnel, their responsibilities, their resources, or organizational structures change, to familiarize new or reorganized personnel with procedures

    ■ When polices, procedures, or infrastructures change

    Source: "Emergency Management Guide for Business and Industry" Federal Emergency Management Agency, August, 1998 and "NFPA 1600 Standard on Disaster/Emergency Management and Business Continuity" National Fire Protection Association, 2000 edition.

26. Which choice below refers to a business asset?

    a. Events or situations that could cause a financial or operational impact to the organization

    b. Protection devices or procedures in place that reduce the effects of threats

c. Competitive advantage, credibility, or good will

d. Personnel compensation and retirement programs

Answer: c

Assets are considered the physical and financial assets that are owned by the company. Examples of business assets that could be lost or damaged during a disaster are:

■ Revenues lost during the incident

■ On-going recovery costs

■ Fines and penalties incurred by the event.

■ Competitive advantage, credibility, or good will damaged by the incident

Answer a is a definition for a threat. Answer b is a description of mitigating factors that reduce the effect of a threat, such as a UPS, sprinkler systems, or generators. Answer d is a distracter. Source: Contingency Planning and Management, "Contingency Planning 101" by Kelley Goggins, March, 1999.

27. Which choice below is an example of a potential hazard due to a technological event, rather than a human event?

a. Sabotage

b. Financial collapse

c. Mass hysteria

d. Enemy attack

Answer: b

A financial collapse is considered a technological potential hazard, the other three are human events. Of the three categories of potential hazards (natural, technological, and human), technological events could include:

■ Hazard material release (HazMat)

■ Explosion or fire (non-arson)

■ Fuel shortage

■ Structure collapse

■ Utility failure

■ Severe air pollution

Source: "NFPA 1600 Standard on Disaster/Emergency Management and Business Continuity," National Fire Protection Association, 2000 edition.

28. When should the public and media be informed about a disaster?

a. Whenever site emergencies extend beyond the facility

b. When any emergency occurs at the facility, internally or externally

c. When the public's health or safety is in danger

d. When the disaster has been contained

Answer: a

When an emergency occurs that could potentially have an impact outside the facility, the public must be informed, regardless of whether there is any immediate threat to public safety. The disaster recovery plan should include determinations of the audiences that may be affected by an emergency, and procedures to communicate with them. Information the public will want to know could include public safety or health concerns, the nature of the incident, the remediation effort, and future prevention steps. Common audiences for information could include:

■ The media

■ Unions and contractors

■ Shareholders

■ Neighbors

■ Employees' families and retirees

Since the media is such an important link to the public, disaster plans and tests must contain procedures for addressing the media and communicating important information. A trained spokesperson should be designated, and established communications procedures should be prepared. Accurate and approved information should be released in a timely manner, without speculation, blame, or obfuscation. Source: "Emergency Management Guide for Business and Industry," Federal Emergency Management Agency, August, 1998.

29. Which choice below is the first priority in an emergency?

a. Communicating with employees' families the status of the emergency

b. Notifying external support resources for recovery and restoration

c. Protecting the health and safety of everyone in the facility

d. Warning customers and contractors of a potential interruption of service

Answer: c

Life safety, or protecting the health and safety of everyone in the facility is the first priority in an emergency or disaster. Evacuation routes, assembly areas, and accounting for personnel (head counts and last-known locations) are the most important function of emergency procedures, before anything else. Once all personnel have been accounted for and emergency teams have arrived to prevent further damage or hazard, family members should be notified of the status of the event. Providing restoration and recovery, and implementing alternative production methods also comes later. Source: "Emergency Management Guide for Business and Industry," Federal Emergency Management Agency, August, 1998.

Chapter 9—Law, Investigation, and Ethics

1. In the legal field, there is a term that is used to describe a computer system so that everyone can agree on a common definition. The term describes a computer for the purposes of computer security as "any assembly of electronic equipment, hardware, software and firmware configured to collect, create, communicate, disseminate, process, store and control data or information." This definition includes peripheral items such as keyboards, printers, and additional memory. The term that corresponds to this definition is:

   a. A central processing unit (CPU)

   b. A microprocessor

   c. An arithmetic logic unit (ALU)

   d. An automated information system (AIS)

   > *Answer:* d
   >
   > In some ways, this terminology harkens back to the days of large mainframe computers, but the term AIS is used in the legal community to refer to a computer system. Answer a, CPU, refers to the portion of a computer that performs arithmetic and logical operations on data. To support these operations, the CPU incorporates a hardware arithmetic logic unit or ALU (answer c). The CPU is synonymous with the word *"processor."* If the CPU is integrated onto a silicon chip, it is called a *microprocessor* (answer b). If the CPU is connected with memory and Input/Output (I/O) through a set of wires called a *bus*, the resulting combination is called a computer. This concept is shown in Figure A.13.

2. In general, computer crimes fall into two major categories and two additional related categories. Which of the following categories is NOT one of these four?

   a. The computer as a target of the crime

   b. Crimes using the computer

   c. Malfeasance by computer

   d. Crimes associated with the prevalence of computers

   > *Answer:* c
   >
   > Malfeasance by computer is an act involving a computer that is technically and ethically improper, but may or may not be illegal. Some of these activities may not be considered illegal by the user and may be unintentional. Examples of such behavior are:
   >
   > - Using a password that you have been given by someone else to have access to their computer and using that password to view files that were not intended for your perusal

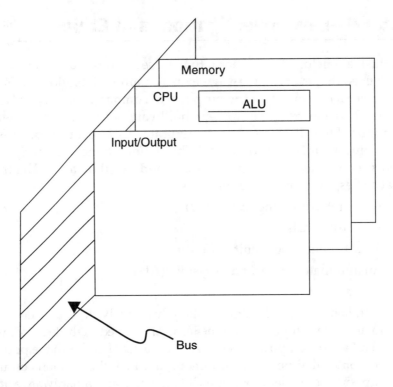

Figure A.13 A computer.

- Giving a copy of a software package that you purchased to a member of your family for personal use (In most instances, this is illegal based on software licenses.)
- Using the computer at your place of employment to store some information related to an outside business activity

Answers a, b, and d are valid categories of computer crime. The fourth category is a crime where the computer is incidental to other crimes. Examples in these four categories are:

The computer is a target of the crime. Sabotage or theft of intellectual property, disruption of business operations, illegal access to government and personal information, and falsifying or changing records.

Crimes using the computer. Theft of money from financial accounts, credit card fraud, fraud involving stock transfers, billing charges illegally to another party, and telecommunications fraud.

Crimes associated with the prevalence of computers. Violation of copyright restrictions on commercial software packages, software piracy and software counterfeiting.

The computer is incidental to other crimes. (In this category, the crime could be committed without the computer, but the computer permits the crime to be committed more efficiently and in higher volume.) Money laundering, keeping records and books of illegal activity and illegal gambling.

3. Which of the following is NOT a valid legal issue associated with computer crime?

a. Electronic Data Interchange (EDI) makes it easier to relate a crime to an individual.

b. It may be difficult to prove criminal intent.

c. It may be difficult to obtain a trail of evidence of activities performed on the computer.

d. It may be difficult to show causation.

Answer: a

EDI makes it more difficult to tie an individual to transactions since EDI involves computer-to-computer data interchanges and this makes it more difficult to trace the originator of some transactions. Answer b is a valid legal issue since it may be very difficult to prove criminal intent by a person perusing computer files and then causing damage to the files. The damage may have not been intentional. Answer c describes the situation of trying to track activities on a computer where the information is volatile and may have been destroyed. In answer d, common law refers to *causation* of the criminal act. Causation is particularly difficult to show in instances where a virus or other malicious code erases itself after causing damage to vital information.

4. The Federal Intelligence Surveillance Act (FISA) of 1978, the Electronic Communications Privacy Act (ECPA) of 1986, and the Communications Assistance for Law Enforcement Act (CALEA) of 1994 are legislative acts passed by the United States Congress. These acts all address what major information security issue?

a. Computer fraud

b. Wiretapping

c. Malicious code

d. Unlawful use of and access to government computers and networks

Answer: b

These laws reflected different views concerning wiretapping as technology progressed. The Federal Intelligence Surveillance Act (FISA) of 1978 limited wiretapping for national security purposes as a result of the record of the Nixon Administration in using illegal wire-taps. The Electronic Communications Privacy Act (ECPA) of 1986 prohibited eavesdropping or the interception of message contents without distinguishing between private or public systems. The Communications Assistance for Law Enforcement Act (CALEA) of 1994 required all communications carriers to make wiretaps possible in ways approved by the FBI.

5. A *pen register* is a:

   a. Device that identifies the cell in which a mobile phone is operating

   b. Device that records the URLs accessed by an individual

   c. Device that records the caller-ID of incoming calls

   d. Device that records all the numbers dialed from a specific telephone line

   Answer: d

   (Electronic Privacy Information Center, "Approvals for Federal Pen Registers and Trap and Trace Devices 1987-1998," www.epic. org). Gathering information as to which numbers are dialed from a specific telephone line is less costly and time-consuming than installing a wiretap and recording the information. There is also equipment that can record the information listed in answers a and b. The device referred to in answer c is called a *trap-and-trace* device. All of the answers in this question are a subset of the category of *traffic analysis* wherein patterns and frequency associated with communications are studied instead of the content of the communications.

6. A device that is used to monitor Internet Service Provider (ISP) data traffic is called:

   a. Carnivore

   b. Echelon

   c. Escrowed encryption

   d. Key manager

   Answer: a

   Carnivore is a device used by the U.S. FBI to monitor ISP traffic. (S.P. Smith, et. al., *Independent Technical Review of the Carnivore System – Draft report*, U.S. Department of Justice Contract # 00-C-328 IITRI, CR-022-216, Nov 17, 2000). Answer b, *Echelon*, refers to a cooperative, world-wide signal intelligence system that is run by the NSA of the United States, the Government Communications Head Quarters (GCHQ) of

England, the Communications Security Establishment (CSE) of Canada, the Australian Defense Security Directorate (DSD), and the General Communications Security Bureau (GCSB) of New Zealand. These organizations are bound together under a secret 1948 agreement, UKUSA, [European Parliament, "Development of Surveillance Technology and the Risk of Abuse of Economic Information," Luxembourg (April 1999), PE 166.184/Part 3 /4]. Answer c is a distracter and is discussed in the questions and answers of Chapter 4, "Cryptography." Answer d is a distracter.

7. In 1996, the World Intellectual Property Organization (WIPO) sponsored a treaty under which participating countries would standardize treatment of digital copyrights. One of the items of standardization was the prohibition of altering copyright management information (CMI) that is included with the copyrighted material. CMI is:

   a. An encryption algorithm

   b. Product description information

   c. A listing of Public keys

   d. Licensing and ownership information

      Answer: d

      The other answers are distracters. The WIPO digital copyright legislation that resulted in the U.S. was the 1998 Digital Millennium Copyright Act (DMCA). In addition to addressing answer d, the DMCA prohibits trading, manufacturing, or selling in any way that is intended to bypass copyright protection mechanisms. It also addresses Internet Service Providers (ISPs) that unknowingly support the posting of copyrighted material by subscribers. If the ISP is notified that the material is copyrighted, the ISP must remove the material. Additionally, if the posting party proves that the removed material was of "lawful use," the ISP must restore the material and notify the copyright owner within 14 business days.

      Two important rulings regarding the DMCA were made in 2001. The rulings involved DeCSS, which is a program that bypasses the Content Scrambling System (CSS) software used to prevent viewing of DVD movie disks on unlicensed platforms. In a trade secrecy case [DVD-CCA v. Banner], the California Appellate Court overturned a lower court ruling that an individual who posted DeCSS on the Internet had revealed the trade secret of CSS. The appeals court has reversed an injunction on the posting of DeCSS, stating that the code is speech-protected by the First Amendment.

      The second case [Universal City v. Reimerdes] was the first constitutional challenge to DMCA anti-circumvention rules. The case involved Eric Corley, the publisher of the hacker magazine *2600 Magazine*. Corley was covering the DeCSS situation and, as part of that coverage, posted DeCSS on his publication's Web site. The trial and appellate courts both ruled that the posting violated the DMCA and was, therefore, illegal. This ruling upheld the DMCA. It appears that there will be more challenges to DMCA in the future.

8. The European Union (EU) has enacted a Conditional Access Directive (CAD) that addresses which of the following?

   a. Access to and use of copyrighted material

   b. Reverse engineering

   c. Unauthorized access to Internet subscription sites and pay TV services

   d. Use of copyrighted material by libraries

   Answer: c

   The focus of the CAD is on access to services as opposed to access to works. As of this writing, the EU is discussing a directive focusing on copyrights, but it has not been finalized. It is anticipated that this directive will be similar to the U.S. DMCA (Question 7). Answers a, b, and d are copyright issues that will be addressed by the EU Copyright Directive or by other related directives.

9. Which of the following actions by the U.S. government are NOT permitted or required by the U.S. Patriot Act, signed into law on October 26, 2001?

   a. Subpoena of electronic records

   b. Monitoring of Internet communications

   c. Search and seizure of information on live systems (including routers and servers), backups, and archives

   d. Reporting of cash and wire transfers of $5,000 or more

   Answer: d

   Wire and cash transfers of $10,000 or more in a single transaction must be reported to government officials. Actions in answers a, b, and c are permitted under the Patriot Act. In answers a and b, the government has new powers to subpoena electronic records and to monitor Internet traffic. In monitoring information, the government can require the assistance of ISPs and network operators. This monitoring can even extend into individual organizations. In the Patriot Act, Congress permits investigators to gather information about electronic mail without having to show probable cause that the person to be monitored had committed a crime or was intending to commit a crime. In answer c, the items cited now fall under existing search and seizure laws. A new twist is delayed notification of a search warrant. Under the Patriot Act, if it suspected that notification of a search warrant would cause a suspect to flee, a search can be conducted before notification of a search warrant is given.

In a related matter, the U.S. and numerous other nations have signed the Council of Europe's "Cybercrime Convention." In the U.S., participation in the Convention has to be ratified by the Senate. In essence, the Convention requires the signatory nations to spy on their own residents, even if the action being monitored is illegal in the country in which the monitoring is taking place.

10. The U.S. Uniform Computer Information Transactions Act (UCITA) is a:

   a. Model act that is intended to apply uniform legislation to software licensing

   b. Model act that addresses digital signatures

   c. Model act that is intended to apply uniform legislation to electronic credit transactions

   d. Model act that addresses electronic transactions conducted by financial institutions

   Answer: a

   The National Commissioners on Uniform State Laws (NCUSL) voted to approve the Uniform Computers Information Transactions Act (UCITA) on July 29, 1999. This legislation, which will have to be enacted state-by-state, will greatly affect libraries' access to and use of software packages. It also will keep in place the current licensing practices of software vendors. At the present time, shrink-wrap or click-wrap licenses limit rights that are normally granted under copyright law. Under Section 109 of the U.S. 1976 Copyright Act, the first sale provision permits "the owner of a particular copy without the authority of the copyright owner, to sell or otherwise dispose of the possession of that copy." However, the software manufacturers use the term license in their transactions. As opposed to the word "sale," the term license denotes that the software manufacturers are permitting users to use a copy of their software. Thus, the software vendor still owns the software. Until each state enacts the legislation, it is not clear if shrink-wrap licenses that restrict users' rights under copyright law are legally enforceable. For clarification, shrink-wrap licenses physically accompany a disk while click-on and active click-wrap licenses are usually transmitted electronically. Sometimes, the term shrink-wrap is interpreted to mean both physical and electronic licenses to use software. The focus of the UCITA legislation is not on the physical media, but on the information contained on the media.

11. The European Union Electronic Signature Directive of January, 2000, defines an "advanced electronic signature." This signature must meet all of the following requirements except that:

    a. It must be uniquely linked to the signatory.

    b. It must be created using means that are generally accessible and available.

    c. It must be capable of identifying the signatory.

    d. It must be linked to the data to which it relates in such a manner that any subsequent change of the data is detectable.

    Answer: b

    The Directive requires that the means be maintained under the sole control of the signatory. This requirement is a particularly difficult one to achieve. One approach is to use different tokens or smart cards for the different transactions involved. The other answers are typical characteristics of digital signatures that can be implemented with public key cryptography.

12. On June 30, 2000, the U.S. Congress enacted the Electronic Signatures in Global and National Commerce Act (ESIGN) "to facilitate the use of electronic records and signatures in interstate and foreign commerce by ensuring the validity and legal effect of contracts entered into electronically." An important provision of the Act requires that:

    a. Businesses obtain electronic consent or confirmation from consumers to receive information electronically that a law normally requires to be in writing.

    b. The e-commerce businesses do not have to determine whether the consumer has the ability to receive an electronic notice before transmitting the legally required notices to the consumer.

    c. Businesses have the ability to use product price to persuade consumers to accept electronic records instead of paper.

    d. Specific technologies be used to ensure technical compatibility.

    Answer: a

    The legislation is intent on preserving the consumers' rights under consumer protection laws and went to extraordinary measures to meet this goal. Thus, a business must receive confirmation from the consumer in electronic format that the consumer consents to receiving information electronically that used to be in written form. This provision ensures that the consumer has access to the Internet and is familiar with the basics of electronic communications. Answer b is, therefore, incorrect. Answer c is also incorrect since the legislation reduces the ability of businesses to use product price unfairly to persuade consumers to accept electronic records. Answer d is incorrect since the legislation is specifically technology-neutral to permit the use of the best technology for the application.

13. Under Civil Law, the victim is NOT entitled to which of the following types of damages?

    a. Statutory

    b. Punitive

    c. Compensatory

    d. Imprisonment of the offender

    Answer: d

    Imprisonment or probation is not a type of punishment available for conviction of a civil crime. Answer a refers to awards set by law. Answer b, punitive damages, are usually determined by the jury and are intended to punish the offender. Compensatory awards are used to provide restitution and compensate the victim for such items as costs of investigations and attorneys' fees.

14. Which of the following is NOT one of the European Union (EU) privacy principles?

    a. Individuals are entitled to receive a report on the information that is held about them.

    b. Data transmission of personal information to locations where "equivalent" personal data protection cannot be assured is prohibited.

    c. Information collected about an individual can be disclosed to other organizations or individuals unless specifically prohibited by the individual.

    d. Individuals have the right to correct errors contained in their personal data.

    Answer: c

    This principle is stated as an "opt-out" principle in which the individual has to take action to prevent information from being circulated to other organizations. The correct corresponding European Union principle states that "information collected about an individual cannot be disclosed to other organizations or individuals unless authorized by law or by consent of the individual." Thus, the individual would have to take an active role or "opt-in" to authorize the disclosure of information to other organizations. The other principles are valid EU privacy principles.

15. Which of the following is NOT a goal of the Kennedy-Kassebaum Health Insurance Portability and Accountability Act (HIPAA) of 1996?

    a. Provide for restricted access by the patient to personal healthcare information

    b. Administrative simplification

    c. Enable the portability of health insurance

    d. Establish strong penalties for healthcare fraud

    Answer: a

    HIPAA is designed to provide for greater access by the patient to personal healthcare information. In answer b, administrative simplification, the goal is to improve the efficiency and effectiveness of the healthcare system by:

    ■ Standardizing the exchange of administrative and financial data

    ■ Protecting the security and privacy of individually identifiable health information

    Answers c and d are self-explanatory.

16. The proposed HIPAA Security Rule mandates the protection of the confidentiality, integrity, and availability of protected health information (PHI) through three of the following activities. Which of the activities is NOT included under the proposed HIPAA Security Rule?

    a. Administrative procedures

    b. Physical safeguards

    c. Technical services and mechanisms

    d. Appointment of a Privacy Officer

    Answer: d

    HIPAA separates the activities of Security and Privacy. HIPAA Security is mandated under the main categories listed in answers a, b, and c. The proposed HIPAA Security Rule mandates the appointment of a Security Officer. The HIPAA Privacy Rule mandates the appointment of a Privacy Officer. HIPAA Privacy covers individually identifiable health care information transmitted, stored in electronic or paper or oral form. PHI may not be disclosed except for the following reasons:

    ■ Disclosure is approved by the individual

    ■ Permitted by the legislation

    ■ For treatment

    ■ Payment

    ■ Health care operations

■ As required by law

Protected Health Information (PHI) is individually identifiable health information that is:

■ Transmitted by electronic media

■ Maintained in any medium described in the definition of electronic media ...[under HIPAA]

■ Transmitted or maintained in any other form or medium

17. Individual privacy rights as defined in the HIPAA Privacy Rule include consent and authorization by the patient for the release of PHI. The difference between consent and authorization as used in the Privacy Rule is:

a. Consent grants general permission to use or disclose PHI, and authorization limits permission to the purposes and the parties specified in the authorization.

b. Authorization grants general permission to use or disclose PHI, and consent limits permission to the purposes and the parties specified in the consent.

c. Consent grants general permission to use or disclose PHI, and authorization limits permission to the purposes specified in the authorization.

d. Consent grants general permission to use or disclose PHI, and authorization limits permission to the parties specified in the authorization.

Answer: a

Answer b is therefore incorrect. Answer c is incorrect since the limits to authorization do not include the parties concerned. Answer d is incorrect since the limits to authorization do not include the specified purposes. The other individual privacy rights listed in the HIPAA Privacy Rule are:

■ Notice (of the covered entities' privacy practices)

■ Right to request restriction

■ Right of access

■ Right to amend

■ Right to an accounting

In August of 2002, the U.S. Department of Health and Human Services (HHS) modified the Privacy Rule to ease the requirements of consent and allow the covered entities to use notice. The changes are summarized as follows:

■ Covered entities must provide patients with notice of the patient's privacy rights and the privacy practices of the covered entity.

■ Direct treatment providers must make a good faith effort to obtain patient's written acknowledgement of the notice of privacy rights and practices. (The Rule does not prescribe a form of written acknowledgement; the patient may sign a separate sheet or initial a cover sheet of the notice.)

■ Mandatory consent requirements are removed that would inhibit patient access to health care while providing covered entities with the option of developing a consent process that works for that entity. If the provider cannot obtain a written acknowledgement, it must document its good faith efforts to obtain one and the reason for its inability to obtain the acknowledgement.

■ Consent requirements already in place may continue.

18. Because of the nature of information that is stored on the computer, the investigation and prosecution of computer criminal cases have specific characteristics, one of which is:

a. Investigators and prosecutors have a longer time frame for the investigation.

b. The information is intangible.

c. The investigation does not usually interfere with the normal conduct of the business of an organization.

d. Evidence is usually easy to gather.

Answer: b

The information is stored in memory on the computer and is intangible as opposed to a physical object. Answer a is incorrect since investigators and prosecutors are under time pressure to gather evidence and proceed to prosecution. If the suspect is alerted, he or she may do damage to the system or destroy important evidence. Search warrants may have to be obtained by law enforcement to search the suspect's home and workplace and seize computers and disks. Answer c is incorrect since an investigation will interfere with the normal conduct of business. Some of the ways in which an investigation may affect an organization are:

■ The organization will have to provide experts to work with law enforcement.

■ Information key to the criminal investigation may be co-resident on the same computer system as information critical to the day-to-day operation of the organization.

■ Proprietary data may be subject to disclosure.

- Management may be exposed if they have not exercised "Due Care" to protect information resources.
- There may be negative publicity that will be harmful to the organization.

Answer d is incorrect. Evidence is difficult to gather since it is intangible and easily subject to modification or destruction.

19. In order for evidence to be admissible in a court of law, it must be relevant, legally permissible, reliable, properly identified, and properly preserved. Reliability of evidence means that:

   a. It must tend to prove a material fact; the evidence is related to the crime in that it shows that the crime has been committed, can provide information describing the crime, can provide information as to the perpetrator's motives, can verify what had occurred, and so on.

   b. The evidence is identified without changing or damaging the evidence.

   c. The evidence has not been tampered with or modified.

   d. The evidence is not subject to damage or destruction.

   Answer: c

   This requirement is a critical issue with computer evidence since computer data may be easily modified without having an indication that a change has taken place. Answer a defines the *relevancy* of evidence, answer b describes the *identification* of evidence, and answer d describes the *preservation* of evidence.

20. In the U.S. Federal Rules of Evidence, Rule 803 (6) permits an exception to the Hearsay Rule regarding business records and computer records. Which one of the following is NOT a requirement for business or computer records exception under Rule 803 (6)?

   a. Made during the regular conduct of business and authenticated by witnesses familiar with their use

   b. Relied upon in the regular course of business

   c. Made only by a person with knowledge of the records

   d. Made by a person with information transmitted by a person with knowledge

   Answer: c

   The business or computer records may be made by a person with information transmitted by a person with knowledge, also. The other answers are requirements for exceptions to the Hearsay Rule.

21. Law enforcement officials in the United States, up until passage of the Patriot Act (see Question 9), had extensive restrictions on search and seizure as established in the Fourth Amendment to the U.S. Constitution. These restrictions are still, essentially, more severe than those on private citizens, who are not agents of a government entity. Thus, internal investigators in an organization or private investigators are not subject to the same restrictions as government officials. Private individuals are not normally held to the same standards regarding search and seizure since they are not conducting an unconstitutional government search. However, there are certain exceptions where the Fourth Amendment applies to private citizens if they act as agents of the government/police. Which of the following is NOT one of these exceptions?

    a. The government is aware of the intent to search or is aware of a search conducted by the private individual and does not object to these actions.

    b. The private individual performs the search to aid the government.

    c. The private individual conducts a search that would require a search warrant if conducted by a government entity.

    d. The private individual conducts a warrantless search of company property for the company.

    Answer: d

    Since the private individual, say an employee of the company, conducts a search for evidence on property that is owned by the company and is not acting as an agent of the government, a warrantless search is permitted. The Fourth Amendment does not apply. For review, the Fourth Amendment guarantees:

    The right of the people to be secure in their persons, houses, papers, and effects, against unreasonable searches and seizures, shall not be violated, and no Warrants shall issue, but upon probable cause, supported by oath or affirmation, and particularly describing the place to be searched, and the persons or things to be seized.

    The *exigent circumstances doctrine* provides an exception to these guarantees if destruction of evidence is imminent. Then, a warrantless search and seizure of evidence can be conducted if there is probable cause to suspect criminal activity. Answers a, b, and c describe exceptions where the private individual is subject to the Fourth Amendment guarantees.

22. One important tool of computer forensics is the disk image backup. The disk image backup is:

    a. Copying the system files

    b. Conducting a bit-level copy, sector by sector

    c. Copying the disk directory

    d. Copying and authenticating the system files

      Answer: b

      Copying sector by sector at the bit level provides the capability to examine slack space, undeleted clusters and possibly, deleted files. With answer a, only the system files are copied and the other information recovered in answer b would not be captured. Answer c does not capture the data on the disk, and answer d has the same problem as answer a. Actually, authenticating the system files is another step in the computer forensics process wherein a message digest is generated for all system directories and files to be able to validate the integrity of the information at a later time. This authentication should be conducted using a backup copy of the disk and not the original to avoid modifying information on the original.

      For review purposes, *computer forensics* is the collecting of information from and about computer systems that is admissible in a court of law.

23. In the context of legal proceedings and trial practice, *discovery* refers to:

    a. The process in which the prosecution presents information it has uncovered to the defense, including potential witnesses, reports resulting from the investigation, evidence, and so on

    b. The process undertaken by the investigators to acquire evidence needed for prosecution of a case

    c. A step in the computer forensic process

    d. The process of obtaining information on potential and existing employees using background checks

      Answer: a

      The key words are legal proceedings and trial practice. Information and property obtained in the investigation by law enforcement officials must be turned over to the defense. For some information that is proprietary to an organization, restrictions can be placed on who has access to the data. Answers b, c, and d are forms of the investigative process. During an investigation, answers b and c are appropriate definitions of discovery.

24. Which of the following alternatives should NOT be used by law enforcement to gain access to a password?

    a. Using password "cracker" software

    b. Compelling the suspect to provide the password

    c. Contacting the developer of the software for information to gain access to the computer or network through a back door

    d. Data manipulation and trial procedures applied to the original version of the system hard disk

    Answer: d

    The original disk of a computer involved in a criminal investigation should not be used for any experimental purposes since data may be modified or destroyed. Any operations should be conducted on a copy of the system disk. However, the answers in a, b, and c are the preferred methods of gaining access to a password-protected system. Interestingly, in answer b, there is legal precedent to order a suspect to provide the password of a computer that is in the custody of law enforcement.

25. During the investigation of a computer crime, audit trails can be very useful. To ensure that the audit information can be used as evidence, certain procedures must be followed. Which of the following is NOT one of these procedures?

    a. The audit trail information must be used during the normal course of business.

    b. There must be a valid organizational security policy in place and in use that defines the use of the audit information.

    c. Mechanisms should be in place to protect the integrity of the audit trail information.

    d. Audit trails should be viewed prior to the image backup.

    Answer: d

    The image backup should be done first in order not to modify any information on the hard disk. For example, the authentication process applied to a hard disk can change the time of last access information on files. Thus, authentication should be applied to a disk image copy.

26. The Internet Activities Board (IAB) considers which of the following behaviors relative to the Internet as unethical?

    a. Negligence in the conduct of Internet experiments

    b. Recordkeeping whose very existence is secret

c. Recordkeeping in which an individual cannot find out what information concerning that individual is in the record

d. Improper dissemination and use of identifiable personal data

Answer: a

The IAB document, *Ethics and the Internet* (RFC 1087) listed behaviors as unethical that:

- Seek to gain unauthorized access to the resources of the Internet
- Destroy the integrity of computer-based information
- Disrupt the intended use of the Internet
- Waste resources such as people, capacity and computers through such actions
- Compromise the privacy of users
- Involve negligence in the conduct of Internetwide experiments

Answers b, c, and d are taken from the Code of Fair Information Practices of the U.S. Department of Health, Education of Welfare.

27. Which of the following is NOT a form of computer/network surveillance?

a. Keyboard monitoring

b. Use of network sniffers

c. Use of CCTV cameras

d. Review of audit logs

Answer: c

CCTV cameras fall under the category of physical surveillance. Answers a and b are forms of active surveillance. These types of surveillance require an organizational policy informing the employees that the surveillance is being conducted. Additionally, warning banners describing the surveillance at log-on to a computer or network should be prominently displayed. These banners usually state that by logging on, the user acknowledges the warning and agrees to the monitoring. Answer d is a passive form of computer/network surveillance.

28. Which of the following is NOT a definition or characteristic of "Due Care?"

a. Just, proper, and sufficient care, so far as the circumstances demand it.

b. That care which an ordinary prudent person would have exercised under the same or similar circumstances.

c. Implies that a party has been guilty of a violation of the law in relation to the subject-matter or transaction.

d. It may and often does require extraordinary care.

Answer: c

Due Care implies that not only has a party not been negligent or careless, but also that he/she has been guilty of no violation of law in relation to the subject mater or transaction which constitutes the cause of action. "Due Care" and "Reasonable Care" are used interchangeably. The definitions of Due Care given in answers a, b, and c are from Black's Law Dictionary, Abridged Fifth Edition, West Publishing Company, St. Paul Minnesota, 1983.

29. The definition "A mark used in the sale or advertising of services to identify the services of one person and distinguish them from the services of others" refers to a:

a. Trademark

b. Service mark

c. Trade name

d. Copyright

Answer: b

For answer a, a trademark is a "distinctive mark of authenticity, through which the products of particular manufacturers or the vendible commodities of particular merchants may be distinguished from those of others." Answer c, a trade name is "any designation which is adopted and used by a person to denominate goods which he markets, or services which he renders or business which he conducts. A trade name is descriptive of a manufacturer or dealer and applies to business and goodwill. A trademark is applicable only to vendible commodities. In answer d, a copyright is "an intangible, incorporeal right granted by statute to the author or originator of certain literary or artistic productions, whereby he is invested, for a statutorily prescribed period, with the sole and exclusive privilege of multiplying copies of the same and publishing and selling them. (These definitions were also taken from Black's Law Dictionary, Abridged Fifth Edition, West Publishing Company, St. Paul Minnesota, 1983.)

30. It is estimated that the Asia/Pacific region accounts for about $4 billion worth of loss of income to software publishers due to software piracy.

As with the Internet, cross-jurisdictional law enforcement issues make investigating and prosecuting such crime difficult. Which of the following items is NOT an issue in stopping overseas software piracy?

a. Obtaining the cooperation of foreign law enforcement agencies and foreign governments.

b. The quality of the illegal copies of the software is improving, making it more difficult for purchasers to differentiate between legal and illegal products.

c. The producers of the illegal copies of software are dealing in larger and larger quantities, resulting in faster deliveries of illicit software.

d. Lack of a central, nongovernmental organization to address the issue of software piracy.

Answer: d

The Business Software Alliance (BSA) is a nongovernmental anti-software piracy organization (www.bsa.org). The mission statement of the BSA is:

The Business Software Alliance is an international organization representing leading software and e-commerce developers in 65 countries around the world. Established in 1988, BSA has offices in the United States, Europe, and Asia . . . . Our efforts include educating computer users about software copyrights; advocating public policy that fosters innovation and expands trade opportunities; and fighting software piracy.

Chapter 10—Physical Security

1. Which choice below is NOT a common biometric method?

    a. Retina pattern devices

    b. Fingerprint devices

    c. Handprint devices

    d. Phrenologic devices

    Answer: d

    Biometrics are commonly used to verify the authenticity of someone attempting to gain access to a secure facility. Biometrics examine each person's unique physiological characteristics to provide positive personal identification. Fingerprints and handwritten signatures have been used in the past for identification, but modern biometric devices use many other physical traits to allow entrance to a facility or access to a system. Several types of biometric devices are common, such as retina pattern devices, fingerprint devices, handprint devices, and voice pattern devices. The effectiveness of these procedures and the impact of false positive and false negative error rates is covered in the Access Control domain.

    Phrenology was a pseudo-science developed in the late 18th century to assign behavior attributes based upon the examination, the shape, and unevenness of a head or skull. It was believed that one could discover the development of the particular cerebral "organs" responsible for different intellectual aptitudes and character traits. For example, a prominent protuberance in the forehead at the position attributed to the organ of "benevolence" was meant to indicate that the individual had a "well developed" organ of benevolence and would therefore be expected to exhibit benevolent behavior. It was thought this could predict criminal or anti-social behavior. Source: *Computer Security Basics* by Deborah Russell and G.T. Gangemi Sr. (O'Reilly, 1992) and John van Wyhe, *The History of Phrenology on the Web* (http://pages.britishlibrary.net/phrenology/), February 8, 2002.

2. According to the NFPA, which choice below is NOT a recommended risk factor to consider when determining the need for protecting the computing environment from fire?

    a. Life safety aspects of the computing function or process

    b. Fire threat of the installation to occupants or exposed property

    c. Distance of the computing facility from a fire station

    d. Economic loss of the equipment's value

    Answer: c

While the distance of the computing facility from a fire station should be considered when initially determining the physical location of a computing facility (as should police and hospital proximity), it is not considered a primary factor in determining the need for internal fire suppression systems. The National Fire Protection Association (NFPA) defines risk factors to consider when designing fire and safety protection for computing environments. The factors to be used when assessing the impact of damage and interruption resulting from a fire, in priority order, are:

- The life safety aspects of the function, such as air traffic controls or safety processing controls
- The fire threat of the installation to the occupants or property of the computing area
- The economic loss incurred from the loss of computing function or loss of stored records
- The economic loss incurred from the loss of the value of the equipment

As in all evaluations of risk, not only fire risk, life safety is always the number one priority. Source: "NFPA 75 Standard for the Protection of Electronic Computer/Data Processing Equipment" National Fire Protection Association, 1999 Edition.

3. Which choice below is NOT an example of a Halocarbon Agent?

    a. HFC-23

    b. FC-3-1-10

    c. IG-541

    d. HCFC-22

    Answer: c

    IG-541 is an inert gas agent, not a halocarbon agent. Halocarbon agents or inert gas agents can be replacements for Halon 1301 and Halon 1211 in gas-discharge fire extinguishing systems. Halocarbon agents contain one or more organic compounds as primary components, such as the elements fluorine, chlorine, bromine, or iodine. Inert gas agents contain as primary components one or more of the gases helium, neon, argon, or nitrogen. Some inert gas agents also contain carbon dioxide as a secondary component. Halocarbon agents are hydrofluorocarbons (HFCs), hydrochloroflurocarbons (HCFCs), perfluorocarbons (PFCs or FCs), or fluoroiodocarbons (FICs). Common inert gas agents for fire extinguishing systems are IG-01, IG-100, IG -55, and IG-541. Source: "NFPA 2001 Standard on

Table A.14 Combustible Materials Fire Class Ratings

FIRE CLASS	COMBUSTIBLE MATERIALS
A	Wood, cloth, paper, rubber, most plastics, ordinary combustibles
B	Flammable liquids and gases, oils, greases, tars, oil-base paints and lacquers
C	Energized electrical equipment
D	Flammable chemicals such as magnesium and sodium

Clean Agent Fire Extinguishing Systems" National Fire Protection Association, 2000 Edition.

4. Which choice below is NOT an example of a combustible in a Class B fire?

   a. Grease

   b. Rubber

   c. Oil-base paints

   d. Flammable gases

   Answer: b

   Fire combustibles are rated as either Class A, B, C, or D based upon their material composition, and this determines which type of extinguishing system or agent is used. Rubber is considered an ordinary Class A combustible. Table A.14 shows the different combustibles and their related classes. Source: "NFPA 2001 Standard on Clean Agent Fire Extinguishing Systems" National Fire Protection Association, 2000 Edition.

5. Which statement below most accurately describes a "dry pipe" sprinkler system?

   a. Dry pipe is the most commonly used sprinkler system.

   b. Dry pipe contains air pressure.

   c. Dry pipe sounds an alarm and delays water release.

   d. Dry pipe may contain carbon dioxide.

   Answer: b

   In a dry pipe system, air pressure is maintained until the sprinkler head seal is ruptured. The air then escapes, and the water is brought into the room. One advantage of the dry pipe system is that the wet pipe system is vulnerable to broken pipes due to freezing. Answer a is incorrect; wet pipe is the most commonly used sprinkler system, dry pipe is second. In a wet pipe system, water is standing in the pipe and is released when heat breaks the sprinkler head seal. Answer c describes a preaction pipe, which sounds an alarm and delays the water release. This allows computer operations to shut down before the release of water. A preaction pipe may or may not be a dry pipe, but not all dry pipes are preaction. Answer d is incorrect, because a dry pipe is a water release system. Source: "NFPA 75 Standard for the Protection of Electronic Computer/Data Processing Equipment" National Fire Protection Association, 1999 Edition and "NFPA 13 Standard for the Installation of Sprinkler Systems."

6. Which choice below is NOT a recommendation for records and materials storage in the computer room, for fire safety?

   a. Green bar printing paper for printers should be stored in the computer room.

   b. Abandoned cables shall not be allowed to accumulate.

   c. Space beneath the raised floor shall not be used for storage purposes.

   d. Only minimum records required for essential and efficient operation.

   Answer: a

   The NFPA recommends that only the absolute minimum essential records, paper stock, inks, unused recording media, or other combustibles be housed in the computer room. Because of the threat of fire, these combustibles should not be stored in the computer room or under raised flooring, including old, unused cabling. Underfloor abandoned cables can interfere with airflow and extinguishing systems. Cables that are not intended to be used should be removed from the room. It also recommends that tape libraries and record storage rooms be protected by an extinguishing system and separated from the computer room by wall construction fire-resistant rated for not less than one hour. Source: "NFPA 75 Standard for the Protection of Electronic Computer/Data Processing Equipment" National Fire Protection Association, 1999 Edition.

7. Which choice below is NOT considered an element of two-factor authentication?

   a. Something you know

   b. Something you do

c. Something you have

d. Something you are

Answer: b

Something you do, is an element of role-based access authentication, but is not an element of two-factor authentication. The most common implementation of two-factor authentication are "smart cards." Some smart cards employ two-factor authentication because they are an example of "something you have," the encoded card, with "something you know," like a PIN or password. "Something you are" describes biometric authentication. Source: *Computer Security Basics* by Deborah Russell and G.T. Gangemi Sr. (O'Reilly, 1992).

8. Which choice below is NOT an example of a "clean" fire extinguishing agent?

a. CO_2

b. IG-55

c. IG-01

d. HCFC-22

Answer: a

Since Halon was banned for use in fire suppression systems, many different chemical agents have been used. Some of these agents are called "clean" agents, because they do not leave a residue on electronic parts after evaporation. CO_2, carbon dioxide, does leave a corrosive residue, and is therefore not recommended for computer facility fire suppression systems. A "clean agent" is defined as an electrically nonconducting, nonvolatile fire extinguishant that does not leave a residue upon evaporation. Answers b and c, IG-55, and IG-01, are inert gas agents that do not decompose measurably or leave corrosive decomposition products and are, therefore, considered clean agents. Answer d, HCFC-22, is a halocarbon agent, which also is considered a clean agent. Source: "NFPA 2001 Standard on Clean Agent Fire Extinguishing Systems" National Fire Protection Association, 2000 Edition.

9. Which choice below is NOT considered a requirement to install an automatic sprinkler system?

a. The building is required to be sprinklered.

b. The computer room is vented to outside offices.

c. The computer room contains a significant quantity of combustible materials.

d. A computer system's enclosure contains combustible materials.

Answer: b

Computer room venting is an element of smoke detection and protection. The room should not be vented to the outside unless damping elements are installed to prevent smoke from the computer room from entering other offices. An automatic sprinkler system must be provided to protect the computer room or computer areas when either:

■ The enclosure of a computer system is built entirely or in part of a significant quantity of combustible materials.

■ The operation of the computer room or area involves a significant quantity of combustible materials.

■ The building is otherwise required to be sprinklered.

Source: "NFPA 75 Standard for the Protection of Electronic Computer/Data Processing Equipment" National Fire Protection Association, 1999 Edition and "NFPA 13 Standard for the Installation of Sprinkler Systems."

10. Which choice below is NOT a type of motion-detection system?

a. Ultrasonic-detection system

b. Microwave-detection system

c. Host-based intrusion-detection system

d. Sonic-detection system

Answer: c

Host-based intrusion-detection systems are used to detect unauthorized logical access to network resources, not the physical presence of an intruder. There are four basic technologies for detecting the physical presence of an intruder:

■ Photometric systems, which detect changes in the level of light

■ Motion-detection systems, which detect Doppler-type changes in the frequency of energy waves

■ Acoustical seismic-detection systems, which detect changes in the ambient noise level or vibrations

■ Proximity-detection systems, which detect the approach of an individual into an electrical field

Of the motion detection types, three kinds exist: sonic, ultrasonic, and microwave, depending upon the wavelength of the transmitters and receivers. Motion detectors sense the motion of a body by the

Table A.15 Common Motion Detection System Frequencies

DETECTOR TYPE	FREQUENCY
Sonic	1500-2000 hertz
Ultrasonic	19,000-20,000 hertz
Microwave	400-10,000 megahertz

change in frequency from the source transmission. Sonic detection systems operate in the audible range, ultrasonic detection systems operate in the high frequency, and microwave detection systems utilize radio frequencies. Table A.15 shows the common frequencies of motion detectors. Source: *CISSP Examination Textbooks, Volume one: Theory* by S. Rao Vallabhaneni (SRV Professional Publications, first edition 2000).

11. Which fire extinguishant choice below does NOT create toxic HF levels?

    a. Halon 1301

    b. Halon 1211

    c. IG-01

    d. HCFC-22

    Answer: c

    HF stands for Hydrogen fluoride, a toxic by-product of hydrocarbon agents after discharge. Answer c, IG-01, is an inert gas, which doesn't contain HFs. Inert gas does, however, create a danger to personnel by removing most of the breathable oxygen in a room when flooded, and precautions must be taken before its use. The inert gas agent IG-541 contains CO_2 as an additive, which appears to allow for more breathable time in the computer facility to allow for evacuation, however CO_2 lessens the agent's use as a "clean" agent. CO_2 and Halon are both toxic. Source: "NFPA 2001 Standard on Clean Agent Fire Extinguishing Systems" National Fire Protection Association, 2000 Edition.

12. Which choice below is NOT permitted under computer room raised flooring?

    a. Interconnecting DP cables enclosed in a raceway

    b. Underfloor ventilation for the computer room only

    c. Nonabrasive openings for cables

    d. Underfloor ventilation to the rest of the offices' ventilation system

    Answer: d

    Underfloor ventilation, as is true of all computer room ventilation, should not vent to any other office or area. HVAC air ducts serving other rooms should not pass through the computer room unless an automatic damping system is provided. A damper is activated by fire and smoke detectors and prevents the spread of computer room smoke or toxins through the building HVAC. Raised flooring, also called a false floor or a secondary floor, has very strict requirements as to its construction and use. Electrical cables must be enclosed in metal conduit, and data cables must be enclosed in raceways, with all abandoned cable removed. Openings in the raised floor must be smooth and nonabrasive, and should be protected to minimize the entrance of debris or other combustibles. Obviously, the raised flooring and decking must be constructed from noncombustible materials. Source: "NFPA 75 Standard for the Protection of Electronic Computer/Data Processing Equipment" National Fire Protection Association, 1999 Edition.

13. Which choice below represents the BEST reason to control the humidity in computer operations areas?

   a. Computer operators do not perform at their peak if the humidity is too high.
   b. Electrostatic discharges can harm electronic equipment.
   c. Static electricity destroys the electrical efficiency of the circuits.
   d. If the air is too dry, electroplating of conductors may occur.

   Answer: b

   Electrostatic discharges from static electricity can damage sensitive electronic equipment, even in small amounts. Even though a static charge of several thousand volts may be too low to harm humans, computer equipment is sensitive to static charges. Dry air, below 40 percent relative humidity, increases the chance of static electricity being generated. When the relative humidity is too high, say more than 80 percent, electrical connections become inefficient. The electrical contacts start to corrode and a form of electroplating begins. The recommended optimal relative humidity level is 40 percent to 60 percent for computer operations. Source: *The International Handbook of Computer Security* by Jae K. Shim, Anique A. Qureshi, and Joel G. Siegel (The Glenlake Publishing Co. Ltd, 2000).

14. Which statement below is NOT accurate about smoke damage to electronic equipment?

   a. Smoke exposure during a fire for a relatively short period does little immediate damage.
   b. Continuing power to the smoke-exposed equipment can increase the damage.

   c. Moisture and oxygen corrosion constitute the main damage to the equipment.

   d. The primary damage done by smoke exposure is immediate.

      Answer: d

      Immediate smoke exposure to electronic equipment does little damage. However, the particulate residue left after the smoke has dissipated contains active by-products that corrode metal contact surfaces in the presence of moisture and oxygen. Removal of the contaminant from the electrical contacts, such as printed circuits boards and backplanes, should be implemented as soon as possible, as much of the damage is done during this corrosion period. Also, power should be immediately disconnected to the affected equipment, as continuing voltage can plate the contaminants into the circuitry permanently. Source: "NFPA 75 Standard for the Protection of Electronic Computer/Data Processing Equipment" National Fire Protection Association, 1999 edition and "NFPA 2001 Standard on Clean Agent Fire Extinguishing Systems" 2000 edition.

15. Which choice below most accurately describes the prime benefit of using guards?

   a. Human guards are less expensive than guard dogs.

   b. Guards can exercise discretionary judgment in a way that automated systems can't.

   c. Automated systems have a greater reliability rate than guards.

   d. Guard dogs cannot discern an intruder's intent.

      Answer: b

      The prime advantage to using human guards is that they can exercise discretionary judgment when the need arises. For example, during an emergency guards can switch roles from access control to evacuation support, something guard dogs or automated systems cannot. While guard dogs are relatively expensive to keep, guards are generally the most expensive option for access control. Answers c and d are distracters. An issue with guards, however, is that they can be socially engineered, and must be thoroughly vetted and trained. Source: *The NCSA Guide to Enterprise Security* by Michel E. Kabay (McGraw-Hill, 1996).

16. Which choice below is an accurate statement about EMI and RFI?

   a. EMI can contain RFI.

   b. EMI is generated naturally; RFI is man-made.

   c. RFI is generated naturally; EMI is man-made.

   d. Natural sources of EMI pose the greatest threat to electronic equipment.

Answer: a

Electromagnetic interference (EMI) and radio-frequency interference (RFI) are terms used to describe disruption or noise generated by electromagnetic waves. RFI refers to noise generated from radio waves, and EMI is the general term for all electromagnetic interference, including radio waves. EMI and RFI are often generated naturally, for example solar sunspots or the earth's magnetic field. Man-made sources of EMI and RFI pose the largest threat to electronic equipment from sources like cell phones, laptops, and other computers. Guidelines to prevent EMI and RFI interference in the computer room should be adopted, such as limiting the use and placement of magnets or cell phones around sensitive equipment. The United States government created the TEMPEST (Transient ElectroMagnetic Pulse Emanations Standard) standard to prevent EMI eavesdropping by employing heavy metal shielding. Source: *The NCSA Guide to Enterprise Security* by Michel E. Kabay (McGraw-Hill, 1996).

17. In which proper order should the steps below be taken after electronic equipment or media has been exposed to water?

_____ a. Place all affected equipment or media in an air-conditioned area, if portable.

_____ b. Turn off all electrical power to the equipment.

_____ c. Open cabinet doors and remove panels and covers to allow water to run out.

_____ d. Wipe with alcohol or Freon-alcohol solutions or spray with water-displacement aerosol sprays.

Answer: b, c, a, and d.

Water-based emergencies could include pipe breakage, or damage to sensitive electronic equipment due to the proper use of water fire sprinklers. The first order of business is shutting down the power to the effected equipment, to prevent shock hazards, shorting, or further damage. Any visible standing water should be removed and allowed to drain from around and the inside the unit. As the room may still be extremely humid, move the equipment, if possible, to a humidity-controlled environment, then wipe the parts and use water displacement sprays. If corrective action is initiated immediately, the damage done to the computer equipment can be greatly reduced and the chances of recovering the data are increased. Source: "NFPA 75 Standard for the Protection of Electronic Computer/Data Processing Equipment" National Fire Protection Association, 1999 Edition and "Electronics and Magnetic Media Recovery" Blackmon-Mooring-Steamatic Catastrophe Inc.

18. Which choice below is NOT an example of using a social engineering technique to gain physical access to a secure facility?

    a. Asserting authority or pulling rank

    b. Intimidating or threatening

    c. Praising or flattering

    d. Employing the salami fraud

    Answer: d

    The "salami fraud" is an automated fraud technique. In the salami fraud, a programmer will create or alter a program to move small amounts of money into his personal bank account. The amounts are intended to be so small as to be unnoticed, such as rounding in foreign currency exchange transactions. Hence the reference to slicing a salami.

    The other three choices are common techniques used by an intruder to gain either physical access or system access:

    Asserting authority or pulling rank.   Professing to have the authority, perhaps supported with altered identification, to enter the facility or system.

    Intimidating or threatening.   Browbeating the access control subjects with harsh language or threatening behavior to permit access or release information.

    Praising, flattering, or sympathizing.   Using positive reinforcement to coerce the subjects into giving access or information for system access.

    Source: *Fighting Computer Crime* by Donn B. Parker (Wiley, 1998).

19. In which proper order should the steps below be taken after electronic equipment or media has been exposed to smoke contaminants?

    _____ a. Turn off power to equipment.

    _____ b. Spray corrosion-inhibiting aerosol to stabilize metal contact surfaces.

    _____ c. Spray connectors, backplanes, and printed circuit boards with Freon or Freon-alcohol solvents.

    _____ d. Move equipment into an air-conditioned and humidity-controlled environment.

    Answer: a, d, c, and b.

    As with water damage, smoke damage can be mitigated with a quick response. Immediately cut power to the equipment to lessen the chance of contaminant plating, and move the equipment to an air-conditioned area free of smoke exposure. Smoke contaminant particles are invisible, so the effected area will contain these articles for a long time. Freon or alcohol-based solvents can remove the initial layer of contaminant particles, then use corrosion-inhibiting aerosols to stabilize the contact surfaces from further corrosion. Like with water damage, if the recovery is prompt and successful, data may be able to be removed from the system after stabilization. Also, like water or other types of damage, the treated systems should never be used again once all usable data has been recovered.

Source: "NFPA 75 Standard for the Protection of Electronic Computer/ Data Processing Equipment" National Fire Protection Association, 1999 edition and "Electronics and Magnetic Media Recovery" Blackmon-Mooring-Steamatic Catastrophe Inc.

20. Which fire suppression medium below is considered to be the MOST toxic to personnel?

    a. CO_2

    b. IG-01

    c. Halon 1301

    d. Halocarbon Agents

    Answer: a

    Carbon dioxide (CO_2) is fatal to personnel when used in large concentrations, like the level required to flood a computer room during a fire. CO_2 is generally used for direct fire suppression at the source. The other three choices can be toxic in that they remove the oxygen from a room to end the fire, but they also remove the breathable air accessible to personnel. Halon 1301 has been banned by the 1987 Montreal Protocol as it contributes to the depletion of the ozone layer. Source: "NFPA 2001 Standard on Clean Agent Fire Extinguishing Systems" National Fire Protection Association, 2000 Edition.

21. Which type of personnel control below helps prevent piggybacking?

    a. Man traps

    b. Back doors

    c. Brute force

    d. Maintenance hooks

    Answer: a

    "Piggybacking" describes an unauthorized person entering a facility through a carded or controlled door by following an authorized person who has opened the door. A man trap is a set of double doors, often with a guard, that is intended to control physical personnel entrance to the facility. Of course, the best protection from this type of intrusion is through security awareness training, to prevent employees from holding the door open or allowing unauthorized intruders from entering.

The other three answers are not personnel or physical controls, but are technical threats or vulnerabilities. Answer b, back doors, commonly refers to Trojan Horses used to give an attacker backdoor network access covertly. Back doors are installed by hackers to gain network access at a later time. Answer c, brute force, is a cryptographic attack attempting to use all combinations of key patterns to decipher a message. Answer d, maintenance hooks, are undocumented openings into an application to assist programmers with debugging. Although intended innocently, these can be exploited by intruders. They are also called "trap doors." Source: *The International Handbook of Computer Security* by Jae K. Shim, Anique A. Qureshi, and Joel G. Siegel (The Glenlake Publishing Co. Ltd, 2000).

22. Which type of physical access control method below is best suited for high-security areas?

   a. Deadbolts

   b. Access token

   c. Key locks

   d. Pushbutton locks

     Answer: b

     Answers a, c, and d are examples of mechanical locks, whereas choice b is an element of an electronic system. An electronic system can be very sophisticated perhaps using smart cards, random keypads, auditing features, and time-operation limits. Deadbolts, keyed locks, and five-button pushbutton locks cannot provide the control and detection features necessary for high-security facilities. Source: *Computer Security Basics* by Deborah Russell and G.T. Gangemi Sr. (O'Reilly, 1992) and *The NCSA Guide to Enterprise Security* by Michel E. Kabay (McGraw-Hill, 1996).

23. Which term below refers to a standard used in determining the fire safety of a computer room?

   a. Noncombustible

   b. Fire-resistant

   c. Fire retardant

   d. Nonflammable

     Answer: b

     The fire-resistant rating of construction materials is a major factor in determining the fire safety of a computer operations room. The term fire-resistant refers to materials or construction that has a fire resistance rating of not less than the specified standard. For example, the computer room must be separated from other occupancy areas by construction with a fire-resistant rating of not less than one hour. Answer a, noncombustible, means material that will not aid or add appreciable heat to an ambient fire. Answer c, fire retardant, describes material that lessens or prevents the spread of a fire. Fire retardant coatings are designed to protect materials from fire exposure damage. Answer d, nonflammable, describes material that will not burn. Source: "NFPA 2001 Standard on Clean Agent Fire Extinguishing Systems" National Fire Protection Association, 2000 Edition.

Notes

1. CSC-STD-001-83
2. Gligor, Virgil D., "Guidelines for Trusted Facility Management and Audit," University of Maryland, 1985.
3. Ibid.
4. The ISO/IEC's web site is at http://isotc.iso.ch/livelink/livelink/fetch/2000/2489/Ittf_Home/ITTF.htm.
5. For more information about BS7799, visit:www.gammassl.co.uk/bs7799/works.html.
6. NCSC-TG-O15, Guide To Understanding Trusted Facility Management [Brown Book].
7. A Guide to Understanding Data Remanence in Automated Information Systems, NCSC-TG-025, National Computer Security Center, September 1991.

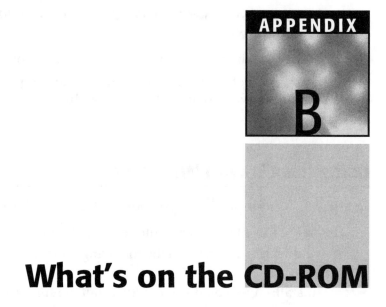

What's on the CD-ROM

This appendix provides you with information on the contents of the CD that accompanies this book. For the latest and greatest information, please refer to the ReadMe file located at the root of the CD. Here is what you will find:

- System Requirements
- Using the CD with Windows
- What's on the CD
- Troubleshooting

System Requirements

Make sure that your computer meets the minimum system requirements listed in this section. If your computer doesn't match up to most of these requirements, you may have a problem using the contents of the CD.

For Windows 9*x*, Windows 2000, Windows NT4 (with SP 4 or later), Windows Me, or Windows XP:

- PC with a Pentium processor running at 120 MHz or faster
- At least 32 MB of total RAM installed on your computer; for best performance, we recommend at least 64 MB
- A CD-ROM drive

Using the CD with Windows

To install the items from the CD to your hard drive, follow these steps:

1. Insert the CD into your computer's CD-ROM drive.
2. A window will appear with the following options: Install, Explore, and Exit.

    Install: Gives you the option to install the supplied software and/or the author-created samples on the CD-ROM.

    Explore: Allows you to view the contents of the CD-ROM in its directory structure.

    Exit: Closes the autorun window.

If you do not have autorun enabled or if the autorun window does not appear, follow the steps below to access the CD.

1. Click Start @@> Run.
2. In the dialog box that appears, type *d*:\setup.exe, where *d* is the letter of your CD-ROM drive. This will bring up the autorun window described above.
3. Choose the Install, Explore, eBook, Links, or Exit option from the menu. (See Step 2 in the preceding list for a description of these options.)

What's on the CD

Included on the CD-ROM is a testing engine that is powered by Boson Software. This program resembles the testing engine that will be used by the testing center where you will be taking your exam. The goal of the testing engine is to make you comfortable with the testing interface so that taking your exam will not be the first time you see that style of exam.

The questions that will be used in the testing engine are those presented in the book, and cover all 10 domains of the exam. When installed and run, the test engine presents you with a multiple-choice, question-and-answer format. Each question deals directly with exam-related material.

Once you select what you believe to be the correct answer for each question, the test engine not only notes whether you are correct, but also provides information as to why the right answer is right and the wrong answers are wrong, providing you with valuable information for further review. Thus, the test engine gives not only valuable simulated exam experience, but useful tutorial direction as well.

Troubleshooting

If you have difficulty installing or using any of the materials on the companion CD, try the following solutions:

Turn off any anti-virus software that you may have running. Installers sometimes mimic virus activity and can make your computer incorrectly believe that it is being infected by a virus. (Be sure to turn the anti-virus software back on later.)

Close all running programs. The more programs you're running, the less memory is available to other programs. Installers also typically update files and programs; if you keep other programs running, installation may not work properly.

Reference the ReadMe: Please refer to the ReadMe file located at the root of the CD-ROM for the latest product information at the time of publication.

If you still have trouble with the CD, please call the Wiley Customer Care phone number: (800) 762-2974. Outside the United States, call 1 (317) 572-3994. You can also contact Wiley Customer Service by e-mail at techsupdum@ wiley.com. Wiley will provide technical support only for installation and other general quality control items; for technical support on the applications themselves, consult the program's vendor or author.

Index

A

acceptability metric, access control, 125
acceptance, false, 137
access control, 12–19, 121–139
    authentication in, 17, 133–134
    authorization in, 133
    base relations (SQL) and, 16, 129–130
    biometrics in, 14, 18, 124–125, 137–138
    call back schemes and, 13, 121–122
    checksums and, 16, 131
    context dependence/independence in,
        14, 125
    criteria for, 18, 134–135
    databases and, 14, 125–126
    enforced paths in, 13, 121
    Enterprise Access Management (EAM) in,
        18, 136–137
    general packet radio services (GPRS) and,
        19, 138
    global system for mobile (GSM) and, 19,
        138–139
    group rights and, 16, 130
    grouped processes and, 13, 122–123
    inference and, 16, 129
    integrity in, 15, 127
    Kerberos and, 15–17, 127–128
    limiting routes in, 13, 121
    log on process and, 13, 122
    mandatory, 130–131
    object-oriented databases and, 17, 132–133
    Open Group and, 17, 131–132
    passwords and, 18, 135–136
    physical controls for, 13–14
    physical security and, for high security
        areas, 96, 309
    protection domains and, 13, 122–123
    reference monitors and, 17, 133–134
    relational databases and, 14, 17, 126, 132–133
    restricted shell and, 14–15, 126–127
    role-based, 16, 130, 197
    rows and columns in, 13, 123–124
    Secure European System for Applications in
        Multivendor Environment (SESAME)
        and, 15, 128–129
    security kernels and, 133
    Security Support Provider Interface (SSPI)
        in, 129
    Simple Security Property and, 16, 130–131
    single sign on (SSO) interfaces and, 17,
        131–132, 136–137
    SQL and, 16, 129–130

C

singlemode optical fiber, in telecommunications and network security, 27, 155

site accreditation, in security architecture and models, 205

Skipjack algorithm, 175

smoke damage, 95–96, 304–305, 307–308

SMURF attack, 147

Snort, 154

social engineering, in physical security, 96, 307

SOCKS protocol, in telecommunications and network security, 25, 149

software capability evaluation, 66–67, 245

software engineering, 65, 239–240

Software Engineering Institute (SEI), 212–213

software piracy, 90, 294–295

software process assessment, 66–67, 245

software process capability, 243

software process maturity, 244

software process performance, 244

software processes, 243

spanning tree protocol, in telecommunications and network security, 23, 141–142

spiral model, in applications and systems development, 66, 243

spoofing attacks, 27, 153–154

sprinkler systems, 94, 301–302

SQL, in access control, 16, 129–130

standards for security management, 4, 101–102

Star Property, in access control, 16, 130–131

star topologies, 154

start bits, 207

stateful inspection firewalls, 153

static random access memory (SRAM), 206

static routing, 158

statistical information, in access control, 16, 129

statistical modeling, 249

stop bits, 207

storage of records and materials, 93–94, 300

store and forward switching, in telecommunications and network security, 25, 148–149

stream cipher cryptography, 42, 192

strong tranquillity property (Bell-LaPadula model), 48, 198–199

structured analysis/structured design (SA/SD), 239

structured walk through test, in business continuity, disaster recovery, 259

subclasses, in applications and systems development, 67, 246

subnet masks, in telecommunications and network security, 30, 162

substitution, in OOP, 239–240

substitution ciphers, 40–41, 187, 189

superscalar processors, 195

surveillance of computer/networks, 89, 293

switched multimegabit data service (SMDS), 156

symmetric key encryption, 170

SYN attack, 153

synchronicity of transmissions, 24, 146

synchronous data transmission, 146, 207

system owner, 7, 111–112

system-high mode of operation, 218–219

system-specific policies, in security management, 7, 110

T

table top exercises, in business continuity, disaster recovery, 259

TCP SYN attack, 147

telecommunications and network security, 21–30, 141–163

  back doors and, 26, 150

  backup methods in, 29, 161–162

  basic rate interface (BRI) in ISDN and, 23, 143

  cut through switching and, 25, 148–149

  denial of service (DoS) attack and, 25, 147

  dial up hacking and, 25, 149

  disk mirroring and, 25, 146–147

  DoD layered network model in, 23–24, 143–144

  dual homed hosts and, 26–27, 152

  dynamic state tables and, 27, 152–153

  email and, 26, 150–151

  Ethernet 100BaseT networks in, 24, 144–145

  Ethernet networks and, 28–29, 156–157, 159

  firewalls and, 26–27, 151–153

  interior gateway protocols in, 24, 145

  Internet Assigned Numbers Authority (IANA), 23, 142–143

  IP addressing and, 23, 26, 28–30, 142–143, 151, 162

  IPSec and, 25, 148

  LAN topologies and, 27, 154

  media access control (MAC) addresses and, 23, 28–29, 141–142

  multimode vs. singlemode optical fiber and, 27, 155

  network address translation (NAT), 143

  Network Layer in, 24, 144

  optical fiber networks and, 28–30, 157, 162

  OSI layered reference model in, 23–24, 141, 144

  packet switching networks and, 28, 156

  passwords in, 26, 149–150

Vigenere cipher squares cryptography, 42–43, 190–191
virtual LANs (VLANs), 28, 155–156
virtual memory, 212
virtual private networks (VPNs), 19, 121, 138
visibility of IT security policy, 9, 117–118
volatile memory, 206
von Neumann architectures, 246
vulnerability assessments, in business continuity, disaster recovery, 78, 268–269

W

walk through drill, in business continuity, disaster recovery, 259
WAP Forum, 179
WAP Identity Module (WIM), 179
war walking/war driving, 149
warm sites, 75, 257–258, 306
water damage, 95–96, 306
water purification, 79, 269–270
waterfall model, in applications and systems development, 66, 242
weak tranquillity property (Bell-LaPadula model), 199
well-formed transactions, 200
wide area networks (WANs), 28, 156
Windows 2000, access control, 16–17, 128–129
Windows NT and passwords, 26, 149–150

wired equivalent privacy (WEP), 41, 187
wireless application protocol (WAP), 187
    access control and, 138
    cryptography and, 37, 177–179
wireless connectivity, telecommunications and network security, 24, 144
wireless LANs (WLANs)
    cryptography and, 41, 187
    telecommunications and network security and, 29, 159–160
wireless personal area networks (WPAN), 144
wireless transaction protocol (WTP), access control, 138
wireless transport layer security (WTLS), 37, 177–179
wiretapping, 83, 279–280
WMLScript Crypto Library, 179
World Intellectual Property Organization (WIPO), 84, 281–282
World Wide Web Consortium (W3C), security architecture and models, 51–52, 209–210

X

X.25, 156
X.52 standard, 40, 185–186
X12 standard in security architecture and models, 51, 207–209
XORing cryptography, 189, 192

Wiley Publishing, Inc.
End-User License Agreement

READ THIS. You should carefully read these terms and conditions before opening the software packet(s) included with this book "Book". This is a license agreement "Agreement" between you and Wiley Publishing, Inc. "WPI". By opening the accompanying software packet(s), you acknowledge that you have read and accept the following terms and conditions. If you do not agree and do not want to be bound by such terms and conditions, promptly return the Book and the unopened software packet(s) to the place you obtained them for a full refund.

1. **License Grant.** WPI grants to you (either an individual or entity) a nonexclusive license to use one copy of the enclosed software program(s) (collectively, the "Software," solely for your own personal or business purposes on a single computer (whether a standard computer or a workstation component of a multi-user network). The Software is in use on a computer when it is loaded into temporary memory (RAM) or installed into permanent memory (hard disk, CD-ROM, or other storage device). WPI reserves all rights not expressly granted herein.

2. **Ownership.** WPI is the owner of all right, title, and interest, including copyright, in and to the compilation of the Software recorded on the disk(s) or CD-ROM "Software Media". Copyright to the individual programs recorded on the Software Media is owned by the author or other authorized copyright owner of each program. Ownership of the Software and all proprietary rights relating thereto remain with WPI and its licensers.

3. **Restrictions on Use and Transfer.**

    (a) You may only (i) make one copy of the Software for backup or archival purposes or (ii) transfer the Software to a single hard disk, provided that you keep the original for backup or archival purposes. You may not (i) rent or lease the Software, (ii) copy or reproduce the Software through a LAN or other network system or through any computer subscriber system or bulletin-board system, or (iii) modify, adapt, or create derivative works based on the Software.

    (b) You may not reverse engineer, decompile, or disassemble the Software. You may transfer the Software and user documentation on a permanent basis, provided that the transferee agrees to accept the terms and conditions of this Agreement and you retain no copies. If the Software is an update or has been updated, any transfer must include the most recent update and all prior versions.

4. **Restrictions on Use of Individual Programs.** You must follow the individual requirements and restrictions detailed for each individual program in the About the CD-ROM appendix of this Book. These limitations are also contained in the individual license agreements recorded on the Software Media. These limitations may include a requirement that after using the program for a specified period of time, the user must pay a registration fee or discontinue use. By opening the Software packet(s), you will be agreeing to abide by the licenses and restrictions for these individual programs that are detailed in the About the CD-ROM appendix and on the Software Media. None of the material on this Software Media or listed in this Book may ever be redistributed, in original or modified form, for commercial purposes.

5. **Limited Warranty.**

    (a) WPI warrants that the Software and Software Media are free from defects in materials and workmanship under normal use for a period of sixty (60) days from the date of purchase of this Book. If WPI receives notification within the warranty period of defects in materials or workmanship, WPI will replace the defective Software Media.

    (b) WPI AND THE AUTHOR OF THE BOOK DISCLAIM ALL OTHER WARRANTIES, EXPRESS OR IMPLIED, INCLUDING WITHOUT LIMITATION IMPLIED WARRANTIES OF MERCHANTABILITY AND FITNESS FOR A PARTICULAR PURPOSE, WITH RESPECT TO THE SOFTWARE, THE PROGRAMS, THE SOURCE CODE CONTAINED THEREIN, AND/OR THE TECHNIQUES DESCRIBED IN THIS BOOK. WPI DOES NOT WARRANT THAT THE FUNCTIONS CONTAINED IN THE SOFTWARE WILL MEET YOUR REQUIREMENTS OR THAT THE OPERATION OF THE SOFTWARE WILL BE ERROR FREE.

    (c) This limited warranty gives you specific legal rights, and you may have other rights that vary from jurisdiction to jurisdiction.

6. **Remedies.**

    (a) WPI's entire liability and your exclusive remedy for defects in materials and workmanship shall be limited to replacement of the Software Media, which may be returned to WPI with a copy of your receipt at the following address: Software Media Fulfillment Department, Attn.: Advanced CISSP Prep Guide: Exam Q&A, Wiley Publishing, Inc., 10475 Crosspoint Blvd., Indianapolis, IN 46256, or call 1-800-762-2974. Please allow four to six weeks for delivery. This Limited Warranty is void if failure of the Software Media has resulted from accident, abuse, or misapplication. Any replacement Software Media will be warranted for the remainder of the original warranty period or thirty (30) days, whichever is longer.

(b) In no event shall WPI or the author be liable for any damages whatsoever (including without limitation damages for loss of business profits, business interruption, loss of business information, or any other pecuniary loss) arising from the use of or inability to use the Book or the Software, even if WPI has been advised of the possibility of such damages.

(c) Because some jurisdictions do not allow the exclusion or limitation of liability for consequential or incidental damages, the above limitation or exclusion may not apply to you.

7. **U.S. Government Restricted Rights.** Use, duplication, or disclosure of the Software for or on behalf of the United States of America, its agencies and/or instrumentalities "U.S. Government" is subject to restrictions as stated in paragraph (c)(1)(ii) of the Rights in Technical Data and Computer Software clause of DFARS 252.227-7013, or subparagraphs (c)(1) and (2) of the Commercial Computer Software—Restricted Rights clause at FAR 52.227-19, and in similar clauses in the NASA FAR supplement, as applicable.

8. **General.** This Agreement constitutes the entire understanding of the parties and revokes and supersedes all prior agreements, oral or written, between them and may not be modified or amended except in a writing signed by both parties hereto that specifically refers to this Agreement. This Agreement shall take precedence over any other documents that may be in conflict herewith. If any one or more provisions contained in this Agreement are held by any court or tribunal to be invalid, illegal, or otherwise unenforceable, each and every other provision shall remain in full force and effect.